MANAGING INSTITUTIONAL ARCHIVES

Recent Titles in
The Greenwood Library Management Collection

Strategic Marketing for Libraries: A Handbook
Elizabeth J. Wood, with assistance from Victoria L. Young

The Smaller Academic Library: A Management Handbook
Gerard B. McCabe, editor

Operations Handbook for the Small Academic Library
Gerard B. McCabe, editor

Data Bases for Special Libraries: A Strategic Guide to Information Management
Lynda W. Moulton

Time Management Handbook for Librarians
J. Wesley Cochran

Academic Libraries in Urban and Metropolitan Areas: A Management
Handbook
Gerard B. McCabe, editor

Managing Institutional Archives

Foundational Principles and Practices

Richard J. Cox

THE GREENWOOD LIBRARY MANAGEMENT COLLECTION

Greenwood Press
NEW YORK • WESTPORT, CONNECTICUT • LONDON

Library of Congress Cataloging-in-Publication Data

Cox, Richard J.
    Managing institutional archives : foundational principles and
practices / Richard J. Cox.
        p.   cm. — (The Greenwood library management collection, ISSN
0894–2986)
    Includes bibliographic references and index.
    ISBN 0–313–27251–4 (alk. paper)
    1. Archives—Administration.   2. Associations, institutions, etc.—
Archives—Administration.   I. Title.   II. Series.
CD950.C69   1992
025.17'14—dc20   91–34470

British Library Cataloguing in Publication Data is available.

Library of Congress Catalog Card Number: 91–34470
ISBN: 0–313–27251–4
ISSN: 0894–2986

First published in 1992

Greenwood Press, 88 Post Road West, Westport, CT 06881
An imprint of Greenwood Publishing Group, Inc.

Printed in the United States of America

The paper used in this book complies with the
Permanent Paper Standard issued by the National
Information Standards Organization (Z39.48–1984).

10 9 8 7 6 5 4 3

Copyright Acknowledgment

Grateful acknowledgment is given for permission to use *Components of a Disaster Plan*,
SOLINET Preservation Program, Southeastern Library, Inc., Atlanta, Georgia. The Program
is partially funded by a grant from the National Endowment for the Humanities, Office of
Preservation.

Contents

Preface

Individuals are likely to approach a book about managing institutional archives with certain presuppositions and expectations. Some individuals will search for a basic text that, in one single volume, answers all of their questions about what constitutes institutional archives and how they should be managed. This book is not intended for this purpose, at least partly because the author does not believe that this is an achievable objective. The body of archival knowledge has grown too large, and the constant change in this knowledge makes this objective difficult to achieve for any type of archival program. Nevertheless, the size and complexity of archival knowledge that should be mastered by any archivist, including institutional archivists, have certainly contributed to the length of this volume.

Others will expect to find a book that digests management theory and principles and relates them to the administration of institutional archives. There have been some noteworthy efforts at achieving exactly this goal in other fields. John Rizzo's text on library management was his "attempt to bring certain aspects of the management field to aspiring and practicing librarians. . . . On the whole the book is more about management than it is about libraries."[1] This book does not take this approach because the author is convinced that there are excellent texts on management readily available to the institutional archivist and because there has been a dearth of efforts to apply in a systematic way basic management theory to archival programs such as those found in institutional settings. Writing a book of this type requires a different approach and much more empirical research than is available.

Some individuals may approach this book hoping to discover what makes institutional archives different from, and similar to, other kinds of archival operations. This purpose is, in effect, what this book has tried to achieve. The purpose of *Managing Institutional Archives* is to articulate, in one place, what the primary foundational principles and practices are for institutional archives. By foundational principles and practices I mean those approaches that are absolutely essential to the adequate performance of an institutional archives. Many of these principles and practices are generic ones that could be applied to any archival or historical manuscript program; the requirements for a professionally trained and experienced archivist or for organizational support for the program are necessary for any kind of archival or historical manuscript repository. But some principles are uniquely important to institutional archives. For instance, it is, in this author's opinion, axiomatic that a successful institutional archives must be closely connected to an organizational records management approach to enable suitable identification of archival records as well as the best maintenance of these records. This necessity is not at all the case with repositories that collect historical manuscripts based on some geographical or topical or other scheme.

Managing Institutional Archives is an effort to serve as a basic beginning point for individuals facing the development of institutional archives or for organizations considering what should be involved in the commencement of internal archives programs. The book provides advice on the basic functions of an institutional archives—administration; appraisal; preservation and security; arrangement, description, and reference; building internal and external support; and cooperative opportunities. All of these have been presented with specific examples from institutional archives. The final part of the book presents three case studies in the initial development of institutional archives that summarize the problems and challenges facing these kinds of programs; the concluding chapter presents some sources for further assistance to the institutional archivist.

Some people might ask why a book that focuses on institutional archives is necessary. The answer here is very simple. Peter Drucker began his classic text on management with the following: "During the last fifty years, society in every developed country has become a society of institutions. . . . On the performance of these institutions, the performance of modern society—if not the survival of each individual—increasingly depends."[2] It is equally true that the archivist's quest to document society is dependent on the formation of viable institutional archives. Collecting repositories do not possess the space and other resources to acquire the voluminous archival records of even a small portion of the important institutions in our society. The modern archival profession must work to persuade these institutions to establish archival programs that meet acceptable professional standards, allow reasonable access to their records to outside researchers, and make a commitment to ensuring the survival of the archival records of these organizations. It is hoped that this book will be a useful tool in this work.

Readers of this volume will note that this book is based largely upon North American, primarily U.S., archival practice. The reason is, of course, the author's professional experience in, and knowledge of, this aspect of archival theory and practice. But there is another reason; there is no clear sense of an archival system in the United States. As a result, in this nation the development of institutional archives is completely voluntary and, in some sectors, a virtual rarity. The archival profession has failed to make persuasive arguments that lead to regulations or, as would be more welcome in the United States, incentives that protect the portion of this nation's documentary heritage located in private and public organizations and institutions. This book is an effort to draw more attention to this issue and need. Archivists from other nations will have to evaluate whether the statements, arguments, and cases in this book are relevant to their own settings. If they are, it is hoped that this book will be useful. If they are not, it is hoped that this book will stimulate discussion that will benefit the international archival community.

This book derives from work that the author has been involved in during his 20-year archival career. His first professional responsibility was in a private historical society charged with the mandate of documenting a state's historical development. During these early years the author was involved most often in salvaging archival records from institutions that had gone out of operation or that viewed these records as "old stuff" needing to be disposed of as expeditiously as possible. These experiences awakened the author to the problems of collecting repositories dealing with the voluminous and complex records of modern institutions.

The author's subsequent work in municipal and state government archives provided other opportunities to consider the nature of modern documentation. For reasons explained in chapter 1, this book does not examine state and local government archives, but there were many lessons learned from working with such documentation that went into the writing of this book. The nature of modern documentation cuts across institutional boundaries.

The most relevant origin of writing this book has been the author's experiences in consulting with a variety of organizations about the creation of records management and archives programs and the preparation of a self-study guide for historical records repositories. Consulting with educational, government, professional, and other kinds of institutions has provided a chance to consider the needs of these organizations in establishing operations that manage their records and information systems in a better way. It has also led the author to conclude that a book of this type would be a useful addition to the archival literature. These consulting lessons are incorporated throughout the text and in chapter 9 on the three institutional case studies. The responsibility of preparing a self-study guide for historical records repositories enabled the author to consider what an archival program is or should be. It was a logical next step to relate what was learned in this process to a specific kind of archival program. The nature of this process has been more directly discussed in chapter 8.

The writing of such a book would not have been possible without the assistance of many individuals. As I mentioned above, the immediate impetus for writing this book derived from my work on the historical records program's self-study guide while at the New York State Archives and Records Administration from 1986 to late 1988. Numerous discussions with individuals such as Bruce Dearstyne, Larry Hackman, and Margaret Hedstrom were extremely helpful in my thinking about such matters. Other archivists through the years have served as useful sounding boards for my thinking, often corrected my ideas that had strayed considerably far afield, and provided useful criticism that has proved helpful to me. At the risk of omitting the names of some of these individuals, I would especially like to thank David Bearman, Ed Bridges, Paul Conway, Charles Dollar, Luciana Duranti, Terry Eastwood, Tim Ericson, Larry McCrank, Avra Michelson, Jim O'Toole, and Helen Samuels. Others have noticed my habit of collecting anything about archival management, theory, and practice and have taken it upon themselves to keep me generously supplied with articles, reports, and studies. Frank Evans has, for example, regularly sent me such materials. Over the past three years encounters with students have also helped me to try to clarify my thinking; while there are too many to thank, a few readily come to mind, including Rebecca Albitz, Naomi Nelson, and Steve Wagner. My brief sojourn at the University of Pittsburgh School of Library and Information Science has also proved to be a most hospitable environment for writing and research. This environment has been even more pleasurable because of individuals like Toni Carbo Bearman, Mary Margaret Kimmel, Stephen Almagno, Christinger Tomer, Tom Wall, Ellen Detlefsen, and Edie Rasmussen. Chapter 7 was given special attention by Anne Wordsworth, an expert on library cooperation and networking. To all of these people, I express gratitude for their willingness to use their time for discussing matters with me.

A special acknowledgment must be made to Lynn and Emma, who continue to be tolerant of the numerous projects I undertake. Both possess an uncanny sense of humor that gets me through the rough spots and times.

NOTES

1. John Rizzo, *Management for Librarians: Fundamentals and Issues* (Westport, CT: Greenwood Press, 1980), xiii.

2. Peter Drucker, *Management: Tasks, Responsibilities, Practices* (New York: Harper and Row, 1974), 3.

1

Why Institutional Archives Are Important

POPULAR CONCEPTIONS OF ARCHIVES AND ARCHIVISTS

In seeing a book about something as seemingly esoteric as institutional archives, many people already have some preconceived notions about the nature of its subject matter. Some of these individuals may also be responsible managers in important corporations and institutions. Their preconceptions may, unfortunately, threaten records that have inestimable value to their institutional creators and to society because of a lack of awareness about the nature and benefits of institutional archives and the specialists that staff such programs.

Without question, archives and archivists conjure up a variety of images in the public mind, not all of them flattering or accurate, fostered by popular literature, motion pictures and television, and other media. Archives are often viewed as records that are old, decaying, and musty. Archives are written in indecipherable, ancient scripts on yellowing scraps of paper. They are perceived to be treasures waiting to be discovered or nuisances, jumbled in basements or piled high in attics. The following exchange between a fictional detective and a suspect in a case captures some of the popular ideas held about archives and their custodians:

"Yes, sir. Of course, sir. I will make inquiries. And then see what sort of records [read archives] we've got downstairs."

"The wrong sort," rejoined Leeyes gloomily. "Bound to be. A note of everyone who's ridden a bicycle without a rear light for the last fifty years or who parked their horse and cart badly and nothing more useful." In a flash the superintendent was astride another hobby horse. "That's the trouble with records. You never know which to keep. File one lot and you've got them cluttering up the place for years. Chuck 'em out and someone wants them the next morning."

"Yes, sir." No one could say that the prospect of a Records job carried much appeal to a working detective inspector.[1]

Archives are associated with other relics of the past and provoke curiosity but have uncertain value except as reminders of a bygone era. In this day of thriving auction houses and astronomical prices for antiques and collectibles, some see archives as revenue sources and hope that a newly discovered letter or diary by an important historical figure will surface. The sensational story of the forgery of the Hitler diaries or the lurid murders surrounding fabrications of Mormon-related documents are recent examples of the unfortunate kind of attention the public often gives historical records or archives.[2] In a public mind filled with images of archaeologists seeking mystical objects and fighting stereotypically evil Nazis, it is not surprising that archivists will stir up confused Hollywood-like notions of stodgy records clerks and scholarly museum curators.

Archivists bring to mind certain other stereotypes. The detective inspector's revulsion at the thought of a records job is not atypical of how archivists are seen by many sectors of the public and individuals in responsible management positions in organizations. They are bookish and introverted. Archivists are elderly and bespectacled. They possess the same musty odor as their records. Archivists worship old things, some have suggested, only because they are old. They long to be in an earlier time and seek company with their records for comfort and solace. They are pack rats, or, as archivist David Gracy found in one *New York Times* editorial, they are "squirrels . . . to pick up and put away the evidence of our passage through the centuries."[3] Archivists, even worse, are invisible! In one of Robert Ludlum's popular thrillers, a federal agent does surveillance disguised as a staff member of the government archives. He wore an "official-looking identification pinned to his breast pocket . . . stamped with the seal of the Department of Archives. No one questioned it; no one knew what it meant."[4]

These popular perceptions of archives and archivists are, of course, disturbingly inaccurate. Archivists and the records they administer are essential to institutions if those institutions desire to be healthy and well managed. A company without access to its historical records is in the same position as a person suffering from memory lapses; while both can function, neither can do so as well as desired. Institutional archives are also crucial to society's ability to understand its development and the nature of current

A Comprehensive Analysis of the Archivist's Image

In a major study of the images held by resource allocators (those who employ and/or control the financial and other resources available for archivists), the following characteristics emerged:

1. Archivists are respected as skilled people with strong motivation.
2. They come from diverse backgrounds. They are generally liberal arts people, often with training in history and library science, particularly; and other course work in the humanities.
3. Courses in archival work would be useful, certification seems less important. Allocators are content with archivists learning by doing.
4. Personal qualities, skills, talents stand out:
   a. Appreciation of history
   b. A detective-like curiosity
   c. Patience with details
   d. A strong sense of organization
   e. Ability to work in solitude and confinement
   f. Desire and ability to serve various people
   g. Skill with preservation and repair
5. Intrinsic work satisfaction is expected to be high.
   a. Important work, touched with immortality
   b. Intellectual challenge
   c. Joy of discovery
   d. Pride in publication
   e. Gratification in being of service
6. Resource allocators say archivists are just people, with varied personalities, BUT . . .
   a. They are scholarly
   b. They have cultural interests
   c. They are apt to be introverted, bookworms, quiet and mousey
   d. They are amazingly good at finding what one wants from the archives
   e. They may be territorial and possessive, ambivalent about sharing and serving.
7. Archivists' impact on organizational policy is thought to be moderate. Archivists are middle range professionals - not oriented to growth positions, management roles, or organizational power.
8. Their status is respected and judged by allocators to be satisfactory. It would be nice if they got more money and recognition, but resource allocators do not see archivists as being dealt with inappropriately.

Summarizing the situation, it may be said that it is one weighted with "niceness" - the archivists having the impotence of virtue, which is expected to be its own reward, leaving the allocators to address themselves to more pressing concerns.

Social Research Inc., The Image of Archivists: Resource Allocators' Perceptions, Study 722/01 (Chicago: Society of American Archivists, 1984), ii-iii.

concerns and issues. Destruction of the sacramental records of a church, as just one example, might rob an individual of the opportunity to discover links in his or her family lineage, negate the possibility of a historical researcher's understanding the significance of religion in an earlier time, or lessen a medical researcher's chances to make important connections in research on a genetically caused disease.

THE VALUES OF ARCHIVES AND ARCHIVISTS

Regardless of their source, popular images of archives and archivists do not properly convey their importance to institutions. Archives, the portion of recorded information that possesses continuing value to its creators and society, are one of the most valuable commodities produced by institutions, even exceeding the costly investment made in their creation. At Nabisco Brands, over 1,600 original oil paintings, watercolors, and other illustrations by American artists such as Norman Rockwell, N. C. Wyeth, and James Montgomery Flagg, originally commissioned for use in advertising the company's products, were discovered in the company's archives; these materials proved to be a boon for the company's public relations department, as well as, of course, being essential for documenting the careers of these important artists.[5] Other companies have found their archives to be important for a variety of reasons. An article in the *Wall Street Journal* described the following:

A major financial-services firm, looking for a new CEO [chief executive officer], spent several months and thousands of dollars collecting and analyzing information on past successful executive searches. This information could have been at management's fingertips in well-run archives. Business archives also provide easier access to critical information needed by management in litigation, sales, acquisitions, and for sound managerial judgment.[6]

Archives are important to institutions because a knowledge of history is essential for internal communications and for solutions to problems. One CEO observed: "It is always hard to communicate any sort of abstract idea to someone else, let alone get any acceptance of it. But when there is some agreement on the factual or historical background of that idea, the possibilities for general agreement expand enormously. . . . Historical work . . . can help provide semantic abbreviations that, in turn, facilitate communication." This same CEO also said that "if you don't have this kind of idea or historical perspective, there is an enormous temptation to make a managerial mistake that could be financially traumatic—and to make it simply by using aspiration instead of reality in the decision framework."[7] The needed historical perspective is possible only if the institution's archives are available for consultation.

The Value of Hospital Archives

The general lack of archival activity in Canadian hospitals can be attributed to a number of causes, most notable of which is the fact that there are far more pressing concerns when attempting to deliver quality health care with diminishing resources . . . . At the same time, the preservation of archival records should not be dismissed out of hand. Some of the information in these records can be used to assist hospital staff in various activities designed to support the provision of quality care.

[V]irtually all possess records of archival value. They exist in various locations, ranging from framed incorporation certificates hanging in the foyer or original board minutes in individual desks, to old policy manuals in the basement and correspondence from government officials in the bottom drawers of filing cabinets. Together, these records document the history of the hospital . . . .

When it comes to the use of archival records, most people understand how history can be used outside the hospital to produce various popular works and academic studies. However, history can be used equally effectively within the institution to the potential benefit of both hospital staff and members of the community . . . .

[M]ost Canadian hospitals use archival records to support various promotional activities . . . . The publication of a hospital history, usually associated with some milestone, would be all but impossible without access to archival records, as would biographies of early medical, nursing and administrative pioneers. Archival holdings . . . are also eminently suited for use in historical displays in support of anniversary celebrations, special events, or simply to generate awareness of the hospital's role in the community . . . .

Perhaps the area in which archives have their greatest unrealized potential is in planning, decision making, and policy formulation . . . . If records are transferred systematically, the archives will preserve a complete picture of the operation of the hospital over time. As a result, the information contained in these records will be of use whenever plans and decisions have to be made.

Robin G. Keirstead, "Hospital Archives Revisited: History at Work," Dimensions in Health Service 65, no. 4 (May 1988): 21-22. Reprinted by permission of the Canadian Hospital Association.

Institutional archives possess a variety of important values for the institution and, indeed, all of society. Archives protect the legal rights of the institution as well as individuals. Institutional archives are used to protect the institution's ownership of property. An international financial institution regularly consults its archives to ensure that it is complying with various government and business regulations. The archival records of hospitals are used to protect themselves from unjust medical malpractice suits. In a litigious society such as ours, this value of institutional archives alone justifies their existence and support.

Institutional archives are also essential to the administrative continuity of an organization. Archives of a religious congregation were used to assist the refurbishing of its historic church building. The archival records of a major hospital were used to track trends in health care and costs in order to project future costs for planning and policy-making. When the head of Wells Fargo and Company was asked why he had established a corporate archives, he said it was a simple decision: "He used to attend meetings and listen to people discuss what they *thought* had happened. He wanted a place he could call to get some facts." He had learned that "one of the facts of corporate life is that people frequently head off in one direction—through transfers, promotions, departures—and the memory and records of what happened on a project head off in another."[8] Not only is institutional or corporate memory important to institutions today, but it was a motivator for the development of ancient archives. Hecataeus, writing a history of the Trojan War, collected reminiscences of the poets and priests as well as local traditions. The first sentence of his 490 B.C. account stated, "I write down what I consider to be true, for the things that the poets tell us are in my opinion full of contradictions and worthy to be laughed out of court."[9] Hecataeus and the CEO of Wells Fargo had a lot in common.

The archival records of institutions are also important for individuals and institutions in their coping with current issues, needs, and problems and provide a sense of institutional and individual place and identity in the modern world. The rebuilding of a major urban area, for example, has turned up the ruins of older, long lost buildings. Institutional records of water utilities have been successfully utilized by urban archaeologists to determine what these older structures were, as well as to protect the historic sites from unnecessary destruction. University archives have been examined to help locate the storage of deadly toxic wastes. The older records of a hospital have been used to conduct studies on the cost of health care and the social and personal impact of these costs. Institutional archives of a large financial firm are used in that organization's new employee orientation program, giving these employees a better sense of the bank's history. The archives of an urban university with a relatively recent date of origin have been drawn upon for a variety of uses because the campus is new and the students seek some sense of tradition.

Institutional archives also contribute to the education and personal enrichment of the organization's employees and of other individuals. Institutional archives have been used for writing and staging plays, making motion pictures, and scripting radio broadcasts. These historical records have also been used for the development of educational packets for use in elementary and secondary schools. "Exposure to primary [archival] sources," wrote one individual experienced in this use of archival materials, "can help students learn the historical, critical thinking, and social skills necessary . . . to prepare students to be informed, thoughtful participants in society."[10] Local history and its reliance on archival records provide individuals with a "sense of identity," important in a society nearly shaken apart in the wake of Vietnam and Watergate.[11] As one cultural historian has written: "The vision of the past and its interpretation do not belong to the historian alone, nor are they simple issues for classroom discussion. . . . In Western society history is culturally important. It will continue to be used, mythically or ideologically, whether we like it or not. Man will insist on a historical view and he will use it, come what may, to help him determine his present and his future."[12] Archives, including those of institutions, are essential for an accurate and informed view of the past.

If none of the above reasons for institutional archives seems compelling, then these operations' importance for identifying and preserving records necessary for historical and other essential research ought to be enough. Not all records with archival value can be collected by historical societies, libraries, and universities. Since such records may be required at any time to meet the needs and interests of individuals and institutions, then the creators of such records must play a greater role in their preservation and management. It has been written that we do not "study history because of its utility or because it can tell [us] how to perform a job or what to do. History . . . is the record of [our] past, and we study it partly out of curiosity, partly out of a deep need to search out our origins, and partly because we feel we should know where we have been to get some idea of where we are going."[13] History cannot help us if there are no records to study and understand it. Without institutional archives, a significant portion of our documentary heritage will be inaccessible, or even lost forever. Whether institutional archives are used to document the history of a specific institution, assist a scholar to understand important historical trends and events, or enable an individual to identify an ancestor or learn the reasons for certain occurrences in his or her local community, institutional archives are vital to our society and its inhabitants.

WHO ARE ARCHIVISTS? WHAT ARE INSTITUTIONAL ARCHIVES?

Institutional records with the kinds of archival values described above will be lost to their creators and to others if institutions fail to establish formal archival programs, hire competent professional archivists, and provide adequate financial and other resources. Both archivists and archival programs will be described in detail throughout this book, but first it is important to mention the qualifications archivists should have and the standards that programs should meet in order to set the proper context for considering the nature, development, and benefits of institutional archives.

Professional archivists have been formally educated in graduate archival education programs generally located in either library and information

The Archives of Advertising Firms

Some records need to be carefully maintained for purely legal reasons. Papers of incorporation, partnership agreements, licenses, contracts, annual reports, board of directors' minutes and the like must be kept as a condition of the incorporation laws of most states. Many of these items must be kept for the life of the company.

Perhaps more importantly, records of an archival nature should be maintained because of their great value to the day-to-day operating management. Records which allow for the easy identification of previous marketing strategies and tactics can serve a number of functions for the account executive or creative teams working on a client's account. They serve as an excellent source of material to rapidly brief a new member of an account team. They permit a long-term continuity of marketing strategy, as opposed to changes in direction with every change in personnel. They can be a source and stimulus for both copy and art ideas. Lastly, and perhaps most importantly, they allow for the accumulation of knowledge about the product, its consumers and its promotion, thereby permitting advertising efforts to become increasingly effective. This accumulated information prevents redundancy of efforts so that researchers need not gather virtually identical information repeatedly, or creative teams need not reinvent the wheel.

These practical uses of material of an archival nature are often overlooked . . . . This ahistorical attitude is especially unfortunate since the potential value of historical case material is underscored by the impact of the relatively high rate of turnover among advertising personnel in both the agency and the client's offices, and by the fact that client company records are often notoriously poor on advertising matters.

Richard W. Pollay, "Maintaining Archives for the History of Advertising," Special Libraries 69 (April 1978): 149. Reprinted from Special Libraries, 69, no. 4 (April 1978): 145-54. c. by Special Libraries Association.

---

science schools or history departments. They have a command of archival principles and practices, and, more recently, many have been certified by the Academy of Certified Archivists. Contrary to what some organizations seem to think, archivists are not institutional employees with seniority, librarians maintaining reference book collections and online information systems, records or files clerks, or public relations staffs.[14] Although all of these individuals are valuable for the management of institutional archives, they are not the professionals that should direct such programs. Graduate archival education programs that prepare individuals to function as professional archivists can be identified by contacting the Society of American Archivists' Office of Education, which maintains a directory of those programs that meet that association's minimum guidelines for such programs, as well as other schools that offer basic, introductory course work.

Archivists are also characterized by their basic knowledge and experience. Among other things, these individuals are able to identify which records possess continuing value and should be retained, arrange and describe these records so that they can be effectively used by their creators and other researchers, ensure that these valuable records are secure and preserved for long-term use, provide access to these records as needed, promote interest in their use, and see that their programs are adequately managed and possess the necessary resources for optimal care of the archival records.

The Academy of Certified Archivists (ACA) is another way to identify individuals who are well educated and sufficiently experienced in archival administration. Although, at this time, individuals certified by this organization will be more likely those that fill middle or upper administrative positions in institutional archives, entry-level archivists will seek certification after a sufficient period of professional experience is added to their academic preparation. Since the ACA has been in existence only since 1989, the hiring of certified archivists will be a difficult process for some time; however, institutions should encourage and support their archivists to prepare for and successfully pass the certification examination as a measure of their competence.[15]

Institutional archives programs have sometimes been considered to be little more than the accumulation of a few select documents, like a company charter or letter written by a famous person, collections of published reports, and institutional mementos, such as the shovel used to break ground for the construction of the corporate headquarters. These are not, of course, "programs," nor are they sufficient for the identification, preservation, and use of institutional records having archival value. The next chapter will provide a detailed description of what an institutional archives operation should consist of, but for now it is sufficient to state that these programs are staffed by professionals, work in conjunction with institutional records managers, librarians, and information systems managers, have sufficient facilities for the storage, preservation, and use of archival records, and are considered to be important to the ongoing operation of the organization. Institutional archives are programs that care for and make available for use the records identified to have value primarily for the institutions; that these programs also serve a broader public role in preserving historical information of more general interest only attests to the value of the archival records.

Institutional archives can be considered to be closest in origin and purpose to what the library profession terms "special libraries." These are libraries with "relatively small collections ... carefully defined clienteles ... [and] an explicit and sharply focused mission." In the United States, these libraries date back to the eighteenth century in hospitals, theological seminaries, law offices, historical societies, scientific and medical societies, universities, businesses, and governments. Their growth has been tremen-

A Definition of An Archivist

What is an archivist?

An archivist is a professional who is responsible for the management of important records. Five basic activities define an archivist's function. Archivists:

Appraise. They determine which records are permanently valuable and should be retained. Often they work closely with key administrators and records managers in making these decisions;

Acquire. After deciding which material should be kept, they add it to the organization's archives;

Arrange and describe. Following established archival principles, archivists refine the order of the files and then prepare finding aids which enable users to locate material;

Preserve. Preservation encompasses a wide range of activities, including the simple storage of materials in safe areas with controlled climates, the transfer of files to acid-free folders and boxes, special handling of individual pages, and consultation with professional conservators on preservation treatment;

Provide access and reference service. Whether the archives are open to the public, to a limited category of researchers or scholars, or only to the staff of the organization, the archivist makes the holdings of the archives available to the individuals who need to use them.

Professional archivists combine the talents and abilities of information specialists, librarians, editors, records managers, conservators, researchers and historians. The archivist . . . should have specific experience related to [the] institution's concerns.

What to look for

Most . . . archivists now working combine a masters degree with work experience and professional involvement. The complexity and requirements of the job will determine the level of experience, education and professional activity necessary . . .

Archivists Round Table of Metropolitan New York and the Mid-Atlantic Regional Archives Conference, Selecting an Archivist (1985).

A Comparison of Institutional Archives and Historical Records Repositories

Institutional Archives		Historical Records Repositories
Administrative Uses to Records Creator	*Purpose*	Cultural, Research, and Educational Uses
Records Management (Retention and Disposition Schedule)	*Acquisition*	Collecting Policy and Program
Focus on Internal Policy and Other Administrative Functions	*Reference*	Focus on Research Community
Varies: Executive Office, Public Relations, Information Management Unit, etc.	*Placement*	Varies: Separate Unit, Part of Library, or Special Collections, etc.

dous since the late nineteenth century, a growth evident by the organization of the Special Libraries Association in 1909 and the flourishing of this association since then. Many of these libraries encompassed the kinds of materials also located in archives. Business libraries started out as accumulations of company records and reports and expanded to include technical and specialized reference works related to the company's particular frame of reference.[16] Not surprisingly, many of these special libraries have expanded to include institutional archives or have been called upon to assist with their organizational archivists and records managers in caring for records. Institutional archivists will need to work with the administrators of special libraries in order to ensure that an organization's information needs are met.

Institutional archives programs are also very close in function to records management operations. Although records management has a long and interesting intellectual origin, the modern form of organizational records management emanated from modern government records needs and concerns about a half-century ago. In fact, records management practices and theories were pioneered primarily by the working archivists seeking means to manage voluminous quantities of documentation and to identify that portion possessing archival value. Despite this intellectual archival parent, the records managers have developed their own professional attributes, and, as a result, in many institutions archives and records management programs have tended to develop independently or in isolation. The need is often, therefore, to bring the two operations together within institutions or to establish and nurture the component that is absent. Institutional archives will find it difficult to function properly without records management, and vice versa.

TYPES OF INSTITUTIONAL ARCHIVES

Although institutional archives share a common mission to identify, preserve, manage, and make accessible the records of their institutions possessing archival value, they vary greatly in structure, resources, conditions, and administrative placement. The institutional archives of businesses, colleges and universities, museums, religious organizations, labor unions, and libraries reflect these similarities and differences.

Business Archives

One of the most readily identifiable institutional archives is the business or corporate archives. These organizational archives date back to the early twentieth century, when the interest in collecting manuscripts documenting the history of business began on a limited basis. The initial efforts were part of a rise of a scholarly business history research community. This community soon realized that collecting by institutions like the Baker Library at Harvard University was not sufficient to preserve the voluminous records created by the corporations. By the late 1930s, there were efforts to convince the companies to establish legitimate corporate archives. A decade later, the first of such institutional archives began to be formed. In 1943, Firestone Tire and Rubber Company established an archives, primarily to document its wartime activities. Other companies, like Time, Inc. and Eastman Kodak, also created archival programs.

Despite the relatively early origins of corporate archives, their growth has been slow and their numbers remain low. Thirty years ago, only 12 large companies employed professional archivists. By the early 1980s there were approximately 200 business archives employing around 60 corporate archivists, still a somewhat small portion of the corporate world as well as of the archival community. The reasons for this slow growth, despite the tremendous values to the companies of preserving such records, are several. The early emphasis on collecting business archival records and on establishing institutional archives consistently stressed their historical importance. Cost-conscious executives were slow to be won over by such limited arguments. Surprisingly, the rise of corporate records management, with its emphasis on cost effectiveness and information retrieval efficiency and its theoretical inclusion of archival administration as a basic function, worked against the development of institutional archives in the business world. Records management came to concentrate its energies on the administration of current or semicurrent records, and the split between the records management practitioners and the archivists in the 1950s and 1960s only accentuated this viewpoint. The more recent growth of institutional archives since the 1970s resulted from the combined rise in historical consciousness derived from the celebration of the American bicentennial, the increasing occurrence of important corporate anniversaries, a more active advocacy by public or applied historians and archivists, the increasing number of lawsuits requiring the use of older records, and the recognition of other uses for archival records in public relations, marketing, and the like.[17]

College and University Archives

Colleges and universities, both public and private, have long been collecting historical records from outside the academy, some amassing major holdings unrivaled in importance for historical research. Ironically, colleges and universities have not devoted as much attention, until recently, to their own institutional records. The first important formal college and university archives programs—acquiring administrative records, the papers of prominent faculty members, the records of student organizations, and the like— were established about half a century ago. These programs were founded as archivists in these institutions, then usually responsible for historical manuscript collecting operations, recognized the need to acquire and preserve their own records. By the mid–1960s over 500 institutions of higher learning had some form of archival operation; by the early 1980s this number had nearly doubled. During this period of growth, college and university archivists became more prominent in national archival affairs, and a literature specifically dealing with the management of these records was developed. Today, colleges and universities represent a major employer of archivists and a source of leadership in the archival profession, despite the fact that these institutional archives are marked by great diversity in conditions, resources, holdings, and staffing.[18]

The nature of college and university archives can be gleaned from the guidelines that the Society of American Archivists adopted for these institutional archives in 1979. Among other things, these guidelines state that college and university archives' core mission is "to appraise, collect, organize, describe, make available, and preserve records of historical, legal, fiscal, and/or administrative value to their institution." Other aspects of the core mission stipulate adequate facilities, information services, a resource for teaching and research, and "efficient records management." The remaining guidelines describe in detail each of the elements of this core mission.[19]

Museum Archives

Museums are well known as essential institutions for the preservation of society's cultural heritage and serve as repositories of historical artifacts and art objects. But the management of their administrative and collection records has been increasingly recognized as necessary for the security and care of their collections, so that the operation of museum archives has

A Profile of College and University Archives

[W]hat generalizations can be made about college and university archives? . . . A typical archives at a public university was established within the last 15 years on a campus whose 1979-80 enrollment was nearly 11,000 students. The archives is staffed by one full-time professional and a few student assistants and has no volunteers or personnel on grant money, but perhaps has a part-time clerical worker . . . .

The archives at this typical public university has slightly less than 1,000 cubic feet of records occupying 80 percent of the available stack space. About 20 percent of the holdings are unprocessed. Included among material housed in the archives are iconography, sound recordings, campus publications, memorabilia, faculty papers, student organization records, alumni papers, and administrative records of the institution. There is an even chance that the archives also is responsible in part for records management. The archives is supervised and open to patrons 40 hours a week with students, faculty, community users, and administrators comprising the major users - in that order . . . . The archives is physically housed in, and administratively reports within, the library . . . . The staff spends most of its time on arrangement and description, reference, and appraisal, and it considers the size of the unprocessed backlog and lack of space to be its main problems.

Archives at private colleges and universities differ in some important respects from those at public institutions. The typical archives at a private institution was established more than 25 years ago on a campus whose 1979-80 enrollment was 3,000 students. While the archives may not be staffed by a fulltime professional, the person in charge of the archives on a part-time basis has more formal education than his public counterpart, but less archival training . . . .

While the size of holdings, percentage of unprocessed backlog, available stack space, and kinds of material collected do not differ from those of public institutions, the ranking of patron usage is different, with students and administrators making nearly equal use of the collections, followed by outside patrons and faculty . . . . Environmental and safety controls are generally comparable with those of public institutions, and, as with public ones, the archives in private institutions report to, and are housed within, the library. The private institution has no records management program. The staff spends most of its time on the same major activities as its public counterparts, but a somewhat larger proportion of time on reference. On other matters private institutions appear to share the same general characteristics as public institutions.

Nicholas C. Burckel and J. Frank Cook, "A Profile of College and University Archives in the United States," American Archivist 45 (Fall 1982): 426-28.

become part of the elements scrutinized for institutional accreditation by the Association of American Museums. Archival records have become recognized as essential for maintaining important ownership information often needed to authenticate items, charting changing physical conditions of collections, insuring the artifacts and art objects, and making it possible to loan collections to other museums. Museums that have also established current records management programs, such as the Detroit Institute of Arts, have realized other benefits; a former archivist of this institution wrote that "some of the most practical benefits of a comprehensive archival management program have included freeing limited office space of inactive records, demonstrating to the staff that its past records will continue to be accessible in the future, consolidating the purchase of filing and copying equipment and helping the staff develop efficient recordkeeping practices."[20]

The Detroit Institute of Arts, in the process of establishing an archives program, also discovered many valuable records "scattered in unexpected places throughout the building," including Diego Rivera's working drawings for some important frescoes. Other museums have also discovered the benefits of museum archives operations. William Deiss's manual on museum archives chronicled such progress:

Over the past several years museum archives have been used by an increasing number of administrators and curators as well as other scholars. In one instance the director of an anthropological museum in a large eastern city used his museum's archives to learn why a municipal appropriation to the museum had been eliminated several years earlier. Armed with the historical data found in the archives the museum administrators planned to try to regain the funding. Curators at the St. Louis Art Museum found that some records dealing with purchases of works of art a few decades ago had not been preserved in the curatorial files. A search of the archives yielded the needed information in ledgers produced by the business office.[21]

Interest in museum archives has been a very recent development. It was only little more than a decade ago that individuals interested in museum records first gathered to discuss plans for remedying the care of these documents. In 1981 the Society of American Archives established its first museum archives task force, three years later published a basic manual for the administration of such institutional archives, and in 1986 authorized the formation of a Museum Archives Round Table as a mechanism for the sharing of concerns and planning by museum archivists and others interested in the welfare of their records. These activities have reflected some growth in the establishment of museum archives and have generated new growth in such institutions as well. Federal funding from archival, humanities, and arts programs has also spurred the development of museum archives.[22]

Religious Archives

Religious archives have, perhaps, the longest history of all institutional archives in the United States. They date back to the mid-nineteenth century, when some of the major denominations established historical societies for the purpose of collecting important documents, publishing histories and biographies, and ensuring that the denomination's traditions and public image were properly maintained.[23] Like all historical societies of this early period, these organizations were indiscriminate and eclectic in their acquisition. Today, there are many hundreds of religious archives, including not only the programs of major denominations but diocesan archives, seminary and academic archives, and individual churches. In general, all of these programs have tended to concentrate on the policy and main organizational records of their institutions.[24]

Like other institutional archives, religious archives are diverse in nature, conditions, and resources. With the exception of some of the major denominations, however, these records programs often tend to be more underfunded and understaffed than most institutional archives. This situation has led to an intense effort by religious archivists to establish their own support network and continuing education programs. Individuals staffing religious archives more often tend to come to their positions first because of their previous association with the church, diocese, or denomination and then seek training in archival administration and records management. The other major difference comes in the nature of their concern with humanity's spiritual condition, a concern that sometimes leads to a preoccupation with future concerns that sometimes works against placing resources in preserving their past or managing current records. Some religious archivists have made great efforts to document functions and activities of their institutions other than merely their governance and to proselytize among the religious organizations to establish more effective and better-supported institutional archives.[25]

Other Institutional Archives

There are, of course, a tremendous number of other types of institutional archives, some more highly developed than others, partly because the preservation of their records has been handled by manuscript-collecting institutions or because their development has been arrested by other priorities. Labor archives, for example, have been more the province of large collecting programs—such as at Wayne State University, Cornell University, Temple University, the State Historical Society of Wisconsin, and Georgia State University—than of institutional archives.[26] The establishment by the AFL-CIO of the George Meany Memorial Archives in 1981 represents a departure, but even its emphasis beyond the organization's

The Nature of Religious Archives

Today there are considerably more than five hundred religious archives and historical institutions functioning at various levels. Some administer large collections, some small. Some offer an excellent range of professional services, others are no more than a closet open to the public for a few hours on an afternoon. Some have developed well-defined systems of collecting, processing, and public relations, and others seemingly still live from hand to mouth.

Diversity among religious archives is partly a legacy of collecting policies of the past. Collections frequently were accumulated by an elected church official, perhaps a secretary or clerk, who by virtue of his office happened to create or possess records. Sometimes the religious jurisdiction required maintenance of certain records. However, as the collections grew larger and their immediate practical value declined, or as one officer succeeded another, the size or geographical dispersal of such collections demanded other provisions.

Sometimes such collections of church officials were transferred to nearby church colleges or seminaries at the time of the death of the officials . . . .

In other cases, private collectors gathered records. Such efforts may have had their roots in personal or family interests. Perhaps a professor of history was engaged in research and endeavored to collect as much as possible on a given subject. . . .

Religious historical societies also contributed to the development of ecclesiastical records collections and archives. Early societies of this type were those established in the 1840s and 1850s by the Reformed Church, Presbyterians, Mormons, Lutherans, and others. All too often the group received only limited financial support from the denomination's membership, and after the first charismatic leader died, the collections fell into neglect.

In some instances, special collections were also gathered at seminary libraries, primarily because of the work or interests of professors . . . .

Collecting practices of religious archives are still diverse, but generally four basic types of agency can be identified.

* A national denominational archives that also collects considerable state or diocesan materials and even some parish records.

* A denominational archives that deals exclusively with the top administrative records of the denomination. This type does not preserve any state, diocesan, or parish records under the assumption that they are preserved on those levels. Regrettably, there is often no liaison or cooperation between such intermediate agencies.

* Active state diocesan archives within a denomination, but no denominational headquarters archives.

* The circuit or parish level, where generally little archival activity takes place.

August R. Suelflow, Religious Archives: An Introduction (Chicago: Society of American Archivists, 1980), 6-7.

administrative records is its serving as a liaison to place the records of other labor organizations in established archival repositories.[27] Library archives, as another example, have remained very underdeveloped despite the strong interest in the history of library administration. Surprisingly, the development of library archives has been somewhat slowed because of the primary interest by these institutions in collecting historical manuscripts, rare books, and other special collections materials.[28] There is, however, every likelihood that labor, library, and other institutions will increasingly establish in-house programs to manage and care for their archival materials.[29]

What about federal, state, and local government archives that manage the archival records created by these political entities? Although these archives can certainly be characterized as institutional archives in one sense, their broader public mandate, governance through legislation, and traditional activities make them far beyond the scope of the other kinds of institutional archives thus far described. Because these records are created as public records for the public good, their management and preservation take on considerably different meanings than the records of businesses and hospitals that are created primarily in the course of daily work. Traditionally such government programs have also seen themselves as public educational and research institutions, promoting the care of historical records nationally and on state and local levels. For reasons such as these, government archives, the topic of a considerable literature in its own right,[30] are beyond the scope of institutional archives being discussed in this book. It is now possible to perceive three major groups of archival institutions: collecting historical records programs, such as historical societies; government archives, such as state archives and municipal archives and records programs; and institutional archives—the subject of this book.

THE PLACE OF INSTITUTIONAL ARCHIVES IN THE ARCHIVAL COMMUNITY AND PROFESSION

Institutional archives occupy an important place in the community of repositories and programs that care for this nation's documentary heritage. Historically, the very concept of archives derives from an institutional setting; the word *archive* is from the Greek *archeion* and the Latin *archivum*, both meaning a government office and its records.[31] Not only are institutional archives, collectively, a prominent portion of the overall number of archival programs,[32] but they administer large quantities of archival records that might otherwise be lost to their institutions, researchers, and society. Although they have developed somewhat later than historical societies and government archives, institutional archives have also significantly contributed to the professional theory, practice, and leadership in the archival profession. The growth of institutional archives also represents

ARCHIVAL REPOSITORIES AND THE ARCHIVAL COMMUNITY

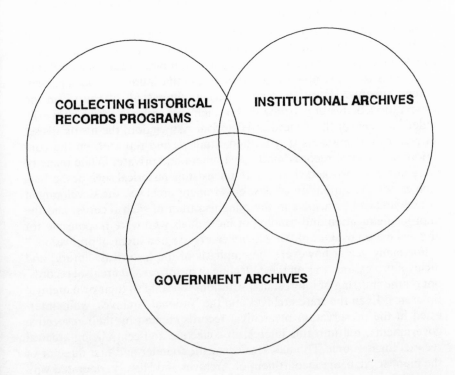

a partial shift away from some of the traditional perspectives and practices of the archival profession, which until more recent years were largely the results of the historical manuscripts and public archives traditions.

There are a number of dates that are given for the start of the American archival profession. Some say it began with the first historical societies; others, with the formation of the library and archives professional associations; and some, with the mid–1930s establishment of the National Archives and the Society of American Archivists. All these events and movements represent, in fact, important influences on the archival profession. The foundation of the first historical society in 1791 and the subsequent burst of growth of such institutions in the early decades of the nineteenth century were the ultimate manifestation of a long interest by antiquarians and scholars in the collecting and preserving of historical records and the general increasing interest in the late eighteenth and early nineteenth century in legitimizing the new nation by giving it a respectable history. All through this period and the remainder of the nineteenth century, however, there was no clear concept of an institutional archives; archives were "ancient" records, were exclusively for historical and anti-quarian research, and were to be collected by historical societies and similar organizations and individuals.

The turn of the last century introduced some important influences that would significantly change the nature of archives and archival programs. The development of professions brought with it new historical and library professions that attempted to introduce scientific study and management to their spheres. Historians were especially interested, of course, in the preservation of historical records for their research. Working primarily under the aegis of the American Historical Association, the historians set up records commissions that located, studied, and reported on the con-dition of historical records, both government and private. While many of these historians worked closely with the existing historical societies, others lobbied for the formation of new government archives, the development of new archival principles in the administration of such records, and the improved education and training of individuals who were responsible for archival materials. Out of this activity emerged a new archival profession.[33]

For many years, however, the emphasis of the historical, library, and archival professions was on the collecting of historical and archival records, not on the spurring of interest in institutions to establish their own archival programs. Even the state archives and the National Archives, while inter-ested in the preservation of archival records created by their respective governments, fell into this interest in collecting and centralizing archival records for research. Thomas M. Owen, the founder and first director of the pioneer Alabama Department of Archives and History, operated with the philosophy of "let the [archival] materials be assembled and the [his-torical] writing will take care of itself"; Owen, exerting great influence on many of the early state archives, argued that the "collection of historical materials was [the archivists'] first duty."[34] It was not surprising that such institutions not only often collected private manuscripts but clearly saw that their responsibility in preserving local government archival records was primarily through removing these records from the localities, where the records were originally created, to the state archives situated in the state capitols. Even the emergence of college and university archives, de-scribed briefly above, was less the result of an interest in preserving the records in these institutions of higher education and more the result of an interest in acquiring research materials for their faculties and the scholarly community in general; as a result, it has been only in recent years that many of these institutions of higher education have begun to try to establish comprehensive records management programs. The collecting impulse of government and other archives has continued to exert a strong influence on their operations and partially accounts for the relatively slowly emerging interest in institutional archives.

The initial establishment of institutional archives in colleges and universities, hospitals, corporations, libraries, and similar organizations resulted from a particular interest by these institutions in preserving at least some of their archival records. Why these records were maintained by the institutions themselves often had more to do with matters such as the celebration of important anniversaries, public relations, concern with confidentiality and other legal issues, or the special interests of one or more key individuals than with the modern archival profession itself. Museums established an archives to ensure that documentation was being maintained about the other collections. Corporations set up an archives to be able to draw upon it for public relations purposes. In fact, it has been only in relatively recent years that the archival profession has begun to stress the importance of the establishment of institutional archives. This relatively new interest by the archival profession has been the result of its realization that not all records with archival value can be "collected" due to their volume and their nature, a topic that will be explored in more detail later in this volume. The important point to remember, however, is that institutional archives are essential to both their parent organizations and society at large; additional evidence for their importance will come in the following chapters. Clearly, the potential growth of institutional archives in the remainder of the twentieth century possibly heralds the culmination of a third archival tradition in the United States, one working side by side with the more established historical manuscripts and public records traditions.

NOTES

1. Catherine Aird, *A Late Phoenix* (New York: Bantam Books, 1971), 829–30.

2. Robert Harris, *Selling Hitler* (New York: Penguin Books, 1987); Steven Naifeh and Gregory White Smith, *The Mormon Murders: A True Story of Greed, Forgery, Deceit, and Death* (New York: Onyx Books, 1988). For a rare analysis of how archives are treated in literature, see Peter Gillis, "Of Plots, Secrets, Burrowers and Moles: Archives in Espionage Fiction," *Archivaria* 9 (Winter 1979–1980): 3–13.

3. David B. Gracy II, "What's Your Totem? Archival Images in the Public Mind," *Midwestern Archivist* 10, no. 1 (1985): 18.

4. Robert Ludlum, *The Chancellor Manuscript* (New York: Bantam Books, 1978), 57.

5. Robert M. Finehout, "Treasure It, Don't Trash It," *Public Relations Journal* 42 (April 1986): 8.

6. Ellen NicKenzie Lawson, "Companies Plumb the Past to Protect the Present," *Wall Street Journal*, January 16, 1989, p.48.

7. Alan M. Kantrow, ed., "Why History Matters to Managers," *Harvard Business Review* 64 (January/February 1986): 82.

8. Harold P. Anderson, "Banking on the Past: Wells Fargo & Company," *Business History Bulletin* 1, no. 1 (1988): 12.

9. Herbert Butterfield, *The Origins of History*, ed. Adam Watson (New York: Basic Books, 1981), 134.

10. Kathleen Roe, *Teaching with Historical Records* (Albany: University of the State of New York, State Education Department, Office of Cultural Education, State Archives, 1981), 3.

11. Fay D. Metcalf and Matthew T. Downey, *Using Local History in the Classroom* (Nashville: American Association for State and Local History, 1982), 2.

12. Warren I. Susman, *Culture as History: The Transformation of American Society in the Twentieth Century* (New York: Pantheon Books, 1984), 49.

13. Louis Morton, "The Cold War and American Scholarship," in *The Historian and the Diplomat: The Role of History and Historians in American Foreign Policy*, ed. Francis L. Loewenheim (New York: Harper and Row, 1967), 138–39.

14. This is not to say that these individuals are sometimes not given archival responsibilities. If this situation occurs, the organization must commit to providing this individual satisfactory training in archival administration. An intelligent individual, with strong knowledge about the organization and additional archival education, can become a very competent institutional archivist.

15. At present, the institution will do best to seek an individual for archivist who has graduated from an educational program that meets graduate education guidelines of the Society of American Archivists or the Association of Canadian Archivists or who has a combination of education (both graduate and continuing) and appropriate experience or who has met the criteria for certification by the Academy of Certified Archivists.

16. The background of special libraries can be seen in Michael H. Harris, *History of Libraries in the Western World: Compact Textbook Edition* (Metuchen, NJ: Scarecrow Press, 1984), 179–83, 258–67 (quote, 180).

17. Christopher L. Hives, "History, Business Records, and Corporate Archives in North America," *Archivaria* 22 (Summer 1986): 40–57 and Julia Niebuhr Eulenberg, "The Corporate Archives: Management Tool and Historical Resource," *Public Historian* 6 (Winter 1984): 21-37 provide an excellent introduction to the development and nature of corporate archives. See also Leon Shkolnik, "The Role of the Archive in the Corporate Structure," *Records Management Quarterly* 24 (October 1990): 18–23, 57–58.

18. For an excellent overview of these programs, refer to Nicholas C. Burckel and J. Frank Cook, "A Profile of College and University Archives in the United States," *American Archivist* 45 (Fall 1982): 410–28 and J. Frank Cook, "Academic Archivists and the SAA, 1938–1979: From Arcana Siwash to the C&U PAG," *American Archivist* 51 (Fall 1988): 428–39.

19. These guidelines were published in the *American Archivist* 43 (Spring 1980): 262–71. For an indication of how well certain of the guidelines have been carried out, refer to Marjorie Rabe Barritt, "Adopting and Adapting Records Management to College and University Archives," *Midwestern Archivist* 14, no. 1 (1989): 5–12.

20. Claudia Hommel, "A Model Museum Archives," *Museum News* 58 (November/December 1979): 68.

21. William A. Deiss, *Museum Archives: An Introduction* (Chicago: Society of American Archivists, 1984), 9–10.

22. See Maygene Daniels, "Developing New Museum Archives," *Curator* 31, no. 2 (1988): 99–105; *Federal Funding for Museum Archives Development Programs: A Report to the Commission*, Commission Reports and Papers no. 2 (Washington, DC:

National Historical Publications and Records Commission, National Archives and Records Administration).

23. See, for example, Richard J. Cox, "The Origins of American Religious Archives: Ethan Allen, Pioneer Church Historian and Archivist of Maryland," *Journal of the Canadian Church Historical Society* 29 (October 1987): 48–63.

24. August R. Suelflow, *Religious Archives: An Introduction* (Chicago: Society of American Archivists, 1980) is a good review of the nature and functions of these archival institutions. There is, as well, a long and diverse literature in archival, historical, and religious journals about religious archives.

25. See, for example, Mark J. Duffy, "The Archival Bridge: History, Administration and the Building of Church Tradition," *Historical Magazine of the Protestant Episcopal Church* 55 (December 1986): 275–87 and *A Heritage at Risk: The Proceedings of the Evangelical Archives Conference July 13–15, 1988* (Wheaton, IL: Billy Graham Center, Wheaton College, 1988).

26. Thomas Connors, "The Labor Archivist and the 'Labor Question': Two Steps Forward, One Step Back," *Midwestern Archivist* 12, no. 2 (1987): 61–72.

27. Stuart B. Kaufman, "Harnessing Labor's Heritage," *American Educator* 12 (Winter 1988): 26–32.

28. See, for example, Richard J. Cox and Anne S. K. Turkos, "Establishing Public Library Archives," *Journal of Library History* 21 (Summer 1986): 574–84.

29. There are many reasons certain institutions will be unable to establish effective archives programs. For an exploration of these reasons, see David J. Klaassen, "The Archival Intersection: Cooperation Between Collecting Repositories and Nonprofit Organizations," *Midwestern Archivist* 15, no. 1 (1990): 25–38 and Dennis E. Meissner, "Corporate Records in Noncorporate Archives: A Case Study," *Midwestern Archivist* 15, no. 1 (1990): 39–50.

30. See, for example, Bruce W. Dearstyne, *The Management of Local Government Records: A Guide for Local Officials* (Nashville: American Association for State and Local Officials, 1988); H. G. Jones, *Local Government Records: An Introduction to Their Management, Preservation, and Use* (Nashville: American Association for State and Local History, 1980); and Ernst Posner, *American State Archives* (Chicago: University of Chicago Press, 1964). There is also a large literature on specifics of government archives in archival and related journals.

31. For an understanding of the origins of the concept of archives, see Ernst Posner, *Archives in the Ancient World* (Cambridge: Harvard University Press, 1972).

32. Academic, business, religious, and museum archives, for example, account for 66 percent of the archival institutions; Paul Conway, "Perspectives on Archival Resources: The 1985 Census of Archival Institutions," *American Archivist* 50 (Spring 1987): 179.

33. For early influences on the development of the archival profession, see William F. Birdsall, "The Two Sides of the Desk: The Archivist and the Historian, 1909–1935," *American Archivist* 38 (April 1975): 159–73, and William F. Birdsall, "Archivists, Librarians, and Issues During the Pioneering Era of the American Archival Movement," *Journal of Library History* 14 (Fall 1979): 457–79.

34. Quoted in Richard J. Cox, "Alabama's Archival Heritage, 1850–1985," *Alabama Review* (October 1987): 291.

2

The Foundation for Administering Institutional Archives

ESSENTIAL ELEMENTS FOR MANAGING INSTITUTIONAL ARCHIVES

As this volume will demonstrate, there are many important and essential aspects to the management of institutional archives. Many of these are common to the administration of all archives programs, indeed, to many other organizational forms, because there are certain common aspects to all management.[1] There is, however, a core group of elements that are absolutely essential to the competent management of institutional archives programs. One archivist has stated that "administration is the art of making things work,"[2] and these elements are essential to making institutional archives work. The purpose of this chapter is to review these aspects; they will also be discussed at various other points throughout this volume, along with other important elements of running such programs.

The essential elements for managing institutional archives (indeed, for all archival programs) are as follows:

- mission statement
- adequate financial resources
- written procedures for caring for the archival records
- professional archivist
- in-service and continuing education commitment

- adequate facility for storage and use of archival records
- cooperative programs with other archival operations.

Not only does acquisition of these elements provide suitable objectives for an institutional archives, but, once implemented, these elements will ensure that the program is properly functioning and the valuable records are being identified, preserved, and made available for use.

The successful acquisition of these elements will also indicate that the institutional archives operation has gained the necessary support from its parent organization and that organization's governing body. It is unfortunate that many organizations set up in-house archives programs that are underfunded and undersupported because of unclear notions of what these programs need or because of inadequate perceptions of their values and appropriate range of activities. The basic elements that are described in this chapter will be gained only if there are clear endorsement and support from the top of the institution; indeed, without such support it is inadvisable for an institutional archives to be established, and the institution should seek some other alternative action for the care of its historical records.[3] Continuance of these elements will occur only if the institution's top managers are able to understand and relate the values and benefits of their archives to the continuing functioning of their organization. One of the chief responsibilities of the head of the institutional archives will be ensuring that this program continues to play an important role and have a prominent profile in the institution; this responsibility will be described in chapter 6.[4] The governing board also has a responsibility because of its concern for the overall management of the organization. The initial establishment of an institutional archives is successful only if the archives program is able to continue in a fashion that guarantees that its archival records will be properly maintained.

The half-dozen areas selected as essential for establishing and maintaining an effective institutional archives program are the result of the author's experience as an archivist in historical, municipal, and state government archives, consulting work with institutional archives, and a general consensus about such matters in the archival profession. The author's involvement with a wide variety of archives, both as administrator and consultant, has served to convince him of the relevance of these particular elements. Other experienced archivists might select other elements as also essential, such as the inclusion of a records management program or specific staffing arrangements, but these have been discussed elsewhere in this volume for reasons that will be explained. Suffice it to say that the elements discussed in this chapter will aid any institutional archives to get off to a good start. The archival profession has also been moving toward a more specific definition of the basics of institutional archives and other archives programs, although there are still a wide range of opinion and needed research necessary for improving the knowledge about such programs. The Society of American Archivists' (SAA) recent completion of the work of the Task Force on Institutional Evaluation, with publication of a self-study manual for archival programs, is best indicative of such needed efforts.[5] The development within the archival profession of an interest in management has also been reflected in the recent establishment of an SAA Management Round Table, expanding number of sessions at professional meetings devoted to management issues, and proposals for management education and training.[6] The entire content of this volume, however, builds on the work of such bodies as this task force, the experience of this author, and the experience of other archivists to lay out an agenda for strengthening institutional archives.

MISSION STATEMENT

A mission statement of any organization, including an archives, is a fairly straightforward matter to describe. This statement is a written expression of the nature, scope, functions, and rationale for existence of an institutional archives. While mission statements can be fairly simple in appearance and brief in length, they serve important purposes for the archives operation and, because of their importance, can be difficult to prepare and approve. Their difficulty in preparation stems not only from the need to possess a clear notion of the program but from the often frequent inability of many individuals to agree about the archival program's main purposes and range of responsibilities. As the SAA self-study guide on archival programs enunciates, a basic principle of administering any archives program is possessing "explicit documentation of an archives' legal status and authority" and "a formal statement of its purpose."[7] In fact, without a carefully thought out, well-constructed mission statement, the chances for the development and functioning of an effective institutional archives program are severely limited. A leading Canadian archivist has stated that "without a clear mandate [mission] statement, an archives cannot function consistently over an extended time. Pressure will constantly be brought to bear on the organization to take on responsibilities which may not have been intended when it was established."[8]

What purposes and benefits does a mission statement serve for the institutional archives? A mission statement should succinctly present the primary reasons for the program's existence, describe the scope and audience of the archives' activities, explain the relationship between the archives and its parent institution, and set forth the reasons for acquiring and maintaining historical records. An institutional archives mission statement should also clearly specify its parameters and relationships with other information managers in the organization; its success in identifying and preserving the information of archival value will be at least partially de-

Example of Mission Statement
for Institutional Archives

Mission statements can be brief and generally descriptive of an institutional archives' purpose and activities. One example for a business archives is as follows:

The Chase Manhattan Archives, established in 1975, is a secure central repository where records of Chase having permanent value are preserved, maintained and made available for research and reference use.

The Archives collection includes non-current records of The Chase Manhattan Corporation, The Chase Manhattan Bank, N.A., and their predecessors, that have lasting administrative, legal, or historical value.

Quoted from the brochure describing the Chase Manhattan Archives.

---

termined by cooperation with institutional librarians, data processors, records managers, and other information professionals.[9] This kind of mission statement is especially important since information, which is the business of the institutional archivist, is at the heart of the organization's operation. To be valid, a mission statement must reflect and fit into the parent institution's broader mission; using the institution's articles of incorporation and policy directives and being aware of its tradition and history will ensure that a relevant statement is produced.

Such a statement is not just an exercise in bureaucratic activity but assists the institutional archives in a variety of important ways. A mission statement provides needed information about the archives' role for the organization's governing board, employees, resource allocators, and the research community. Since the governing board must approve such a mission statement, the board's involvement should clarify its notion of intended scope and likely resources it will receive or should be able to request. Communication about the institutional archives by publicizing the mission statement to the organization's employees will not only make these individuals aware of the archives' resources for ongoing work but may help to uncover important accumulations of institutional records or bring the archivist into the planning of organizational information systems that can guarantee the preservation of information with archival value.

A mission statement also provides the necessary groundwork for setting goals and objectives for the institutional archives, especially in the often difficult task of considering the validity of new programmatic possibilities. Because so many archival programs, institutional or otherwise, operate on limited budgets, the administrators of these programs are tempted to latch

Excerpted Policy Statement of a Medical Archives

The Medical Archives of the New York Hospital-Cornell Medical Center shall serve as a depository for all the institutions of the Center .
. . .

Any records or papers generated or received by the administrative and academic offices of the Center in the conduct of their business are the property of the Center and constitute potential archival material. These records include all paper and correspondence regarding the functioning of the office, minutes of meetings, committee files, record books, reports and studies, official printed material, architectural and engineering plans. The private papers of faculty and staff are included hereunder . . . .

All administrative officers as well as members of the faculty and staff who possess files and records relating to their official duties are requested to observe the following rules:

1)   Institutional papers may not be destroyed or placed in "dead" storage without the approval of the Committee on Records Disposition. It is the responsibility of the officer in charge of each administrative office to notify the Medical Archivist regarding the need for evaluation of these institutional papers by the said Committee.

2)   Records are to be considered for transfer to the Medical Archives when they are no longer in active use in their originating office. Materials designated by the Committee for preservation shall be transferred to the Medical Archives for processing and care.

The Medical Archives will actively seek the personal papers and other non-official records of those people connected with the Center and its institutions . . . .

All photographs, other visual material, and artifacts and apparatus significant to the Center and its institutions will be welcome in the Medical Archives as a part of the collection of iconography and of the "museum" collection . . . .

The purpose of the Medical Archives of the New York Hospital-Cornell Medical Center is to collect, organize, and preserve the records of the Center so as to make these records available for use. The Medical Archives is open for the service of all qualified researchers both within the Center and elsewhere. In view of this, the Medical Archivist shall consult with a representative of the originating office and with other interested parties to determine any restrictions that need to be placed upon the use of confidential records. Additionally, access will not be permitted to records which are less than twenty-five years old.

From Jana Bradley, ed., Hospital Library Management (Chicago: Medical Library Association, Inc., 1983), 392-93. Copyright of the Medical Library Association, 1983. Reprinted by permission of the publisher. No portion of this work may be reproduced in any form without written permission from the publisher.

onto any activity that may bring with it additional or potential sources of new funding. Without a mission statement that sets the archival program's parameters and major goals, the result of such action can be chaotic, leading to an undermining of the institutional archives' major responsibilities. A mission statement should be able to keep the program on track and provide the information needed for assessing the value and relevancy of new programmatic possibilities. Periodic review of the mission statement, annually or certainly no less often than every three to five years, by the archives staff and institution's governing board should help not only to keep the mission statement current but to lead to needed reevaluation of the archival program.

What should a typical institutional archives mission statement look like? At the least, it should accomplish three things. First, it should clearly state the program's main purposes. Because the primary purpose of an institutional archives is always to identify, preserve, and make accessible for use the archival records of the institution, this purpose will be the focal point of the statement. How this responsibility is stated depends, of course, on the nature of the parent institution. Other purposes, such as the potential use of the archival materials for the public relations of the institution and the institution's roles in the community, are also typical of the kinds of matters that a mission statement might address. Individuals responsible for institutional archives programs should not downplay the public relations benefits of their programs and the records administered by them; in many institutions, both for-profit and non-profit, concern for public image is extremely high and can be an important asset for the archivist.[10]

Second, the mission statement should clearly state the institutional archives' acquisition scope. For an institutional archives to be effective, it should have a mission that gives it responsibility—and of course the necessary authority—to care for all the institution's archival records. This requirement does not mean, however, that all the archival records must be physically centralized; the nature of certain records might dictate their remaining in the office of origin, although security copies of their information are generally called for in such circumstances. Depending on the complexity of the institution, however, it may be necessary to describe specifically the nature of the institution and whether and how the archives will handle the records of a large, far-flung corporation. The institutional archives might also have responsibility for acquiring archival records that are not legally owned by the organization but that are so closely related to the organization's development and activities that these records supplement knowledge about the institution. Collecting should never be the main responsibility of the institutional archives, however; a more logical responsibility of the archives would be seeing that such records go to appropriate collecting archives.[11]

Third, a mission statement should clearly spell out the relationship between the institutional archives and the parent organization of which it is a part. As Michael Swift has well stated, "[The] archival administrator must have an unequivocal statement of his responsibilities in this area. The mandate statement of the archives should leave no doubt about the extent of the archives responsibility and staff members must know the breadth of its authority."[12] The breadth of the programs of the institutional archives is important to know, as are the administrative placement and its main source of authority. If an institutional archives is to serve a more limited role only within the organization or, in contrast, have greater responsibilities for public outreach and service to a wider constituency, the nature of these responsibilities should be carefully indicated. The most effective institutional archives will, in most cases, have the broadest mandate and authority.

ADEQUATE FINANCIAL RESOURCES

Discussing the amount of funds needed for managing an institutional archives is, at best, a tricky business. Probably every archival manager would state that funds are inadequate for what the program requires or for new programmatic initiatives that the manager would like to undertake. This problem is additionally complicated by the fact that institutional archives vary greatly in size, scope, activities, and responsibilities, as briefly described in this volume's first chapter. Nevertheless, every archivist responsible for an institutional archives should also be able to identify crucial aspects of financial management necessary for the well-being of his or her programs.

Adequate financial resources are the quantity sufficient to enable basic arrangement, description, and preservation of, and access to, the archival records of an institution. Being able to determine what is adequate presupposes a number of things. An institutional archives must have the means to acquire finances and to monitor and evaluate the use of money. In most institutions, especially for-profit corporations or those that follow zero-based budgeting programs, archivists will be regularly called upon to justify the continuing value of their activities and the effectiveness of their use of funds to carry out those activities. All archival activities should be able to be measured on a cost basis. William Maher, an archivist who pioneered in the measurement of archival costs, wrote:

If an accurate estimate of the cost of archival services is to be obtained, the archivist will have to examine carefully the basic archival operations to isolate the cost of each of his activities. Such an analysis should focus on three principal items supported by the budget—staff, equipment or supplies, and space. These factors must be studied in relation to the three main activities of archives—appraisal, including records management; processing; and reference use.[13]

There have been many other estimates about the portion of budgets provided for certain archival functions; preservation managers estimate, for example, that at least 15 percent of an archives budget should be set aside for preservation activities. There is a common principle regarding the financial and other support of any institutional program at work here. This principle has been stated in terms of corporate archives:

Corporations will eventually discover that a corporate archives . . . will be productive (or nonproductive) in direct relation to the support it receives. If an archives is given a definite mandate, appropriate staff, and staff consistent with its function and the amount of material to be preserved, it will be effective. If it fails to be effective, management should subject the archives to the same analysis given to any problem department within the corporation.[14]

The necessary context of financial monitoring and evaluating is an appropriate, realistic mission statement. The archival manager must also maintain careful information on how his or her program's funding is used and should, as well, perform analyses on the costs of performing certain types of basic archival functions. The maintenance of other kinds of statistics—for example, regarding reference use, records removed to the archives, and visitor rates at public programs—is also important for justifying the continued existence of the archives and periodic expansion in certain new areas and the monies needed to support these activities.

What are the major areas of costs involved in operating an institutional archives? For most institutional archives, salaries and wages, along with benefits and payroll taxes and other such related costs, will constitute the major portion of the continuing budget. Salaries and benefits must be kept as competitive as possible in order to attract the most qualified archivists and support staff. The archival facilities, driven by the need for high-quality, environmentally controlled storage space and space for reference work and staff processing, will certainly be the next major portion of the archives' budget. Supplies and equipment will also constitute a large cost to the program. Archival storage and display, in-house conservation and cleaning, and other similar activities require the use of expensive supplies and equipment, as well as representing activities that cannot be short-changed without serious threats to the important archival materials. Services, such as for insurance, legal, and auditing purposes, will also be important areas of costs, although many institutional archives will probably have part or all of such services supplemented or borne completely by the general activities of the parent institution. Some services, such as for conservation consultation and activity, will be specific expenses of the institutional archives and can quickly mount up. Institutional archives should also not skimp on staff development costs for professional education, memberships, subscriptions, and book purchases or for education and special

Examples of Typical Expenditure Categories
for An Institutional Archives

Salaries and Wages
    Archivists
    Clerical and Other Support Staff
    Technical Staff

Benefits and Payroll Taxes

Supplies and Equipment
    Archival Storage
    Archival Display
    Preservation Management
    Office Supplies, Furniture, and Equipment

Services
    Auditing/Legal Services
    Insurance
    Contracts for Equipment
    Consultation

Facilities
    Rent/Mortgage
    Property Taxes
    Utilities and Heat
    Telephone
    Security
    Maintenance and Repairs

Travel and Education
    Professional Development and Education
    Memberships, Subscriptions, Book Purchases

Outreach and Special Projects
    Publications
    Exhibitions

---

projects that enhance the archives' profile within the institution and the general public as well; cutting costs in such activities will, in the long run, harm the growth and performance of the archival program.

The question of responsibility for supporting such costs as above is an issue that needs to be briefly addressed as well. Many archivists are expected to look to outside funding sources for basic operations. It is, however, the responsibility of the institution either to support adequately the archival operation or to make some other provision for the preservation and access to the organization's historical records; unfortunately, lack of interest in funding institutional archives generally betrays a lack of sense of importance of the archival records and leads to their neglect and, sometimes, deliberate destruction. One archivist has noted that "each [record] brought into the institution is accompanied by ethical and economic responsibilities," and further noted that a "repository ethically cannot acquire materials it cannot care for and make available."[15] The archivist must, of course, constantly work to demonstrate the continuing importance of the archival program to the institutional parent if the institutional records are to be well maintained. External funding sources are appropriate for special projects, research and development that benefit the archival community, or consultancies that enable assessment of new programmatic initiatives. For all of these, however, the institution will undoubtedly be expected to contribute cost sharing. Even agreements with collecting historical repositories to take on responsibility for the institution's archival records might and should, in fact, require the records creator to provide financial and other administrative support.

In order for the appropriate level of financial resources to be available to the institutional archives, the archival manager must also be in a position that provides him or her a significant voice in the development of budgets for the program. Only the archival manager will be able to indicate how funds have been spent, where they can best be used, and where the essential needs are for the institutional archives. Without the opportunity to participate in the budget process, it is unlikely that the institutional archives will have sufficient funds for basic services or necessary special initiatives. Not only will the institution lose because of the possibility of inadequate archival management, but the ongoing work of the institutional archives will be hampered.

ARCHIVAL PROCECURES

An institutional archives needs written procedures for the administration of every phase of its program. The exercise of preparing such procedures is a necessary one for relating the program's activities and responsibilities to its mission and the mission of its parent institution. This effort should also have as an objective the preparation of procedures that are accepted and proven archival methods; it is easier to assess the reliability of the procedures when they are written and can be evaluated by appropriate experts. Finally, written procedures will ensure a measure of continuity for the institutional archives. They will provide introductory and continuing information for new employees and others as the program evolves and as staff changes occur naturally with the passage of time.

In the past, many archives and manuscripts programs developed manuals for the administration of their programs by starting from scratch. The consequence of such efforts was manuals that reflected well the nature of a specific operation but also described at times considerably differing procedures (differing from common archival practice) for the carrying out of

<u>An Example of An Institutional Archives
Processing Manual</u>

The contents of the MIT archives processing manual are as follows:

Introduction
> A Bird's Eye View of Processing a Collection
> Levels of Processing

Background Research
Survey and Analysis of the Collection
Appraisal and Separation of Records
Confidentiality and Access to Records
Intellectual Ordering of the Collection
Physical Arrangement of the Collection
Description of the Collection
> Writing the Inventory
> Elements of the Inventory

Duplication, Distribution, and Publicity
Paperwork and Forms
Preservation
Use of Student Assistants
Appendices
> Bibliography
> Institute Archival Policy
> Access Policy
> Collection Policy (Archives and Manuscripts)
> Book Collection Policy
> Useful Abbreviations
> Conversion of Boxes to Linear Feet

Karen T. Lynch and Helen W. Slotkin, <u>Processing Manual for the Institute Archives and Special Collections MIT Libraries</u> (Cambridge, MA, 1981), 5.

---

basic archival functions. Since there are now a larger number of basic archival standards and reliable guidelines, the purpose of preparing written procedures for an institutional archives—or any archives program—should be to reaffirm the reliance on accepted archival practices and standards while identifying elements (such as institutional mission and internal staff policies and procedures) unique to the institution. Going through the preparation of such a set of procedures is, of course, an excellent manner in which to make sure that the program's internal policies and procedures are in conformity with those of the parent institution and basic archival practices and standards.

A set of written procedures for any institutional archives should consist of at least three basic components. The first should always be descriptions of the general setting and purpose of the program, providing the basis for the actual work with the institutional records. This component should include the program's mission statement, long-range planning documents, administrative structure description, position descriptions for staffs and volunteers, and staff policies and procedures such as for leave, attendance at professional meetings, and the like. Many of these documents will be policies generic to the entire institution. An additional benefit of preparing such a document is what will be learned about the parent institution that can later be utilized in analyzing its records.

The second part of the written procedures should focus specifically on the administration of the institution's archival records. This part should always include statements of acquisition and accession policies, appraisal guidelines, preservation procedures, a plan for disaster preparedness, security procedures, microfilming and photoduplication guidelines, arrangement and description methods, research and access policies, exhibition and loan policies, and copyright regulations. It should be fairly obvious that these sections will draw heavily on existing professional publications; it is advisable either to include copies of these publications in the institution's policies and procedures or, at the least, to cite the availability of these while summarizing their specific application within the archival program. Some of these, however, will require statements unique to the institutional program, even though they might be based on useful generic models from the archival profession. These statements will include, of course, the acquisition policy, disaster preparedness plan, security procedures, and research and access policies. This part of the written procedures will help to remind all staff and volunteers of the institutional archives that they are also part of a larger archival profession with established standards and practices.

The final component of written procedures should include statements on professional conduct. The Society of American Archivists' statements on ethics, reproduction of archives and manuscripts for reference use, and access to original research materials are all examples of this component and should be helpful to the operation of any institutional archives.[16] The purpose of this section is to remind both the institutional parent's administrators as well as the managers and staff of the archives that there is acceptable professional conduct, as well as practice and theory, that needs to be adhered to in order to guarantee the running of an acceptable archives operation. It is not possible to emphasize such concerns too strongly in a society rampant with employee theft, security problems, forgeries, and similar problems. Ignorance of these kinds of statements of professional guidance might lead to problems in the administration of the archives program, not the least being a possibility of presenting a flawed institutional and public image of the institutional archives.

Once the institutional archives has prepared its set of written procedures, it must establish a way of regularly reviewing and revising or expanding the procedures. Each part of the policies and procedures ought to be numbered and dated for easy revision or additions. A loose-leaf binder is probably the most acceptable manner of managing the written procedures, especially if there has been other outside publications and materials added into the procedures; however, the ease of use and updatability of word processors might allow another arrangement to suffice, such as regular publication and reissue annually or as needed (there is, for example, software available on the market specifically for the purpose of creating and maintaining employee handbooks and related materials). One individual within the archives should be responsible for maintaining the record copy of the written procedures, as well as making suggestions for revisions, additions, or deletions as they are needed. A committee of review, operating within the administrative structure and system of the parent institution, needs to be responsible for final decisions about such changes. It is also advisable that all staff and volunteers working within the archives be involved in discussion about the changes to any existing policies, procedures, and practices; this provision will be valuable not only in making sure that the written procedures are as good as they need to be but in aiding the communication about the procedures and building support for their adherence.

PROFESSIONAL ARCHIVAL STAFFING

In the first chapter of this volume, there was a brief discussion about the definition of archivists, their educational backgrounds, responsibilities, knowledge and experience, and related matters. It is not the purpose to reiterate this discussion in this section, but it is essential to reinforce why institutional archives require professional staffing.

Given that the largest portion of archival program budgets generally goes to personnel, it should not be difficult to imagine the importance of having the best qualified individuals staffing the programs. It has long been the case that archival repositories are very closely identified with the staff that operates them and, additionally, that the success of the program greatly depends on this staff, especially with smaller archival programs, and the majority of institutional archives fall into this category. Not having at least one well-educated, experienced, competent archivist in the program severely weakens the ability of the archives to function in a way that benefits the parent agency. Defining and evaluating archival competence are a shared responsibility of the employing institution and the archival profession. The profession, through its main professional association, the Society of American Archivists, needs to set guidelines and standards that enable employing institutions to develop exemplary position descriptions and find suitable candidates for such positions. The present guidelines for graduate archival education programs describe a set of knowledge and skills of which any professional archivist ought to have command.[17] Employers of archivists might also find requiring individuals to be certified by the Academy of Certified Archivists to be an excellent means by which to locate individuals for midlevel and advanced positions within institutional archives programs, although the recent establishment of the ACA still makes certification an uncertain venture; archival administrators and employers ought to keep abreast with the development of the ACA. The ultimate responsibility of the employing institution is to hire individuals with professional competence and, in addition, to use means of evaluating their work that are in conformity with professional archival practices and standards. These institutions should not merely designate a current employee to assume archival responsibilities without providing that individual the opportunity to gain additional education and training. Organizations with institutional archives should also have salaries and benefits sufficient to assure a professional staff and personnel policies that not only reflect institutional tradition but ensure that professional archival expertise can be acquired and maintained.

A professional archivist is needed to carry out a variety of tasks. This individual must work to ensure that proper policies, procedures, and practices are being used in the repository for administering the archival records. To do this work, of course, the archivist must be knowledgeable about such things and current with the archival literature and studies as well as with other fields that affect archival work. The archivist must also be familiar with the increasing sophistication, as well as number and breadth, of standards and guidelines that govern archival practice. To attempt to do archival arrangement and description in the United States without using the US Machine Readable Catalog (MARC) Archives and Manuscript Control (AMC) Format, as just one example, is to risk the violation of standard practices and to minimize the institution's capability of being able to participate in information networks that they might find of advantage to them. This latter need is especially important as institutions increasingly turn to online information systems to enhance their more traditional library operations; both for- and nonprofit organizations need to learn that there is considerable information of current value readily available to them in such systems for their ongoing work.

The professional archivist protects the institution's investment in an archives program, as well as the irreplaceable records that the institution has placed under this individual's care. The professional archivist will be in a better position to know how to use effectively the financial resources that he or she has been provided. Moreover, this individual will also be able to create the best environment and program for training volunteers and others in basic archival work, develop opportunities for beneficial cooperative endeavors with other archival programs, and improve the institu-

Examples of Position Advertisements for Institutional Archives

Archivist Kappa Kappa Gamma Fraternity. Kappa Kappa Gamma Fraternity, founded in 1870, is one of the earliest Greek-letter fraternities for college women. Total membership is over 140,000, with 121 chapters at colleges and universities in Canada and the United States and 450 alumnae groups worldwide. The Fraternity Headquarters are located in Columbus, Ohio. RESPONSIBILITIES: As the organization's first professionally trained archivist, this person will inventory, catalog, arrange, and preserve fraternity archives dating from 1870. This opportunity will include design of physical facilities and the development of systems and policies governing access and acquisition. Some research and reference work will be required. QUALIFICATION: An advanced degree or formal archival training with an undergraduate degree in American history, women's studies, or library science. SALARY: Based on qualifications and experience, $18,000-22,000 with benefits . . . .

Director of Archives Maryknoll Mission Society. Seeking an experienced professional archivist to facilitate the consolidation of the Archives of the Maryknoll Fathers and Brothers (Catholic Foreign Mission Society of America) and the Archives of the Maryknoll Sisters (Maryknoll Sisters of St. Dominic) into one facility and to be Director of the combined repository, The Maryknoll Mission Archives. RESPONSIBILITIES: Administer all aspects of archival administration, direct research, reference, and outreach services for the Maryknoll Mission Archives. Supervise staff of four FTE's. Involvement in long-term planning for the archives and records management program. QUALIFICATIONS: Advanced degree in history, library science, or related discipline with training in archival administration; 3-5 years experience in archives and records management; strong writing skills; ability to work with both professional and clerical staff required. Knowledge of American church history, the requirements of scholarly research, and word processing.

SAA Newsletter, January 1990, 22; November 1989, 28.

---

tional archives' chances of securing outside funding when such funding is desirable.[18]

IN-SERVICE AND CONTINUING EDUCATION COMMITMENT

Making a commitment to having an institutional archives is not a onetime decision. Establishing a program, hiring staff, securing a facility, and related activities require continued support, review, and nurturing. Nowhere is such nurturing quite as important as with the staff—professional, support, paraprofessional, and volunteer—of an institutional archives program. Not only does the staff represent the largest continuing financial obligation of

A Model Statement for an Institutional Archives Continuing Education Policy

Archival staff of the institutional archives are encouraged to participate in continuing education opportunities to maintain and improve their skills for ongoing responsibilities. The following guidelines for staff attendance in continuing education programs are in effect:

1. Each staff member may attend one national professional association meeting that includes training sessions relevant to his or her general responsibilities.

2. Each staff member may attend professional association meetings for which he or she is on the program or holds elected or appointed office.

3. Each staff member may apply to attend other professional association meetings in special institutes, workshops, or courses that are important to his or her ongoing responsibilities.

4. Each staff member may attend professional association meetings or short-term institutes or workshops in close geographic proximity to the repository and that are relevant to his or her responsibilities.

All of the above are dependent upon prior approval by the staff member's supervisor, the availability of funds, and the carrying out of staff responsibilities without serious interruption.

Adapted from Strengthening New York's Historical Records Programs: A Self-Study Guide (Albany: New York State Archives and Records Administration, 1988), 26.

---

most institutional archives, but the success of these programs is generally dependent on the knowledge of these persons. Although basic archival principles have been relatively stable through the years, ways of applying these principles are quite fluid. Increasing uses of electronic records and audiovisual materials in nearly every office and institutional setting are also stretching the application of the basic archival principles and suggesting new concepts, topics that will be described in some of the following chapters. An institution with an archival program must support its staff in keeping up with archival administration methods, research, and ideas or risk the possibility of having less than the most optimal archival operation.

There are two basic means by which organizations can make such commitments to their archival staffs and programs. The first is by providing financial and other support, such as released time, for staff to engage in continuing education opportunities for professionally trained archivists or basic education for paraprofessionals and volunteers. Continuing and basic education opportunities in archival administration derive from many sources and come in many forms. The most regular offerings come from national and regional professional associations, primarily the Society of American Archivists, which maintains an education office staffed by a professional archivist and offers a continuing series of basic and advanced workshops and seminars at its annual meetings and at other sites throughout the country. Regional archival associations also offer many opportunities for continuing education, ranging from formal papers at meeting sessions to multiday basic and advanced workshops and institutes. Institutions with needs in this area should also inquire at local colleges and universities about whether they have courses on archival topics; even though the number of full-fledged, multicourse graduate archival programs is rather limited in number and geographic availability, many history departments and library and information science schools offer one or two basic courses in archival administration, records management, preservation, and related areas. Since many colleges and universities have strong continuing education operations in other (often related disciplines), it might also be possible to persuade them to attract one of the Society of American Archivists workshops or related short courses to the area, provided a sufficient demand is shown. Finally, institutions might see whether it is possible to place an employee with an already established archival program in a kind of internship. Such internships have not often been done, but the possibilities for success here are quite good. Some such training has occurred in library preservation programs, in which experienced librarians are given the opportunity to gain basic and advanced training in library preservation management perspectives and practices at other institutions that possess established preservation programs.

The second major area of commitment in providing continuing education for staff is by development of a formal or regular in-service training program within the institutional archives. There were such programs prior to the fuller development of graduate archival educations, but such internal training programs are still necessary if the archives utilizes a number of paraprofessionals and volunteers. The purposes of these internal programs are not to replace graduate or advanced archival education but to help individuals gain an understanding of the corporate culture of this particular institution and its archives. Such programs should include introductions to the history of the institution and its archival program, as well as introductions to basic archival functions such as appraisal, arrangement and description, preservation, and reference, using examples from the institutional archives. Even if these individuals are not working directly with any or all of these functions, their own work should be enhanced by having a broader knowledge of archival work and how the various basic functions fit together to form a comprehensive program. These in-service programs will be most useful for paraprofessionals and volunteers, and as such they will need to focus on established policies, directives, and the specific range of functions that these staff members will be concerned with in this archives.

FACILITY FOR THE STORAGE AND USE OF ARCHIVAL RECORDS

No matter how good the institutional archives program is, it will fail in its ultimate mission if it lacks an adequate facility for the storage and use of the archival records. Whatever investment is made by an organization in establishing and staffing an institutional archives will be lost if the facilities do not allow for the optimum care of the records themselves. What is meant by *adequate*? Archival records must be stored in an environment that retards deterioration, provides for their security, and enables their use in a manner that prevents damage to, or theft of, the records. While these elements will be described in fuller detail in chapter 4, some brief comments need to be made in this section that emphasize the essentiality of providing such care for the records as one of the crucial components of an institutional archives.

An archival facility must consist of an environment that provides consistent, controlled temperature, relative humidity, and air quality and protects the records from the ultraviolet radiation found in light, from unforeseen fire and water damage, and from human handling. Moreover, the facility must be secure, as well as conveniently located to the institution that requires use of the records. Storage of the records must be able to be done in a manner that reduces their wear and tear, primarily on shelving and records containers that place no stress on the stored archival materials. Special format records—such as audiovisual recordings, large-scale engineering drawings and cartographic renderings, and electronic records— must also be able to be accommodated by the archival facility. Accommodating such records may require planning for special storage areas within the archival facility.

The institutional archives must take into account ergonomic factors as well. The facility must have well-designed work spaces for the archives staff for receipt of the records, their processing, and other similar staff functions. There must also be suitable space for the reference services. There needs to be a segregated space for researchers to work in, and this space needs to be comfortable, well lighted, secure, and accessible to copying and other such services. No matter how small the institutional archives program may be, reference to, and storage of, archival materials must not occur in the same room; allowing this situation to occur will eventually only cause problems, mainly because it lends to a laxity in the protection of the archival materials.

Requirements for a Records Center/Archival Storage Facility

The following requirements for such a facility are modified from a set of guidelines for local government records centers. These requirements are in line with those needed by an institutional archives, especially those that store archival and non-current records together. These guidelines were prepared for local governments that were considering the renovation of an existing facility for records storage, a situation that is apt to be common for most institutions establishing records management and archival administration programs.

Each [institution] should set its own parameters in consideration of its needs and own definitions of "suitability" of a facility for use as a records center. The following criteria and standards are suggested:

* It must be of a physical/structural nature to have the potential to be improvable to a "true" records center.

* It must be as close as possible to the [institution's headquarters]. The closer it is, the more it will be used.

* It must be of sufficient capacity to satisfy at least the [institution's] short-term needs.

* It should be located on the ground floor because of weight constraints and to maximize accessibility and transport of records and equipment. If a basement must be used, it must be made secure against possible water damage.

* If storage of archival material, vital records, and magnetic tape discs is contemplated, temperature and humidity should be in the 70 degree-50 percent range.

* Its construction should be fire-resistant and a sprinkler system and a fire detection system installed.

* The storage area should be secure against unauthorized access.

* Its improvement to serve as a records center must be practical and represent a wise use of [institutional] funds as compared to other alternatives.

From A. K. Johnson, Jr., comp., A Guide for the Selection and Development of Local Government Records Storage Facilities, NAGARA Local Government Records Technical Publication Series, no. 1 (Albany: National Association of Government Archives and Records Administrators, November 1989), 11.

Acquiring such an adequate facility is not necessarily an easy task for the institutional archives because many such programs will be housed within the organization's main structure, which is being used for other activities; some, if not many, of these activities may be counter to the preservation of archival records. Some institutional archivists might be able to build upon the fact that data-processing operations have gained environmentally stable conditions for both their hardware and software considerations. In any event, the institutional archives must seek a facility that provides optimum storage and security for the irreplaceable archival records.

COOPERATIVE PROGRAMS WITH OTHER ARCHIVAL PROGRAMS

Cooperation is another topic that will be given a fuller treatment later in this volume (see chapter 7), but it too must be emphasized as a basic element for successful institutional archives programs. Cooperation has a relatively long history, over 20 years of discussion and experimentation in the archival profession. Concern with cooperation initially emanated from the statewide networks of regional or local repositories organized in some states, usually administered by the state archival institution and largely funded with state funds. Experimentation with cooperation in this manner led to some substantive contributions on the subject to the archival literature.[19] Much of the writing and discussion, however, has been focused on networks, first statewide and now national, at the expense of considering the positive impact of cooperative ventures on individual archival repositories. These networks provide for the physical centralization of the records, however, a possibility that many institutional archives will not be interested in, as they require the control of their own records.

Archival cooperation can be defined in a number of ways, but for the purpose of this volume it is limited to the involvement of two or more archival programs working together to achieve an improvement in the performance of their basic functions. There are many ways in which cooperative efforts can benefit archival programs. Joint purchasing of archival supplies to lower unit prices, building or renovating joint storage facilities, publishing multi-institutional archival guides, hiring consultants for similar evaluation activities, and developing disaster preparedness plans are but a few of the potential activities that can be undertaken in a cooperative manner.

Some may think that institutional archives should not cooperate because such operations are primarily the responsibilities of the parent institution. While the parent organizations should not abrogate responsibilities or lessen resources as a result of savings caused by cooperation, there are no reasons why institutional archives should not seek cooperation with other archival repositories when it is to their benefit. Cooperation can aid the

The Archival Mission and Archival Functions

Mission	Archival Functions
Identify	Appraisal & Acquisition
Preserve	Preservation Management
Make Available	Arrangement & Description
	Reference
	Public Outreach

taking on of work that is beyond the resources of a single institution, increase the availability of archival and other needed expertise through the sharing of staff, and improve public awareness by higher profile, multi-institutional projects. The potential problems with such cooperative activities must also be carefully considered.

CONCLUSION

All of the elements described briefly in this chapter will provide any archival program a good foundation for growth and success, provided the institutional archives is appropriately placed in the organization. Good mission statements, excellent facilities, qualified staff, and adequate financial resources can all be for naught if the archives is administratively placed in a manner that makes every one of its tasks, no matter how simple, a major chore. The institution's archivists must not only have good access to the top-level administrators but be able to work freely and, often, equally with the organization's records managers, librarians, managers of information systems, financial officers, and legal advisers. Most institutions have now come to recognize the value of information to their daily functioning. What they need to be convinced of is that the information they value often encompasses older information found in archival records. Charles McClure noted that "if one defines decision-making as that process whereby information is converted into action, then decision-making has largely to do with the process of acquiring, controlling, and utilizing information to accomplish some objective."[20] Information from the institution's archives is vital to decision making and must be properly maintained and managed.

The next several chapters of this volume will provide a more detailed explanation of the missions of most institutional archives as they relate to basic archival functions. The mission of the archival profession—to identify, preserve, and make available the records of continuing value—can be very easily organized to encompass the most crucial archival work of appraisal, preservation management, arrangement and description, reference, and building internal and public support for the archival programs.

NOTES

1. Barbara Floyd, "The Archivist as Public Administrator," *Midwestern Archivist* 15, no. 1 (1990): 17–24.

2. Peter J. Parker, "The Administration of Historical Records: An Overview," in *A Manual of Archival Techniques*, rev. ed., ed. Roland M. Baumann (Harrisburg: Pennsylvania Historical and Museum Commission, 1982), 1.

3. David J. Klaassen, "The Archival Intersection: Cooperation Between Collecting Repositories and Nonprofit Organizations," *Midwestern Archivist* 15, no. 1 (1990): 25–38 might provide some insight about these difficulties.

4. The differences, similarities, and relationship between institutional archivists and records managers will be described later in this chapter and at selected points throughout this volume.

5. Paul H. McCarthy, ed., *Archives Assessment and Planning Workbook* (Chicago: Society of American Archivists, 1989). See also Richard J. Cox and Judy Hohmann, *Strengthening New York's Historical Records Programs: A Self-Study Guide* (Albany: New York State Archives and Records Administration, 1988).

6. Susan E. Davis, "Development of Managerial Training for Archivists," *American Archivist* 51 (Summer 1988): 278–85.

7. McCarthy, *Archives Assessment and Planning Workbook*, 16.

8. Michael Swift, "Management Techniques and Technical Resources in the Archives of the 1980s," *Archivaria* 20 (Summer 1985): 96.

9. The importance of such activity is fully presented in Richard M. Kesner, *Information Systems: A Strategic Approach to Planning and Implementation* (Chicago: American Library Association, 1988).

10. For a corporation, an archives program might be a means for stressing its importance in, and to, its local community. Use of archival materials in exhibitions and local press releases can stress this connection. Even nonprofits can make similar uses of their historical records. One prominent educational institution for which this author consulted had developed a strong tradition of service and was drawing on its historical records for publicity and other public events; such use of records was a strong motivation for an archives program.

11. Institutional archives that are part of larger archival programs that include collecting manuscripts, such as a college or university archives or museum archives, will not face this dilemma. Acquiring such records could be done through the manuscript or special collections operation. The challenge is for such operations to determine their overall priorities.

12. Swift, "Management Techniques," 96.

13. William Maher, "The Importance of Financial Analysis of Archival Programs," *Midwestern Archivist* 3, no. 2 (1978): 7.

14. Douglas A. Bakken, "Corporate Archives Today," *American Archivist* 45 (Summer 1982): 285.

15. David Hoober, *Manuscript Collections: Initial Procedures and Policies*, American Association for State and Local History, Technical Leaflet 131 (October 1980), 2.

16. A complete list of such statements and policies can be obtained from the Society of American Archivists.

17. "Guidelines for Graduate Archival Education Programs," *American Archivist* are worth perusal by any prospective archival employer. The society's 1990 directory of graduate programs indicates which meet these guidelines.

18. Some of the federal funding programs require that the institution have a full-time archivist or, if the grant is for a planning project or start-up funds, require that the institution make a commitment to the continuation of the project or program.

19. See John A. Fleckner, "Cooperation as a Strategy for Archival Institutions," *American Archivist* 39 (October 1976): 447–59 and Frank G. Burke, "Archival Cooperation," *American Archivist* 46 (Summer 1983): 293–305 are the most important writings on this topic.

20. Charles McClure, "Planning for Library Effectiveness: The Role of Information Resources Management," *Journal of Library Administration* 1 (Fall 1980): 4.

3

Identifying and Selecting Records with Continuing Value

ARCHIVAL APPRAISAL: ITS SCOPE AND IMPORTANCE

In the first chapter of this volume, the general values of archives were briefly discussed. Institutional archives were depicted as essential for internal decision making, public relations, sustenance of the corporate culture, legal matters, administrative continuity, and a variety of other matters. The value of archival records to their institutional creators is dependent, however, on a careful identification, evaluation, and selection process, which is, unfortunately, not always present in organizations that have institutional archives. As has been mentioned earlier, there is the tendency sometimes to view only the oldest records as archival. Worse yet, often the discovery by administrators of records they believe have archival value to the institution or the haphazard identification of what records should be housed in the archives determines the holdings of institutional archives. Such views reveal, of course, basic misconceptions of what an archival program is and should be; it is not the repository of ancient, seldom referred to informational relics, but rather a vital aspect of an organization's operation and use of information to sustain that operation. Since the identification and selection of records possessing archival value, what professional archivists call appraisal,[1] also determine or, at least, greatly affect all other aspects of the archival program—arrangement and description responsibilities, preservation needs, and reference functions, as well as the program's potential visibility and relevance to the organization—it is important that the appraisal of institutional records be a systematic, carefully administered, and orderly process.[2]

Archival appraisal has been defined as the "process of determining the value and thus the disposition of records based upon their current administrative, legal, and fiscal use; their evidential and informational or research value; their arrangement; and their relationship to other records." Through the years, this basic definition has been expanded and refined in both techniques and perspective,[3] but it remains the basic beginning point for any discussion of the nature of this basic archival function. This statement is especially true for institutional archives, which focus on their own records rather than collecting from other institutions and individuals and which often support a records management program, concentrate on systems analysis, and utilize the retention or disposition schedule as a basic tool. These programs will be vitally concerned with the life cycle of records or information, a concept that simply reflects the fact that all records are created for a specific purpose, have periods of time of current use in the creating office, and reach a point where the records can either be destroyed or sent for retention in an archives. An institution that lacks a systematic approach to archival appraisal will not be able to possess an adequate or strong archival program, since the records that it receives will be more prone to chance than through deliberate, comprehensive evaluation and purposeful selection.

There are a number of essential elements that must be in place for an effective archival appraisal program. First, there must be a clear comprehension of the basic informational values that archivists generally ascribe to as essential for documenting institutions and the broader society in which these institutions are immersed. Second, the archival administrators must possess a thorough knowledge of the institution's mission, administrative structure, historical development, and present issues and concerns. Without this knowledge, the archivists will not be able to apply their understanding of the basic informational values of archival records. Third, the institutional archivist must understand the various archival appraisal techniques and practices that have developed to assist the selection of information that is archival. Determining that a voluminous series of records has archival value may not mean that the entire series should or could be preserved; understanding how an archival technique such as sampling could be applied in this situation is an essential skill for the successful operation of an institutional archives. Fourth, institutional archives must operate as part of, or in tandem with, institutional records management and management of information systems programs. The changing nature of recorded information requires, in many cases, that archivists be as close as possible to the point of creation of these records in order to ensure that the archival documentation can be identified and saved; it is another reason

ARCHIVISTS AND THE LIFE CYCLE OF RECORDS

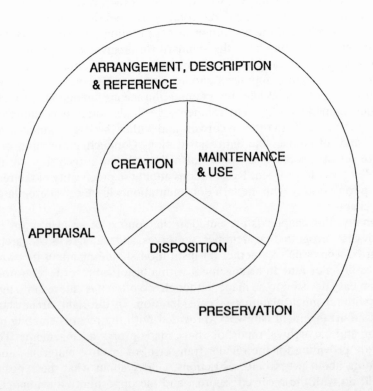

why the archivist should keep in mind the records life cycle concept. All of these elements will be discussed in full in this chapter and referred to in other places in this book.

Before the discussion of archival appraisal, two important archival concepts must be mentioned here. The main focus for all appraisal—as well as arrangement and description work—is the archival series. The series is a file unit or set of documents "arranged in accordance with a filing system or maintained as a unit because they relate to a particular subject or function, result from the same activity, have a particular form, or because of some other relationship arising out of their creation, receipt, or use."[4] Archivists will nearly always appraise records as series, because series are fully meaningful only in their aggregate. Furthermore, efforts to deal with documents individually would require far too much intensive labor. In most institutional settings, records series will always be at least several cubic feet and can accumulate as much as thousands of cubic feet of documentation.

The other basic concept is the record group. The record group has been defined as a "body of organizationally related records established on the basis of provenance [the principle that records of an administrative office or unit should not be mingled with those of another] with particular regard for the administrative history, the complexity, and the volume of the records and archives of the institution or organization involved."[5] While the record group has long been the standard for archival descriptive work, it also plays an important role in the appraisal of institutional records. Records that are being appraised should always be examined within their context of creation. While this examination means looking at the records in their immediate office environment, it will also often necessitate comparing the records to other records found within the larger administrative units and, of course, the entire institution. Conducting appraisal of the entire set of records that would normally make up a record group is an excellent way to proceed. Reservations about the practicality of the record group for working with modern documentation will be considered later in this chapter.

Finally, this chapter is presented in the context of an institution committing to a program that identifies, preserves, and manages its own archival records. The issue of whether an institution should maintain its own archives or enter into an arrangement with a historical records repository is not an easy decision to be made, although too often it is entered into lightly and without much planning or consideration. In the right circumstances such an arrangement can work, provided both the records-creating institution and the archival repository have made proper arrangements. These include providing for the regular transferral of inactive materials, understanding about access and restrictions, clarity about what the repository would do with the received records, and the opportunity for nonarchival materials to be returned.[6]

IDENTIFYING ARCHIVAL INFORMATION

There are many different ways in which archivists have described the values of records. In this section, these values will be introduced. Although there has been some debate about whether appraisal is art or science and whether appraisal can be effectively quantified or reduced to a set of basic heuristic principles, there is no intention here to provide a simplified method by which archivists and/or records managers can document their institutions by preserving certain records or check off certain conditions and logically deduce that certain records provide the best documentation. Individual corporate cultures, institutional histories, personal managerial styles, and chance and accident make such environments too complex to be able to apply simplified formula. There is also some inherent contradiction in the present status of archival appraisal. As archivists have examined and reexamined their appraisal practices in the United States, the concepts, principles, and applications of appraisal have become more in-

Chart of Basic Archival Values

	Evidential	Informational
Administrative	XX	x
Fiscal	XX	x
Legal	XX	x
Research	x	XX
Documentary	x	XX
Intrinsic	XX	XX

This chart is an effort to reflect relative weights of archival values according to the broadly defined evidential value (which has the most relevance to institutional archives) and informational value.   XX indicates a strong relationship, while x indicates a weaker connection. The various terms are defined and described in the text.

tricate. What follows is meant only to introduce the topic, present some issues, and lay a foundation for the ongoing important work of appraisal undertaken by institutional archivists. These archivists must make every effort to stay abreast of new work in this area. It is possible that, despite the increasing complexity of appraisal, the identification of heuristic principles will lead to computerized expert systems that will greatly aid archival appraisal, and institutional archivists should keep track of such developments.

Archivists have traditionally talked about four basic values guiding their identification of records that merit preservation in archival programs from the larger information universe. All values are different aspects of records that have continuing or, as some would prefer, enduring value to the records creator and, often, to society in general.[7]

Administrative value is applied to those transactional records that are important for understanding institutional policy formulation and implementation, contain data accumulated that is essential to the daily functioning of the organization, and usually reflect the interactions between the records creators and the creators' major constituencies. For institutional archives, this value may well be the one that is most important to the program's ongoing operation and the easiest and best to discuss as part of the justification for the archives' existence. With this value the archival program's role as corporate memory is the most pronounced and most readily identified. The records that are maintained for this purpose are the ones most likely to be sought when institutions are considering major changes and desire some historical understanding of why they have functioned in the manner they have to that point. Of course, archivists must be careful not to overemphasize this value at the expense of other values that might inadvertently lead to the destruction of other important records.

For a long time, archivists and institutional historians perceived the identification and preservation of such records to be a fairly straightforward matter. Minutes of governing bodies, published and unpublished reports, and the administrative files of key individuals in the managerial hierarchy of institutions were often seen as sufficient for documenting the basic functioning of any institution—private, public, nonprofit, or for-profit. Archivists and others have now recognized that capturing the administrative value of records is one thing and documenting the administrative functioning of the organization is quite another. Historian JoAnne Yates has shown, in a penetrating analysis of communication systems in modern American businesses, that traditional archival approaches have often been inadequate. For example, she noted:

Many archivists respond to the dilemma of the increasing bulk of business records and the inadequate guidance provided by archival theorists by taking a "tip-of-the-iceberg" approach to appraising institutional records. They retain sets of files almost exclusively from offices and individuals at the top of the organizational chart. Some archivists may supplement these files with systematic samples of homogeneous runs of low-level documents. Both processes ignore the dynamics of communication, which operates as a coherent system of flows, in favor of looking for static information about the organization and its employees.[8]

This kind of problem opens up the need for new archival appraisal approaches, some of which have begun to be developed and will be discussed below.

Fiscal and legal values, the two main companions to administrative value, have been less discussed by the archivist and have been more the focus of the records manager. Fiscal records are those information sources needed for documenting financial transactions, obligations, and authorizations and for continual auditing of the institution's programs. Since audit requirements are often very short-term in practice, generally no more than three years, the emphasis on financial records has tended to be made by records managers rather than archivists. A loss of information about the financial history of an institution will, however, generally ensure that that institution's historical development and present nature will be relegated to an imperfect understanding by organization managers and those studying its history. One archivist, writing on the topic of modern financial records,

Examples of Records According to Appraisal Categories

Appraisal Criteria	Categories of Records	Specific Types of Records
Evidential	**Administrative Records** Without a proportion of policy files records which document the details of administration the creators of the records (or their successors) could not operate. It would not be possible to plan, organize, and make decisions or to ensure consistency and continuity.	policy files statements of functions organization charts procedures and instructions minutes of meetings
Evidential	**Records of Legal Value** These records form proof of an event or agreement. Obligations, commitments, rights, and delegations of authority fall into this category. Without these records there is no security or foundation for decision making.	contracts leases original acts and regulations instruments of appointment agreements wills
Evidential	**Records of Financial Accountability** These records document the honest and responsible conduct of financial affairs and financial standing and obligations. These records are essential to understand and transact business.	financial returns financial reports final budgets audit reports estimates of gross expenditure and income major reports on losses
Informational	**Records of Historic Interest for Public Relations and General Interest Purposes** Records of this type allow the context of the creator to be understood. The social, political, economic, educational, and recreational activities and the relations to the wider community are documented through these records.	all of the above diaries letters photographs posters post cards souvenirs catalogues

Barbara Reed, "Acquisition and Appraisal," in Ann Pederson, ed., <u>Keeping Archives</u> (Sydney: Australian Society of Archivists, 1987), 83.

stated that the "first principle is that a sufficient combination of accounting records should be kept so as to document completely the revenues, expenses, and net financial picture of the business at any point in its existence, and also to document the accounting methods used by the business." This archivist also suggested other basic principles when examining these records, including that retained record series "should each encompass the broadest range of the company's activities and the longest time span possible," that the information "they contain is [not] available in more complete or compact form in some other record," that there are "no two accounting systems [that] function in precisely the same way," and, finally, that they will be "quite small" in volume if dated before 1900.[9] Using these and other archival appraisal principles, the archivist will be able to determine in any specific institutional setting what financial records should be saved; some of these records must be saved, however, to ensure a thorough documentation of the organization.

Legal values are generally called upon to ensure the preservation of information that is needed for the legal protection of the institution, the civil and other rights of individuals associated with the institution, and a variety of other such jurisprudential concerns. These values conjure up all sorts of potential problems for the archivist and the institutional archives. There are many popular press articles advocating that records should be immediately disposed of when they can be legally destroyed in order to prevent the institution from being embroiled in unnecessary lawsuits and other legal problems. This position is, obviously, the result of living in a litigious society, and this environment is often not conducive to the archivist's being able to persuade the organization about the importance of preserving certain kinds of archival records that are of potential historical value to the institution and others. One of the current authorities on record-keeping requirements captured the tension in this issue:

A good records management program protects the organization in case of litigation. The program ensures that records that should exist, do in fact exist, and that records that should not exist, do in fact not exist. It also ensures that records prepared by the organization can readily be admitted into evidence to support the organization's claims. A records management program also puts you in charge of records previously maintained outside the scope of normal business activities and which may later prove detrimental in litigation.[10]

In laboring in the legal area, the archivist should be fully prepared to receive the brunt of a variety of strong reactions, but he or she must be involved in documenting the legal aspects of the institution since this documentation is also essential to a well-rounded understanding of the organization. More information about legal issues affecting access will be provided in chapter 5.

Archivists also, of course, look for historical or, more broadly stated, *research values* of the records. For a long time, most archivists seemed predisposed in appraisal to emphasizing historical value because they assumed that their main clientele was the scholarly historian. An increasing portion of researchers at all archives has included genealogists and family historians, lawyers, political scientists, medical researchers, community activists, and a wide diversity of individuals and groups who need access to archival records to understand the issues and concerns in which they are interested. The same group of archival records may be used by such a broad range of individuals, although for very different reasons, and archivists must understand the potential variety of uses in order to carry out appraisal work effectively. A group of records maintained in a municipal archives relating to the acquisition of property for an urban renewal project could be important to the local government for documenting original decisions relative to the creation of the project and for demonstrating that the city performed the project in appropriate ways; to historic preservationists and historians seeking information about structures that were torn down for the project; to individuals concerned about the displacement of original residents and the social and economic viability of such mass urban renewal efforts; and to current residents of the project seeking a community identity through some knowledge of the location's history. The potential broad range of use of archival materials is typical of archival records. Archivists have resorted, then, to discussing research or archival values rather than the more limited historical sense. This perspective is especially important for the staffs of institutional archives.

The research values of institutional records include information that is both essential for an understanding of the institution's development, its present corporate culture, and its current policies and practices and needed by researchers seeking understanding of broader societal issues and concerns or searching for specific bits of information—such as data on an individual associated with the institution that the institutional records may contain. Institutional archivists, then, have a dual concern for maintaining important information both for the institution and for a variety of potential outside users; in many cases, of course, the same records serve all these purposes and bring no extra expense to the institution itself concerned about such matters. The wider significance of institutional records will always depend on the importance of the organization itself and the individuals associated with it. But it should be always remembered that any institution will possess records that it will want to maintain for its own continuing work.

Archivists have come up with more precise definitions of the potential internal and external values of records created by an institution and use these generally to organize the four basic values previously described (although admittedly some archivists will describe archival records as having

two basic values and use the four described earlier as subsets of these two);
in fact, one recent discussion of appraisal referred to the evidential and
informational values as the "cornerstone" of this basic archival function.[11]
Evidential value is the value of records to their creator needed to provide
information about the organization's purpose, structure, and functioning.
Charters, minutes of governing bodies, basic statistical data, and other
similar sources are records that are generally saved for their evidence about
the institution. Such records also include the documentation vital for the
ongoing administration of the institution, especially those records that contain information essential to the personnel, legal, and fiscal operations.
Informational value is the value of records required for purposes other
than those for which they were created, primarily records that are needed
for understanding the historical development of the institution and the
broader society of which it is a part. Here the urban renewal records
described earlier are again an example of records possessing informational
value. In all cases, the primary responsibility of the institutional archivist
is ensuring that the records with evidential value are first identified and
preserved. The institutional archivist and the institution he or she works
for, however, must also be responsible for records possessing general informational value. The deliberate or inadvertent destruction of such records represents a grievous loss to society and can do public relations or
other damage to the institution once such a loss becomes known.[12]

Closely related to the informational value is the *documentary value* of
institutional records. Documentary value is a relatively new, somewhat
untested archival concept. This value, extracted from the notion of the
documentation strategy model, which is discussed below in greater detail,
makes an effort to ensure that institutional records with essential information for an understanding of the institution's business or other societal
trends and concerns or the geographical region in which it is located are
all preserved and available for use in some way. This value suggests that
for many modern activities and trends their documentation cannot be effectively gained unless very carefully planned research and collecting projects are conducted in which the documents of many records creators are
examined. Some examples will explain this documentary value. An industrial company might be the primary employer in a geographical area. Its
records then take on greater value to an understanding of that area. Records rightly thought to be useless for the company itself might be important
as a source of information, filling in documentary gaps for the region.
Conversely, what records an institution determines to save about specific
projects and activities might be highly affected by its joint work in these
areas with other institutions. It is likely that many high-technology companies in one geographical area or across the country might have worked
closely on specific federal government-funded projects; the records of one
institution might be virtually incomprehensible without knowledge of the

records of other institutions or the essential information duplicated in other sources that have already been deposited in an archival repository.[13]

A final value, which all archivists should be aware of, is the notion of *intrinsic value*. This concept, developed by the staff of the National Archives, is a useful barometer for ascertaining which archival records must be maintained in their original form. It guides an archivist in determining which records, if reformatted (such as through microfilming), will lose essential portions of their information. Records with intrinsic value are normally those records that have a physical form that might be the topic of study; for example, they may reflect a technological change; possess unusual aesthetic or artistic quality; have unique or curious physical features, like wax seals and watermarks; be of a certain age that makes them unique as a documentary source; be useful for exhibitions; be of questionable authenticity, date, or authorship; contain a direct association with a historically significant person or event; or have direct significance as legal documentation for the establishment and continuing operation of an institution. While such records will always represent a minuscule portion of the archival records of an institution, their possible loss could be great.

APPRAISAL AND INSTITUTIONAL UNDERSTANDING

Effective appraisal work cannot be done without an understanding of the institution's origins, development, and current practices and activities. In fact, all of the above values and their understanding make sense only if the creator of the records is known as well. The reason is quite simple. Archival appraisal carried out within an institutional setting, such as described in this book, is primarily for the identification of the records that have continuing or enduring value to the institution's ongoing administration. Being able to make this connection requires, of course, a thorough understanding of the business that the institution is in and the kind of information that it requires to stay competitive (or effective in its services, if it is a nonprofit operation). Archival appraisal is also intended to document the institution's work and, more broadly, its place in society. Looking at appraisal as a documentation exercise requires a thorough knowledge of the institution's evolving activities.

There are many ways in which to think about such institutional understanding. The most common way is to comprehend the administrative structure of the organization, which could be hierarchical, functional, product-oriented, or structured for client or customer services or in any other number of ways. This approach has been, in fact, the dominant one followed by archivists, partly because it has been seen as essential to the archival arrangement, descriptive, and reference functions as well and partly because archival principles in this country developed in coordination with the classical school of management theory that emphasized rationality, individualism, and production.[14] In one model of archival appraisal in the university setting, determining the informational value of specific series or groups of records was started off with questions such as: What is the position of the generating office in the institutional hierarchy?, in a given office, What are the principal functions of the particular unit (or individual) that generated the records?, and in the context of the unit activities, What is the significance of the records?[15] Asking such questions reveals the archivist's dual role of seeking an understanding of the nature of the organization and, thus, the reasons records are being created in the first place, as well as analyzing the contents and assessing the actual informational values of the records themselves.

Much of the archival literature on appraisal has focused, therefore, on the administrative history aspects of the institutional records creator. This focus has led to some problems. It became easy for archivists to make a transition from using their knowledge of the administrative structure of the institution to aid the selection of archival records to equating the main records that fit into the structure as thoroughly documenting the institution. For example, the first records that archivists often searched for in appraising any part of the institutional structure were minutes of governing bodies, official reports and studies reflecting the unit's activities, and the files of the chief administrators; in other words, archivists have been actually identifying the key individuals and organizational bodies on the pyramidal administrative structures creating the records as the main elements determining the records that should be saved. Preserving these records has become equated with documenting the institution, an equation that is not always the case. While preserving such records is probably a good idea in most institutions, the realization that much of the decision making and other activities of an institution are not handled in the "official" channels and structures of the organization should direct the archivist to look at other sources of documentation, or even to create documentation (such as through the recording of oral interviews). The introduction of information technology, especially the advent of the personal computer and the increased use of these machines for things such as electronic mail, has tended to flatten out traditional institutional hierarchies, and has muddled for the archivist the precise decision-making processes that have been in operation. Compensating for these trends should be the result of the archivist's increased understanding of the institution itself.

What should archivists do to develop an adequate knowledge of the organization in order to conduct good appraisal? Without question, the first thing they must do is realize it is a difficult process at best and requires careful development of the overall institutional archives program and its position within the organization. Being able to examine the institution's universe of documentation requires participation in a process that is like

Institutional Understanding and Appraisal

[In high-technology corporations] it is important to be attentive to the peculiarities of how things actually happened, rather than how they should have occurred. For example, different functions and support services may coexist in the same department in the corporate hierarchy. Moreover, although the stages are typical of most high-technology industrial activity, the structure of the organization in which they take place varies over time, with company size, and with company maturity . . . .

[I]t will be easier to identify records associated with a function if the organizational units can be matched to their corresponding function. Knowledge of corporate organization may allow one to guess where records of relevant functions are most likely to be found . . . .

[T]he task of assessing the value of records will be aided by considering the flow of information in modern companies. Communication flows in several different directions . . . .

Sometimes historians and archivists view the records of upper-level management as the core of information about a company. After all, it is at the apex of a hierarchy that important decisions are most often made. However, the activities of a functionally organized or multidivisional corporation cannot be properly documented or understood from centralized upper-management files alone. Information is not merely summarized as it moves up the hierarchy; much of it disappears as decisions are made at lower levels. Other information never gets into the vertical flow in the first place, because it is operational in character and does not need to move to a higher authority . . .

The availability of historical records and the resources that may be used to preserve them varies greatly from company to company. Record series judged to be invaluable in one situation might be viewed as insignificant in another . . . . . If the records-keeping practices of each company were exactly the same, specific recommendations on each type of record could be made. Since this is not the case, . . . it is the archivist's task to understand the universe of documentation that is likely to be found, identify those issues and activities that seem to have historical relevance, and find the records or artifacts that best document them.

Bruce H. Bruemmer and Sheldon Hochheiser, The High-Technology Company: A Historical Research and Archival Guide (Minneapolis: Charles Babbage Institute, University of Minnesota, 1989), 11-13. This publication is distributed by the Society of American Archivists.

the one normally used for standardization. Carl Cargill has recently written that "an internal standards program [in any area] is one of the more difficult corporate functions to manage and make effective. . . . Standardizing a process [which is precisely what archival appraisal requires] requires an understanding of the company, its management, its operating structures and strictures, and its culture."[16] In appraising the records, then, the archivist should know the following:

- the basic outline of origins, development (including significant events, issues, and concerns), and present main issues of the institution
- the major functions of the institution and how those functions are administratively handled
- the existing universe of documentation that has been created and is being created by the institution
- the external influences on the documentation, indicating as well, potential other sources of documentation that might supplement and be important to that created by the institution
- the internal influences on the ways that policy decisions are made and programs are initiated and administered, and how such influences are reflected in existing documentation or not
- individuals knowledgeable about the institution's history either because of their experience in working in the institution or because of research they have conducted about the institution

Knowing such information will greatly assist the archivist to appraise the records of the institution and to help make the institutional archives a viable part of the ongoing work of the institution.

APPRAISAL PRACTICES AND TECHNIQUES

There is a well-developed set of archival appraisal practices and techniques that have proved their effectiveness in identifying and preserving important archival information through the years. These range from efforts to look at specific documents to determine the degree of their informational value found in their physical structure (intrinsic value described earlier) to multi-institutional and multi-disciplinary efforts to determine what should be documented about a particular topic, movement, or geographic area (documentation strategy). With all of these techniques, the most important thing for the institutional archivist to know is how they should be utilized within the institutional setting and in conformity with the institutional mission. The purpose of this section is to discuss briefly some of the more important archival appraisal practices and techniques for the work of institutional archivists.

Acquisition or collecting policies are generally only used by manuscript

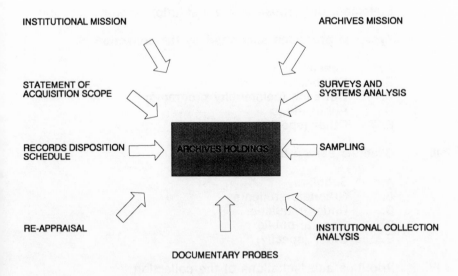

INFLUENCES ON APPRAISAL DECISIONS IN INSTITUTIONAL ARCHIVES

INSTITUTIONAL MISSION

ARCHIVES MISSION

STATEMENT OF
ACQUISITION SCOPE

SURVEYS AND
SYSTEMS ANALYSIS

RECORDS DISPOSITION
SCHEDULE

ARCHIVES HOLDINGS

SAMPLING

RE-APPRAISAL

INSTITUTIONAL COLLECTION
ANALYSIS

DOCUMENTARY PROBES

collecting repositories such as historical societies or academic library special collections units. It is advisable, however, for institutional archives to have similar statements of their acquisition scope, even if limited to records created by the institution. These statements will help to reemphasize the archives' mission statement (described in chapter 2) and to publicize the necessary work of the archival program among the institution's staff. Since many individuals in the institution may well equate the scope of the archives with only "older" or obsolete records, not with records with continuing value to the organization and certainly not with records in electronic form, the development of a collecting policy will be a useful promotional item for the institutional archives. Faye Phillips's scheme for a manuscript collecting policy—purpose statement, programs supported by the collection, clientele served by the collection, priorities and limitations of the collections, cooperative agreements affecting the policy, a resource sharing policy, a deaccessioning policy, procedures guiding the policy's implementation, and procedures for evaluating the guidelines—could be easily adapted for use within an institutional setting.[17]

There is, of course, another reason for an institutional archives' staff

A Structure for a Model Collecting Policy

I.   Statement of purpose of the institution and/or collection.

II.   Types of programs supported by the collection

    A.   Research
    B.   Exhibits
    C.   Outreach (community programs)
    D.   Publications
    E.   Other (specify)

III.   Clientele served by the collection

    A.   Scholars
    B.   Graduate students
    C.   Undergraduates
    D.   General public
    E.   Other (specify)

IV.   Priorities and limitations of the collection

    A.   Present identified strengths
    B.   Present collecting level
    C.   Present identified weaknesses
    D.   Desired level of collecting to meet program needs
    E.   Geographical areas collected
    F.   Chronological periods collected
    G.   Subject areas collected
    H.   Languages, other than English, collected
    I.   Forms of materials, other than manuscripts, collected
    J.   Exclusions

V.   Cooperative agreements affecting the collecting policy

VI.   Statement of resource sharing policy

VII.   Statement of deaccessioning policy

VIII. Procedures affecting collecting policy and its expedition

IX.   Procedure for monitoring development and reviewing collection development guidelines

Faye Phillips, "Developing Collecting Policies for Manuscript Collections," _American Archivist_ 47 (Winter 1984): 39.

thinking about a more traditional collecting policy: whether the institutional archives will acquire noninstitutional records or not. In some cases, an institutional archives might stress the need to collect noninstitutional records because there are important informational sources that fill in gaps found in the institutional records. For example, the personal papers of individuals associated with the organization might be valuable ancillary sources for understanding the historical evolution and present nature of the institution. A collecting policy should be in place for this kind of activity, because it is important to limit the realm of such work. Otherwise, it might become too easy for the archivist to put resources into such an activity and lessen work on the main purposes of the archives to take care of the records formally created by the institution. At best, such collecting should be kept to a minimum. A better arrangement might be that the institutional archives works with a historical manuscripts repository within the same geographical area to see that these manuscripts of importance to the institution are acquired, preserved, and available for consultation; in most cases, these collecting repositories would welcome such advice and assistance, especially when they lead to important historical sources that they might not be aware of and that might fit into their existing collections.

The most common appraisal tool used by all archivists, institutional and otherwise, including records managers, is the records *survey*. A records survey has been defined as

a systematic procedure ... to gather information about records and papers not in their immediate custody. Most surveys are conducted as part of broader archival programs to create research tools, to aid in collection building, to promote preservation of archival materials, or otherwise to contribute to the goals of their sponsors. Information gathering in these projects is a basic step, instrumental in accomplishing these more extended goals.[18]

As can be surmised from this definition, the records survey has become a standard practice by archivists for a variety of reasons, is often employed as one of the initial starting points for any records or archives program, and is periodically used for special initiatives, mainly, in the latter fashion, by collecting repositories. The focus of the records survey is the series, and generally such surveys are conducted with the use of inventory forms that gather data about the records series, creator of the series, and administrative uses of the series.

There are a number of basic uses of a survey for the institutional archivist. A survey of the records of the institution can be used to determine the range of existing documentation, the volume of records, the condition of the records, and the various information media that the archivist will have to contend with to develop criteria for appraisal and eventual designation of certain records as possessing archival significance. All of these benefits

Records Inventory and Analysis Worksheet

(1) Department | Division | Section

(2) Title of records series

(3) Location of records

(4) Description of records series (Content, purpose, etc.)

(5) Earliest date/Latest date | **(6)** Records still created? | **(7)** Volume | **(8)** Annual accumulation

_____ _____ | YES ☐   NO ☐ | _____ cu. ft. | _____ cu. ft.

(9) Record series characteristics (Check appropriate boxes)

TYPE: ☐ PAPER   ☐ CARD   ☐ BOUND VOLUME   ☐ MICROFILM   ☐ MACHINE READABLE
☐ OTHER (Specify)_____

SIZE: ☐ LETTER   ☐ LEGAL   ☐ OTHER (Specify) _____

STATUS: ☐ ORIGINAL   ☐ COPY

FORMAT: ☐ TYPEWRITTEN   ☐ HANDWRITTEN ☐ OTHER_____

ARRANGE-
MENT: ☐ CHRONOLOGICAL   ☐ ALPHABETICAL BY_____ ☐ NUMERICAL BY_____ ☐ OTHER _____

(10) Reference frequency (Check blocks, insert numbers, circle appropriate words)

_____Times, daily, weekly, monthly, yearly for _____ months, years   Never after _____

(11) Information available elsewhere? | **(12)** Microfilmed?

YES ☐   NO ☐   If yes, where?_____ | YES ☐   NO ☐   If yes, explain_____

(13) Are records indexed?

YES ☐   NO ☐   If yes, identify _____

(14) How stored?

☐ Filing Cabinets ☐ Shelves ☐ Boxes ☐ Other_____

(15) Condition of records

_____Poor _____ Fair _____ Good   (Explain any problems)_____

(16) Records on retention and disposition schedule?

YES ☐   NO ☐   If yes, Schedule No. _____ Item No. on Schedule _____
If no, suggested retention period and justification _____

(17) Condition of storage area (Security, fireproof, alarms, environment, etc.)

☐ Good ☐ Poor   State any storage problems _____

(18) Additional comments

(19) Name of person completing inventory | Date

(20) Action taken

☐ Records disposed of, date _____   ☐ Microfilmed, date _____

☐ Sent to inactive records center, date _____   ☐ Retain permanently, sent to archives, date _____

☐ Other (Explain) _____

are most often gained when a records survey is done in the beginning of the development of an institutional archives. Information gained through such a survey will often have a great influence on the nature of the institutional archives, including the staff size of the program, the storage needs for the archives, and the nature of commitment to such basic concerns as preservation and reference facilities.

If conducted at an early stage in the life of an institutional archives, records surveys possess some other potential values as well. Records surveys will help provide important information about the administrative structure and that structure's operation because such surveying will bring the archivist into contact with all aspects of the institution; the information gained will often be an important supplement to other evidence regarding the historical evolution and present functioning of the organization. Surveys can be used to identify potential obstacles in both individuals and administrative structures and to establish or improve the institutional knowledge of, and support for, the program. Institutional archivists can employ the records survey to aid in training individuals throughout the institution about how they need to view the records that they create and maintain; contacts made through surveys and sustained afterward will often turn out to be essential sources of support for the institutional archives.

There are some disadvantages to the ways that records surveys have been used or are seen by those who utilize them. The main problem is that archivists have often confused the records survey with a broad documentation of the institution itself. The existing records are often insufficient to understand an institution or even to meet an institution's continuing information needs from its own records. What needs to be known by the institution about its own operations, policies, and procedures might not be adequately reflected in its own records. These problems can be rectified by the archivist's being able to distinguish such questions and concerns from the best uses of the records survey or by understanding the different uses of a records survey in the establishment of a program (such as the later use of a survey to determine how effectively key aspects of an institution are being documented). Archivists in collecting institutions have developed the concept of institutional collection analysis, which is close to the latter value of the records survey. Collection analysis, described later in this chapter, is a detailed quantitative and qualitative analysis of a repository's existing holdings to determine its strengths and weaknesses in light of broader programmatic objectives.[19] An institutional archives could use such a technique in conjunction with a resurvey of the records and information systems throughout the institution.

Other problems exist with the use of records surveys beyond those described above. Records surveys are extremely labor-intensive efforts, sometimes resulting in efforts that stop short of accessioning archival materials into the repository or bringing control to the records with continuing research and administrative values. More importantly, records surveys conducted by institutional archives must be done in conjunction with an existing institutional records management program, a program that has good control over its *records disposition schedules.*

A records disposition or retention schedule is a "document that authorizes and provides for the transfer and disposition of all records of the organization."[20] *Transfer* means the removal of institutional records from the creating office to a records center or archives, while *disposition* refers either to the destruction of records or to the maintenance of records as part of the institutional archives. These schedules reflect the records life cycle. Schedules are the basic tools of the records management program (which will be discussed below in more detail), but they are also obviously essential to the work of the institutional archivist. Schedules culminate from surveys of records, although these are documents that interpret the raw data of the surveys into a meaningful analysis of an institution's use of information. A glance at the schedules should provide the institutional archivist and/or records manager an understanding of the universe of information within the institution and enable reliable disposition decisions to be made.

A records retention schedule seeks to gather information about the circumstances of any one records series: the creating unit; nature of the records contained within the series; the arrangement of the files and their form; function being reflected by the records; time span of the records; whether the records are still being created or not; and the degree of use within the creating office; and other legal, fiscal, administrative requirements regarding the records. For the records manager, focusing on the current value of the records, the schedule is intended to guide the records through their normal life cycle of value to the organization. For the archivist, such schedules are necessary for effective review of an institution's records in order to determine what records will be maintained for long-term research and other values. For the institution, records retention schedules are published policy statements that communicate to the various individuals and units the need to manage their records and how those records should be managed. While an acquisition policy guides an institution in what archival records it desires to preserve, records surveys and records disposition schedules are tools that are used to analyze the records themselves and determine what records have continuing value to the organization.

There are other tools that are utilized by the institutional archivist to reevaluate internally the archival records. These tools are sampling, reappraisal, and institutional collection analysis (the latter already mentioned above). All three tools are used within the institutional archives to determine whether certain archival records will continue to be maintained, whether they will be reduced in volume, or whether they fulfill adequately

RECREATION

PARKS, RECREATIONAL PROGRAMS AND CIVIC CENTERS

1. **Participation, attendance, or enrollment records** for park, recreational facility, civic center, or club

   a. Summary record or report: — 6 years

   b. Records of original entry, including worksheets, used admission tickets and ticket stubs: — 6 years, or 1 year after posting to summary record or report, whichever is shorter

   c. Statement of disposition of unused tickets, when a fee is charged: — 6 years

2. **Park, recreational facility, civic center, or club permits,** granted to individual or family, including application, affidavit, and copy of stub or license

   a. When a fee is charged: — 0 after invalid, but not less than 6 years

   b. When *no* fee is charged: — 0 after invalid, but not less than 1 year

3. **Parental consent records** allowing child's participation in recreational activities: — 6 years, or 3 years after child attains age 18, whichever is longer

4. **Planning and development records** covering such topics as facility construction, improvement and usage

   a. Final reports and studies: — PERMANENT

   b. Background materials and supporting documentation used to produce reports and studies: — 6 years

5. **Special event file**

   a. Official copy of any program or promotional literature, or photographs of events or performances: — PERMANENT

   b. Background materials and supporting documentation: — 6 years

6. **Athletic program records:** — 6 years

   NOTE: These records may have continuing value for historical or other research, and SARA suggests they be retained permanently.

MENTAL RETARDATION AND DEVELOPMENTAL DISABILITIES (M.R.& D.D.) RECREATIONAL PROGRAMS

1. **Master summary record** of participants in M.R. & D.D. recreation program: — 6 years after last entry

the intended functions of the archival program for the institution. While all three are also fairly labor-intensive exercises, they are necessary to the efficient functioning of the institutional archives. The key to the use of these appraisal tools is to know when to employ them.

Sampling is a technique utilized by archivists for nearly a half-century, although it has been used sporadically, at best, because it is a labor-intensive effort and requires careful planning and execution and considerable archival knowledge and experience. Sampling is generally considered to occur after initial appraisal. It is an effort to reduce the quantity of records that have already been deemed to have continuing value, because the archivist has determined both that the bulk of records might reduce their utility to researchers and that the homogeneity of the records allows reduction without destroying any of the research values of the records. Sampling is also used more directly as an appraisal approach to select the most valuable portions of large series of records that are difficult to deal with because of their volume, necessary resources for support, and other factors. Both applications seem possible in an institutional archives situation where archivists face large runs of modern records and where archivists have intimate knowledge of the institution's inner workings that allows sampling to be applied effectively and safely.

Sampling is also generally accomplished through rigorous statistical methods or, at times, more subjective approaches. The statistical effort can be accomplished through numerical sampling that relies on random number tables. Each file in a records series is given (or might already have) an identification number, and the tables are used to ensure that a truly random selection of the records is made.[21] Other archivists have suggested variations in statistical sampling and argued that such sampling can be effectively applied only by analysis of the total records and mixing the sample at different points to achieve a true portrait of the nature of the records.[22] The more subjective sampling by the archivist occurs when the archivist reduces a records series by removing duplicate material or assessing that some material in the series may be extraneous or of little value. It is akin to the weeding done by librarians of book collections, although it is open to more problems because of the irreversibility of the archivist's destruction of archival records. Still, such subjective sampling may be necessary at times as the archivist faces the prospects of large quantities of records to administer and limited space and other resources to care for the records.

The most difficult aspect of archival sampling is when to apply it. Margery Sly, an archivist with experience in the sampling of records, has developed a good set of questions that can be followed in determining when to use a sampling technique:

1. *What are the records?*
2. *Are they homogeneous—concerned with one function only and essentially similar*

Example of an Archival Sampling Project

The records of Hannah Lay and Company, of Traverse City, Michigan, are an excellent example of the archival problems encountered in attempting to preserve and organize large volumes of documents for historical research . . . .

After the collection's forty years of drift from archives to archives with limited use, logic seemed to dictate that a rational discarding was necessary and indeed beneficial to the life of the collection . . . .

How to weed the bulk efficiently, systematically, and intelligently became our chief problem. In devising a system for the selective weeding we adopted two overall goals: (1) to have enough material readily available for the casual researcher to provide a good overview of the structure and scope of Hannah Lay and Company without having to pour through the entire collection, (2) to retain enough material to provide more serious scholars with sufficient material to get a sense of the complexity and importance of the operations of the company at the various stages of its development.

It was a relatively simple task to isolate records which would provide a quick overview of the nature of the company. The complete minutes of the director's meetings . . . were saved . . . . We also saved the surviving correspondence which provides selective but detailed information regarding the general nature of Hannah Lay's daily activities. There were selective reports on such matters as sales, Great Lakes shipping, annual reports, and departmental reports, which provided important aggregate information . . . . However, to have chosen only those records would have destroyed the research value of the complete set and deprived the serious student of business history with hard data on the development of Michigan's lumber industry . . . .

We first considered saving complete runs of some records and discarding others . . . . In surveying the contents of these records, we concluded that no single run would be of much significance without supporting data from other material, and thus this solution was rejected . . . .

We then explored a sampling approach. Since the contents of the general runs of ledgers, daybooks, and journals were quantitative, we figured that the only way significant conclusions could be drawn from the material would be through a quantitative approach to the sources, and that approach would require selective use of the material . . . .

We selected the census years 1860-1930. Although this was arbitrary decision, it was based on the fact that information in the records for these years could be matched with available census data for larger studies of specific individuals or locations . . . .

Had all runs of journals, daybooks, and similar book records been complete and of uniform quality, the scheme would have given complete samples of the records for the eight census years which occurred during the company's existence. However, most of the series did not cover the entire history of the company, particularly the material on relatively short-lived branches. More important, as accounting techniques evolved over time and became more formal, much of the research value of this type of record diminished . . . . As a result we decided to save the mid-decade years as well, which would provide fifteen total sample years for the company's seventy-five year history.

Larry Steck and Francis Blouin, "Hannah Lay & Company: Sampling the Records of a Century of Lumbering in Michigan," *American Archivist* 39 (January 1976): 15-18.

---

in character—or are they individual and variable in nature? If they are the latter, these records will not be a good candidate for sampling.

3. *Is it possible to retain the essence of the records through sampling?* That is, will a sample of the records lose so much of the evidential and informational characteristics that it will be hard to relate the sample to the original function, nature, and use of the records? If so, these records will not be a good choice for sampling. Other questions to consider are, Will the records serve the user after sampling? and How will the user approach and access the holdings?

4. *What is the correlation between amount of research value and bulk?* If there seems to be a likely use of the records, a use that is discouraged by the records volume, then sampling should be seriously considered, provided the reasons for the research demand will not be undermined by reduction in quantity.

5. *What is the method of arrangement and organization?* If the records arrangement is inadequate for sampling, mandating that they be rearranged prior to sampling, then the time and expense of this work must be factored in as a consideration. The research value and other considerations will have to be very high for sampling to be a good use of resources. Sly also adds related questions, such as: Have the records been properly maintained? Is the filing system adequate and consistent throughout? and What is the method of indexing? All of these questions relate to the condition of the records before sampling is considered.

6. *Do ancillary sources of information exist?* The issue here is whether there are other, more convenient and manageable bodies of records that might be relied on rather than undertaking sampling. This matter relates to other basic questions as well, such as, For what purpose would these records be sampled?; Are the records being retained for evidential or informational purposes or both?; and Are there any acceptable alternatives other than sampling? Such questions demonstrate that sampling must be applied where there is considerable knowledge about the universe of information.

7. *Will anticipated use justify cost of storage?* What resources are available in the owner repository to appraise and process these records? These questions raise the matter of the availability of resources and institutional priorities in the use of such appraisal techniques as sampling. Since sampling is extremely time-consuming and expensive, it must be used judiciously. Temporary storage of bulky records with known archival values might often be the best approach. Later sampling, fitting in with overall priorities and needs, can be generally accommodated.[23]

Utilizing a set of questions such as these will help the institutional archivist to know when to use sampling in appraisal work.

Reappraisal is similar to sampling in that it is done after initial appraisal work and that its most difficult aspect is determining when to apply it. Reappraisal is the process by which records previously appraised as possessing archival values and already accessioned into the archival facility are periodically reexamined to determine whether they should be continued to be maintained as part of the institutional archives. The period of time that has been suggested for reappraisal is 20 or more years. Such an interval would allow time for the repository to publish and circulate descriptions of these records, to prepare guide entries and inventories, and otherwise to serve notice of their existence and availability. It would allow time to analyze what uses, if any, are made of the records. Where samples or selections are periodically accessioned, this analysis would be particularly useful in determining whether the actual uses of these samples and selections were those on which the sampling or selection schemes and percentages were based.[24]

Reappraisal is predicated on several basic notions. First, the archivist's estimation of the value of records can change as a result of the passage of time, which provides additional insights about the functions, issues, events, policies, and other matters that certain records document. Second, additional records can emerge and be accessioned into an archival facility that prove to be better sources of documentation for the specific event, topic, or function for which other records might earlier have been saved. Third, lack of use by researchers, especially those from within the institution, over a lengthy period of time should cause reconsideration to be given to the continued, expensive maintenance of archival records. As has already been suggested, the application of reappraisal must be very carefully considered and administered, since the destruction of archival records is a final act.[25]

Institutional collection analysis, or just *collection analysis,* is a relatively new archival technique for selection of archival materials. It has been developed and experimented with by several statewide historical records programs, whose staffs became concerned (and curious) about whether their actual holdings matched their acquisition policies and what they

A Reappraisal Case Study

In 1946, while the [Wage Adjustment Board] was still in existence, a competent archivist appraised its records. The appraisal, in accordance with the archival thinking of the time . . . , called for the accessioning by the National Archives of almost 700 feet of records, with more to come. These were of enduring value as "the basic record of the policies, procedures, and operations of the Board, and as the principal source of information regarding labor-management relationships and wage stabilization efforts in the key building and construction industry during World War II." But later there were, apparently, some second thoughts. By the time the records were accessioned the quantity had been reduced to 175 feet.

Thirty years ago, as a new archivist, I prepared an inventory of these records. This inventory was published in 1954. Twenty years later, while a member of the Records Appraisal Staff, I asked an archivist on rotation there to look at these records and, if she thought it called for, to reappraise them. She did, and reduced the 175 feet to 24 feet.

In the late 1940s, not long after the records came to the National Archives, two former public members of the board . . . wrote a history of the board, . . . published in 1950. Only their service on the board and their intimate knowledge of it accounts for . . . writing a book about such an obscure agency . . . .

A recent reexamination of the remaining twenty-four feet of the board's records convinces me that something less than half that amount would include whatever worthwhile evidence and information there is.

Leonard Rapport, "No Grandfather Clause: Reappraising Accessioned Records," American Archivist 44 (Spring 1981): 148.

---

thought was represented by their collections. In the best essay relative to this technique, collection analysis has been defined as

a method to assess a repository's holdings in specific categories, [providing] a profile of an institution's collection at a particular time. Archivists can use such concrete knowledge of their holdings to make informed decisions about collecting priorities. Collection analysis has two parts: (1) a quantitative phase in which specific characteristics of a repository's holdings are enumerated and (2) a qualitative phase in which these findings are analyzed and placed in a larger conceptual framework. Along with other considerations, such as the universe of documentation and the realistic collecting possibilities in particular fields, collection analysis can be used by a repository to revise or refine an acquisitions policy or to gauge its success at meeting collecting goals.[26]

The tests of this technique have used broad topical schemes that define the universe of activity in their state or region in order to measure existing collections against such topics. Strengths and weaknesses are thus both identified.

Collection analysis is, obviously, primarily designed for the collecting historical records organization rather than the institutional archives. Still, the basic premise of collection analysis could be adapted and used in the institutional setting. The institutional archivist could determine what his or her archives should have and should be documenting about the institution, relative to both informational and evidential values described above. Once the archivist has determined these documentary goals, an analysis of the holdings of the archives could be completed. Strengths of the holdings would be better known. More importantly, weaknesses would emerge. The archivist could then ascertain why such weaknesses exist and how these weaknesses can be corrected. Is it because significant records have been disposed of, for whatever reason, or is it because the crucial information is not being captured in the transactional records because of the corporate culture and environment of the organization? Once the archivist has a better grasp of these issues, then it will be possible for the archival operation to be better positioned or reoriented for fulfilling its institutional mission.

A similar appraisal tool has been suggested by one of the discipline history centers concerned with documenting science and technology. A *documentary probe* is a "product study that generates diverse historical, organizational, and documentary information from all facets of a company in order to aid in the selection of historically valuable records." The probe makes use of records surveys, interviews, research into the institution's development, and description of other activity in order "to identify how well those issues are represented by extant documentation and to identify other areas needing to be documented." This technique is an effort to rectify some of the traditional problems that occur when the institutional archivist sets out to document an organization through records surveys and other approaches that focus only on extant records rather than posing important questions to be answered or activities and events to be documented.[27]

The concept of a documentary probe, which is focused on one institution's environment, has been adapted from another recently developed concept, the multi-institutional *documentation strategy*. The probe works through a series of steps that do not concentrate solely on the existing records generated by a single institution but that try to mix concerns and information from knowledgeable sources and other settings. Again, the

COLLECTION ANALYSIS

The following worksheets were part of the materials developed for use in a multi-institutional effort to determine how well Milwaukee is being documented by the city's archival repositories. The first form is a simple worksheet that can be used to analyze the topical content of manuscript collections and institutional records series. The second item is the beginning of the guide sheet used to direct the definitions of topics.

COLLECTION ANALYSIS WORKSHEET

Call #: _____

Main Entry: _____

Title: _____

Inclusive Dates: _____

Form: _____

Total Linear Feet: _____

Subject	%	Lin. Ft.

	00	10	20	30	40	50	60	70	80	90
17										
18										
19										

FRAMEWORK FOR TOPICAL ANALYSIS OF COMMUNITY HISTORY

1. **AA ART & ARCHITECTURE**
   a) Individual artists, writers, performers, architects
   b) Institutions (foundations, museums, schools)
   c) Entertainment companies & cultural organizations
   d) Architectural and other arts-related business

probe recognizes that the goal of documentation might not always be achievable through the traditional archival appraisal techniques. The documentation strategy has been born out of the same concerns and issues.

As one of the pioneers in the development of documentation strategies, Helen Samuels has written that the strategy concept was created because archival appraisal carried out solely within one institution "is insufficient to support the decisions archivists face. Individuals and institutions do not exist independently.... Government, industry, and academia—the private and public sectors—are integrated through patterns of funding and regulations." Even an individual's papers have been created by "multiple hands."[28] A documentation strategy is a

plan formulated to assure the documentation of an ongoing issue, activity, or geographic area.... The strategy is ordinarily designed, promoted, and in part implemented by an ongoing mechanism involving records creators, administrators (including archivists), and users. The documentation strategy is carried out through the mutual efforts of many institutions and individuals influencing both the creation of the records and the archival retention of a portion of them. The strategy is refined in response to changing conditions and viewpoints.[29]

How are documentation strategies used by institutional archives? How do documentation strategies affect institutional archives? First, documentation strategies might be employed by an institutional archives. This situation could occur when it realizes that an aspect of its organization that should be documented is cooperative in nature, meaning that important sources of information are held by other organizations. The institutional archives could start an effort to bring together records creators, administrators, and users to determine the best means by which to ensure adequate documentation. Second, an institutional archives might be asked to participate in a documentation strategy effort by an outside actor who believes the archives has an essential role to play in this documentation. This situation could occur as the result of efforts to document either the geographical area in which the institutional archives resides or a topic for which the archives might be in the best position to document.[30] In either way, the documentation strategy is an approach that can assist the institutional archives achieve its mission of preserving records valuable for the institution, even though those records lie outside the immediate control of the records creator the program serves.

Documentation strategies round off the array of appraisal techniques that need to be employed by the institutional archives. These techniques, however, must also be used within the setting of an archival program that is closely tied to an organizationwide records management (or information resources management) operation. Without this connection, the archives will suffer in striving to identify and preserve those records that have long-term value to the organization.

DOCUMENTATION STRATEGY PROCESS MODEL

The following schematic diagram shows the series of steps involved in developing documentation strategies. The diagram is from Larry Hackman and Joan Warnow-Blewett, "The Documentation Strategy Process: A Model and a Case Study," American Archivist 50 (Winter 1987): 19.

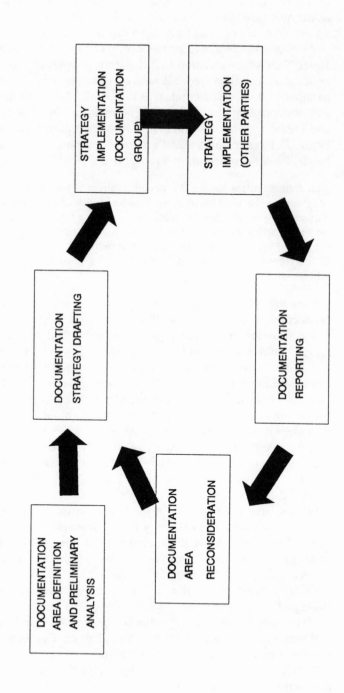

THE INSTITUTIONAL ARCHIVES AND RECORDS MANAGEMENT

Records management has traditionally been concerned with current records' cost-efficient administration and effective access. A typical definition of records management as used in a standard textbook in this field states that it is the "application of systematic and scientific control to all of the recorded information that an organization needs to do business."[31] Built around the life cycle concept of records, the scope of records management has been traditionally viewed as encompassing records from their creation through use in the office of creation to final disposition, which can include destruction or transfer to an archives for permanent preservation—the life cycle of records discussed earlier in this chapter. To manage records, a variety of records management subfunctions has been normally viewed as part of such programs, including records inventorying and appraisal, records scheduling (described earlier), caring for vital records (records identified as essential to the functioning of an organization), micrographics operations, the administration of records centers for the storage of inactive records (records no longer having frequent current use to their creators), an archives for those records possessing historical and other research values, and the control and management of forms, correspondence, mail, reports, directives, and reprographics.

This traditional concept of records management has been challenged through the emergence in the past decade of information resources management (IRM). As one individual has informally defined IRM, it is the view that "information is an organizational resource, technology needs to be managed, and people need to effectively handle both of them."[32] IRM includes the effort to manage the entire range of information resources—computer hardware and software, telecommunications equipment, office automation equipment, and reprographics machinery, as well as the information transmitted through this equipment and the people. IRM includes, as well, a variety of techniques that are very similar to those employed by records managers and built around the life cycle concept. The major difference between IRM and records management is the broader, self-defined scope of IRM. Records management has been primarily oriented to paper records, treating newer forms of electronic records within the scope of the scientific and systematic management of records. IRM sees itself as a melding of many disciplines, including data processing, records management, and related fields, all of which have some stake in the creation and use of information.

Archivists have had a variety of reactions to the records management (or IRM) functions and the profession that supports them. Some archivists have viewed the two fields as completely separate, a characteristic that has certainly been borne out by the last 30 years. The records management field emerged from the archival discipline in the 1950s and through the years has become a separate discipline. An individual can become either a certified records manager or archivist or both, but the structures supporting these designations are completely separate, with very distinct histories. There are also separate professional associations and publications, as well as differing educational programs with their own standards. Others have seen the records management program as an essential tool for effective institutional archives programs, while, curiously, records managers have tended to perceive archival administration as a subfunction, although not an essential one, of their programs. Records management enables the archivist to have a comprehensive view of an institution's documentation while also providing some cost-effective and efficiency arguments that can help to counterbalance the expensive foundations of an archival operation. In a recent assessment of the relationship between the two disciplines, an archivist forthrightly noted that "while the two professions generally require different training and skills, they are in fact mutually dependent upon each other for complete success, and share a common concern for the identification and preservation of records essential to the ongoing operations of their institutions."[33] Finally, other archivists have seen records management as a partial solution to some of the challenges that they face in their institutions. A recent analysis of records management in college and university settings has suggested that records management is an "elusive" objective because for some "it is the wrong goal because it disregards the traditions of those college and university archives that have developed out of an historical manuscript tradition and because it requires greater institutional support than many college and university archives are given." The major aspects of records management that promise cost effectiveness or efficiency are not utilized because these archives "adopt and adapt selected records management techniques that will allow them to maintain more efficiently cultural facilities focusing on the preservation of records for research use."[34]

Still, an institutional archives program must be closely linked with a records management operation in order to ensure that all the records that have archival value are identified, preserved, and made available for use. This need is built upon a very old archival concept. A half-century ago, Philip C. Brooks stated that the "archivist looks upon current records as future archives, and it is a legitimate part of his function to make available counsel on how they [the current records] can be best handled."[35] Because an increasing portion of information is being created, stored, and accessed electronically, it is very important that archivists be as close to the point of creation of these records as possible. The fragility of these electronic media and the ease by which their data bases are erased or altered require that the archivist be available to ensure that the integrity of the archival record is maintained. The previous notion under which archivists operated, that the records should be transferred to their facilities long after their initial creation and use by the creators, is no longer tenable in the electronic environment. The scheduling function of records management also provides an orderly transfer of records to the archives. Records identified as having archival value on the schedules can be regularly sent to the archives as stipulated, a process that also serves the purpose of providing a continual reminder to the institution's employees and administrators that there are archival records in their midst and that resists the notion that archival records are only old or unwanted parts of the institution's documentation. Finally, the inclusion of archival records in the records management loop provides an opportunity for archivists to counterbalance the costs associated with the maintenance of their records, although it is important not to overemphasize such costs savings in certain environments.[36] Archival records can be seen both to be part of a natural process that saves the institution financial resources as well as to protect a valuable information resource.

PUTTING IT ALL TOGETHER

Knowing all the various potential archival values of records does not ensure that an institutional archives will administer an effective appraisal function. Several important structural elements, in addition to the knowledgeable archivist supervising the process, must be in place.

First, the institutional archives should have an advisory committee that provides input into the appraisal decisions. At a minimum this committee should include the organization's executive, legal, and fiscal officers or their representatives—all individuals who have knowledge of the inner workings of the institution and its information requirements and systems—along with one or two external representatives, perhaps historians or other archivists who possess working experience with the kinds of records that the institution represents or the topical matter that the records relate to and who can assist in the appraisal of certain of the organization's records. This advisory committee can be an informal body that changes according to the nature of the appraisal work needed to be completed, although the institutional archivist will probably (and should) have a formal body that approves the final disposition of records or, at least, participate in such a body if the archivist is administratively part of the institution's records management or other information management program.

Second, the institutional archivist must be administratively situated so as to work equally with all the information workers in the organization. This need has been discussed more fully in the second chapter of this volume, but it is worth reemphasizing that the archivist must be able to work with data processors, librarians, records managers, managers of information systems, and other such professionals in order to ensure that the essential documentary record of the institution remains intact. The overall objective of the archivist should be to educate these individuals about the importance of the archival record as an informational, administrative, and cultural resource of the organization.

Finally, the institutional archives must have a good rapport with other institutional archives and collecting repositories located in the immediate geographical area and with relevant discipline history centers if the organization falls into one of the sciences like chemistry or physics. Thorough documentation of any single institution is virtually not achievable with that institution's records because of the interrelatedness of the records with other records creators, regulatory agencies, and funding bodies. This fact suggests that cooperative efforts to ensure that archival documentation outside the institution but important to the institution should be maintained. Furthermore, institutional archives might need to work with other historical records and archival programs to ensure that relevant archival records are preserved. This effort might work if institutional archivists inquire about the potential value of records slated for destruction for a thorough documentation of a region or topical area. Institutional archivists might also learn of the availability of privately held archival records with value to their organization that they might wish to see another institution acquire so that the records are available for consultation.

The complexity of archival appraisal is a given, calling for great knowledge, careful assessment, increased cooperation, and new approaches. While some of these issues might seem to be counter to the best interests of the organization, new means and new approaches are essential for the effectual documentation of institutions. Issues of confidentiality, access, and financial costs and other important matters will be considered in later chapters in this volume.

NOTES

1. The term *appraisal* should not be confused with appraisal of historical records for monetary purposes, such as for tax purposes when manuscript collections are donated to a historical records repository. The long-accepted definition of archival appraisal has been that of the process for ascertaining the informational value of records and whether the records should be preserved in an archival repository or destroyed.

2. For an assessment of the relationship of archival appraisal to other archival functions and continuing research needs in this area, refer to Richard J. Cox and Helen W. Samuels, "The Archivist's First Responsibility: A Research Agenda to Improve the Identification and Retention of Records of Enduring Value," *American Archivist* 51 (Winter/Spring 1988): 28–42.

3. A convenient introduction to some of the changing notions of archival appraisal can be gained by referring to Nancy E. Peace, ed., *Archival Choices: Managing the Historical Record in an Age of Abundance* (Lexington, MA.: Lexington Books, 1984).

4. Frank B. Evans, et al., "A Basic Glossary for Archivists, Manuscript Curators, and Records Managers," *American Archivist* 37 (July 1974): 430.

5. Evans, "A Basic Glossary," 428.

6. See, for example, James W. Geary, "Catholic Archives in a Public Institution: A Case Study of the Arrangement Between Kent State University and the Diocese of Youngstown, Ohio," *American Archivist* 46 (Spring 1983): 175–82 and, for a broader treatment, David J. Klaassen, "The Archival Intersection: Cooperation Between Collecting Repositories and Nonprofit Organizations," *Midwestern Archivist* 15, no. 1 (1990): 25–38.

7. There is debate within the archival profession about the notion of whether archival records possess "continuing" or "enduring" value. Institutional archivists should adopt whatever term is most appropriate in their organization for developing viable archival programs. See David Bearman, *Archival Methods*, Archives and Museum Informatics Technical Report, 3 (Spring 1989), chapter 2 and James M. O'Toole, "On the Idea of Permanence," *American Archivist* 52 (Winter 1989): 10–25 for an introduction to the debate.

8. JoAnne Yates, "Internal Communication Systems in American Business Structures: A Framework to Aid Appraisal," *American Archivist* 48 (Spring 1985): 156.

9. Dennis E. Meissner, "The Evaluation of Modern Business Accounting Records," *Midwestern Archivist* 5, no. 2 (1981): 75–77.

10. Donald S. Skupsky, *Recordkeeping Requirements: The First Practical Guide to Help You Control Your Records . . . What You Need to Keep and What You Can Safely Destroy!* (Denver: Information Requirements Clearinghouse, 1989), 23.

11. Frank Boles and Julia Marks Young, "Exploring the Black Box: The Appraisal of University Administrative Records," *American Archivist* 48 (Spring 1985): 122.

12. If an institution's archival records can be used for public relations efforts, it stands to reason that the loss of such records can have more negative results. All the publicity about Mark Hoffman's forging and dealing of manuscripts concerning Joseph Smith brought negative publicity to the Mormon church when it became more widely known that the church was striving to purchase and conceal documents it believed were negative to its founders and fundamental religious beliefs.

13. A good example of the close relationship of one institution's records to other institutions can be seen in Philip N. Alexander and Helen W. Samuels, "The Roots of 128: A Hypothetical Documentation Strategy," *American Archivist* 50 (Fall 1987): 518–31.

14. Admittedly, this connection has not been analyzed well by the archival profession, but it is certainly evident by even a cursory glance at the archival literature.

15. Boles and Young, "Exploring the Black Box," 138.

16. Carl Cargill, *Information Technology Standardization: Theory, Process, and Organizations* (N.p: Digital Press, 1989), 59.

17. Faye Phillips, "Developing Collecting Policies for Manuscript Collections," *American Archivist* 47 (Winter 1984): 30–42.

18. John A. Fleckner, *Archives & Manuscripts: Surveys*, Basic Manual Series (Chicago: Society of American Archivists, 1977), 2.

19. See Judith E. Endelman, "Looking Backward to Plan for the Future: Collection Analysis for Manuscript Repositories," *American Archivist* 50 (Summer 1987): 340–53.

20. Mary F. Robek, Gerald F. Brown, and Wilmer O. Maedke, *Information and Records Management*, 3d ed. (Encino, CA: Glencoe, 1987), 10.

21. Eleanor McKay, "Random Sampling Techniques: A Method of Reducing Large, Homogeneous Series in Congressional Papers," *American Archivist* 41 (July 1978): 281–89.

22. Frank Boles, "Sampling in Archives," *American Archivist* 44 (Spring 1981): 125–30.

23. Margery N. Sly, "Sampling in an Archival Framework: Mathoms and Manuscripts," *Provenance* 5 (Spring 1987): 58–59.

24. Leonard Rapport, "No Grandfather Clause: Reappraising Accessioned Records," *American Archivist* 44 (Spring 1981): 145–46.

25. See, for example, Karen Benedict, "Invitation to a Bonfire: Reappraisal and Deaccessioning of Records as Collection Management Tools in an Archives—A Reply to Leonard Rapport," *American Archivist* 47 (Winter 1984): 43–49.

26. Endelman, "Looking Backward to Plan for the Future," 341–42.

27. Bruce H. Bruemmer and Sheldon Hocheiser, *The High Technology Company: A Historical Research and Archival Guide* (Minneapolis: Charles Babbage Institute, Center for the History of Information Processing, 1989), 4–5.

28. Helen Samuels, "Who Controls the Past," *American Archivist* 49 (Spring 1986): 111.

29. Samuels, "Who Controls the Past," 115.

30. See Alexander and Samuels, "The Roots of 128," 518–31, and Richard J. Cox, "A Documentation Strategy Case Study: Western New York," *American Archivist* 52 (Spring 1989): 192–200.

31. Robek, Brown, and Maedke, *Information and Records Management*, 5.

32. Sharon S. Dawes, "You Can't Tell the Players Without a Program," in *Gateways to Comprehensive State Information Policy*, ed. (Lexington, KY: Chief Officers of State Library Agencies through the Council of State Governments, 1990), 43.

33. Karen Dawley Paul, "Archivists and Records Management," in *Managing Archives and Archival Institutions*, James Gregory Bradshaw ed. (Chicago: University of Chicago Press, 1989), 35.

34. Marjorie Rabe Barritt, "Adopting and Adapting Records Management to College and University Archives," *Midwestern Archivist* 14, no. 2 (1989): 6, 10.

35. Philip C. Brooks, "The Selection of Records for Preservation," *American Archivist* 4 (October 1940): 223.

36. As Gail L. Blount has noted: "Today's profit-conscious executives are pretty shrewd when it comes to distinguishing 'soft' dollars from hard savings. . . . Despite continuing, universal attempts to totally cost-justify records management programs, many of the cost savings tend to be somewhat soft" ("If Records Management Is Such a Neat Idea—Why Is It So Tough to Sell?" *Records Management Quarterly* 19 [October 1985]: 14.)

4

Preserving and Protecting Institutional Archival Records

PRESERVATION AND SECURITY: ESSENTIAL ACTIVITIES TO PROTECT INSTITUTIONAL ARCHIVES

Although preservation has become something of a trendy topic in the archives and library professions, it might well represent one of the most difficult areas in which the institutional archivist must gain support. Just as archivists conjure up certain popular stereotypes, preservation tends to suggest specific kinds of images for many. For the institutional archivist, advocating that funds be set aside for preserving the organizational records may bring bewildered glances from executives and middle managers. Preservation is a task that is reserved for valuable artwork and museum specimens, they may think, not the ordinary transactional records of the organization. How can records that are less than 100, 50, or even 20 years old require the care of a preservation specialist? Even if successful in gaining the necessary support for basic preservation management of the institutional archives, the archivist may have inadvertently reenforced the notions that his or her program is totally involved with "ancient" records, interesting curiosities but useless for the continued functioning of the organization.

Preservation is a basic archival function—the central element in the mission to identify, preserve, and make available for use the archival rec-

A Definition of Archival Preservation

The following is a "three-part definition of archival preservation that synthesizes leading opinions in the archival and library literature."

Archival preservation is the acquisition, organization, and distribution of resources (human, physical, monetary) to ensure adequate protection of historical and cultural information of enduring value and access for present and future generations.

Archival preservation encompasses planning and implementing policies, procedures, and processes that together prevent further deterioration or renew the usability of selected groups of materials.

Archival preservation, when most effective, requires that planning precede implementation, and that prevention activities have priority over renewal activities.

Paul Conway, "Archival Preservation: Definitions for Improving Education and Training," Restaurator 10 (1989): 47-60.

ords—that has undergone tremendous change in the past several decades. Preservation encompasses the range of actions taken to retard or prevent the deterioration of, or damage to, archival records. Preservation is necessary because the inherent character of all recording media is such that records deteriorate: paper deteriorates because it is often acidic, because of the sizing agents used, and weak, because of the fibers in the paper; all other media, such as magnetic tape or optical disks, also have inherent flaws that lead to their eventual destruction if there is no intervention. Preservation can include efforts to transform a document back to its original appearance (restoration) or to treat the document so that it no longer deteriorates (conservation), both ranges of actions requiring specialized skills. The principal part of archival preservation is the concept of preservation management, which entails the control of the records' physical environment, including their security, in order to arrest the elements that encourage the destruction of the records. All are important aspects of the essential task of ensuring that the archival records are being adequately preserved for current and future use.

Preservation is now viewed as a vital part of any archival program's management. In a sense, of course, this view has always been the case. For years, archivists contended that the preservation of historical and archival records was their primary responsibility, while consistently making it the lowest in funding priorities. This seeming contradiction was partly due to the fact that archivists used to think of the preservation of their records as consisting of little more than the process of bringing the records into their facilities, which often did not possess proper environmental and security controls, and placing them in acid-free storage materials. Following such activity, it was thought, would provide permanent protection to the records.

Now, archivists question even how they should define permanency, indicative of the fact that preservation has become viewed in a much more sophisticated manner.[1] Archivists at least realize that their records will probably not last forever, that preservation is a costly affair with no simple solutions, that considerable damage to the archival materials was being inadvertently inflicted on them by their own staffs because of improper handling procedures, and that their programs needed to make stronger commitments to preservation of the archival records through staffing changes, development of new priorities, new educational initiatives, and experimentation with new mass preservation techniques (such as mass deacidification). Most important, however, preservation is a function to be incorporated into virtually every aspect of an archives' operation. Every staff member is to share some of the responsibility for preserving the records. As one state archivist remarked at a 1987 conference, "We must make certain that preservation is a major ongoing, substantially supported, core function—not merely a special project. To continue to acquire materials while providing no assurance for their survival must become unacceptable for us all."[2] Likewise, it makes little sense for an institution to establish an archival program if it will not provide adequate support for the basic preservation of the archival records.

The new preservation management milieu is something that can, indeed must, be incorporated into the work of the institutional archives. For institutions that have already invested considerable financial and staff resources in the production of information and the technology to utilize that information, retarding the deterioration of these information sources should be a major priority; for organizations that have already adopted records management, information resource management, or archival philosophies, it should be a natural progression to adopting the preservation management concept. Although the areas where records are stored must be environmentally stable and secure, the preservation of archival records should start while the records are still located in their creating offices; records that have been determined to possess archival value must be treated accordingly while they are still in their current mode of use. Furthermore, even in the institutional archival facility, preservation is not a segregated activity. Archivists conducting appraisal should note the physical condition of records; archivists working on the arrangement and description of records should confirm and provide more specific details regarding the preservation needs of the records; and archivists providing reference services to the records should monitor their condition to identify any changes that merit special attention or that signal larger problems in the archives. Even researchers who use the archival materials should be brought into the preservation process by being made aware of how to handle the records properly and how to inform the archivists if they detect any preservation problems.

Preservation management is an effort to deal with one of the inherent contradictions in archival administration, the maintenance of valuable records and the encouragement of their use. As some well-known international archivists have stated: "If we could keep our documents . . . untouched, in an inert atmosphere and with controlled lighting, conservation would pose no problem to the archivist. . . . However, such conditions exist so rarely that we can safely ignore them."[3] This chapter is a fuller treatment of how to develop this preservation mentality in the institutional archives; it starts with the environmental and security conditions and then proceeds to describe various techniques that institutional archivists should employ to preserve their records.

THE INSTITUTIONAL ARCHIVES ENVIRONMENT

Many institutions in the first stages of establishing archival programs will use any available space for the storage of these records. This approach most often happens out of expediency, as well as from the conviction that the centralization of the organization's archival records is essential in enabling the archival program to develop in an adequate way and to possess a satisfactory institutional profile (issues that were considered more fully in the second chapter of this book). Too often, however, "temporary" storage areas become the permanent homes of archival operations and threaten to undo the hard-won battles of the archivist in identifying and consolidating the archival records of the institution.

This section needs to be introduced with two conditions. First, what follows is a very general description of basic preservation procedures that institutional archives should seek to follow. The important concept that is being introduced here is that preservation must be a continuous process of the archival program, an indisputable aspect of the institutional archives staff outlook and basic practices. More detailed information about preservation techniques can be found in other volumes that are described in the final chapter of this book, although, as one conservator has remarked, "Deterioration is an extraordinarily complex process, one which even scientists find difficult to understand;[4] the content of this chapter is, then, a simple set of descriptions, explanations, and advice. Second, the assumption being made here about the institutional archives program is that it will be located in the organization's building or, at the least, share space in one of a larger organization's buildings; this assumption has been made because it is the most common practice and because archival operations are often seen as showpieces for their parent institutions, as they possess exhibition space for displays that can provide publicity for the organization. Separately designed archival facilities usually can have distinct advantages over spaces of older structures that have been renovated or adapted for use by the archives program. Sometimes, an institutional archives will also have the opportunity (or necessity, because of limited space) to place certain of its records in other, more secure facilities or commercial operations that provide inexpensive storage of records; discussion of how such decisions should be made will be discussed later. Regardless of where the archival records are stored, the location should have certain characteristics that ensure the records' preservation.

There are a number of important features that the archival storage areas of any institutional archives should possess. Temperature should be maintained at a fairly constant level, generally given as plus or minus 2 degrees from 67 degrees Fahrenheit. Equally important is the regulating of the relative humidity, by plus or minus 2 percent from 47 percent.[5] The regulation of temperature and relative humidity will help to resist the growth of microorganisms (such as fungi and bacteria) and reduce changes in the inherent structures of the documents themselves caused by fluctuations in temperature and humidity, both extremely important elements in the effort to prevent the deterioration of archival records. Regulating such conditions will require, of course, significant cooperation from the institution's staff that maintains the structure, as well from the top-level administrators to support the extra costs that might result from such controls. Without such controls, however, environmental conditions can result that undo most of the other efforts to preserve the records. In planning for an institutional archives program, therefore, working to ensure that optimum storage space is available should be a high priority. Communicating needs such as this can also help to emphasize to the organization's executives the importance of the archival records maintained by the program. This may be especially difficult for an institutional archives that is situated within a large building in which environmental conditions may be altered for holidays and weekends. Monitoring changes (using thermometers, hygrometers, psychrometers, or hygrothermographs) in the environment to demonstrate the extent of the problem after all efforts have been made to regulate humidity, temperature, and ventilation can usually be used to build cases that lead to improvements.

Other elements are also essential for preventive measures to retard deterioration of the documents. The storage areas should be equipped with filtration screens that retard the entry of harmful gases (sulfur dioxide, hydrogen sulfide, and nitrogen dioxide, which are leftovers from the use of fossil fuels and industrial waste), dirt, and other air pollutants that harm the valuable records by creating environmental conditions that can encourage mold growth, increase acidity of the paper, and contaminate the

Determining Strengths and Weaknesses of
Archival Storage Facilities

Institutional archivists can turn to a number of guides, self-study questionnaires, and other references that will assist them to analyze the attributes of their facilities in which important archival records are located. Because there are many similarities between the storage of archival records and museum collections (many of which are archival in nature), institutional archivists can turn to sources in this field as well for helpful information.   One example of this variety of source is The Conservation Assessment: A Tool for Planning, Implementing, and Fundraising, jointly published by the Getty Conservation Institute and the National Institute for the Conservation of Cultural Property in 1990. This reference provides detailed checklists and self-study questions on the following aspects:

Institutional Profile: The type of institution, date of establishment, and governance structure.
Collections and Exhibitions: The kinds of collections held, the nature of exhibitions, and the nature of collection policies.
Building(s): The nature of the facility and how collections are stored.
Building Use: How the facility is used.
Environmental Controls: The types of controls provided.
Staff: The size and responsibilities of the staff.
Emergency Preparedness: How the institution is prepared to respond to any emergency situation that threatens the collections.
This publication also has an accompanying bibliography for additional study and preparation by an institution and its staff. Institutional archivists can find such sources of great help as they assess the effectiveness of their preservation and security procedures and policies.

---

materials stored in archival facilities. The areas where archival records are stored should also be protected from light with ultraviolet and infrared rays, which can cause paper and other records to deteriorate more quickly than normal by changing their molecular structures, discoloring inks, and causing various chemical reactions. Other equipment expenditures that must be made include those for automatic fire detection and suppression and for detection of water intrusion. Fire detection and suppression systems are important for every archives. Water detection systems will be essential only for those archival facilities that are located where flooding can occur from natural (rivers or heavy precipitation conditions) or man-made (the building's plumbing or external water drainage or wastewater systems) causes; ideally, the archival storage areas should be placed away from such potential problems, but this placement is not always possible. Careful planning for the placement and monitoring of such equipment is also necessary so that their costs are not wasted and a false sense of security given. Nothing can be more discouraging than problems that result because expensive and sophisticated apparatus is improperly installed or used.

The materials used to store the archival records, such as shelving and containers, are as important as ensuring environmental controls. All of these precautions work in tandem in providing the proper conditions to slow the deterioration of the records. Having perfect environmental conditions but using acidic containers and folders for the records would be an imperfect situation. Archival records should be placed on heavy-duty shelving, constructed of materials that do not contain harmful materials, that do not force any stress on the records, and that are able to accommodate standard archival and records center cartons. Records that are oversized or of nonpaper media, such as magnetic tapes, should be placed in containers that are proved not to harm them in any way; oversized records, such as maps or engineering drawings, should be stored in flat file cases that allow the documents to be unfolded and easily accessible in a way that will lessen wear. All storage containers should be constructed of acid-free materials, and plastic containers, where they must be used, should be composed of polyester, polyethylene, polypropylene, triacetate, or other materials that will not react with the enclosed records. Archivists should obtain advice on any storage material if they are uncertain of its suitability for archival preservation. Above all, institutional archivists should be prepared for some difficulty in convincing the organization's procurement staff that the more expensive archival materials are necessary, since many such archival supplies look very similar to other standard office supplies.

As institutional archives programs evolve, certain better operational guidelines can be developed and implemented that may eliminate or lessen preservation problems caused or exacerbated by the use of poor storage materials. In other words, archivists should be concerned with the storage conditions of all potential records wherever they are located in the institution's facilities. Archivists should take every action they can to reduce the amount of work that they will face with the records once they get to the archives. Once they have determined that records possess archival value, archivists could seek to have the archival records produced on acid-free paper, stored in acid-free folders, reproduced on archival-quality microfilm, or managed in some other similar action that is appropriate to the record format and its continuing use in the office of creation. This action will lessen the amount of work that the institutional archivist faces when the records are transferred to the archives, as well as provide better guarantees that the records will arrive in good condition. The most efficient manner in which this result can occur is in tandem with a records management program that has an organizationwide records retention and disposition schedule that can be annotated with preservation-related instructions.

There are other more basic, less expensive, and more routine actions that can be taken to provide stable environments for the institution's archival records. These same storage areas must be regularly cleaned and inspected so that food and drink (generally a problem with staff) are kept out and bibliophagous insects (such as silverfish, cockroaches, and beetles) and rodents do not attack the records. All staff with access to these locations should be trained to detect the appearance of problems in their early stages. Especially important is ensuring that nonarchival or records management staff, such as maintenance supervisors and cleaning staffs, that have access to these areas are also trained to know how to respect the important records that are stored there. A better procedure is to have professional archivists accompany such individuals into the storage locations to provide security for the records and to develop a sense of the importance of the records for the institution; such occasions can be used to train the nonarchives staff about certain actions it should be responsible for (such as ensuring that the process of cleaning floors does not result in water damage to records stored on the lower shelves) and to teach the professional staff about the construction and maintenance of the facility. Similarly, other basic actions can be taken that will reduce the risk of records destruction or damage, such as keeping records away from overhead water and gas pipes, air-conditioning units that might leak moisture, and areas in buildings where water seepage or flooding may or has occurred. Steps as simple as keeping records four or more inches above the floor can prevent considerable damage to the irreplaceable institutional archives in the event of a physical disaster.

Equally important for a proper environment for the maintenance of the institutional archives is the storage areas' security. Most archival operations require security because many of the records for which they are responsible have monetary value and are tempting targets for theft. While an institutional archives might have some records with such value, it is more likely that they will be concerned with security because of their storage of records that are sensitive to the organization and have restricted access or that are essential to the continued operation of the institution. Archivists want to know who has access to the archival records and be able to ensure that the organization's guidelines in access are being carried out. Lapses in security can seriously harm an archival program's support within an institution and reduce the trust that the organization has in placing its valuable records in the archival facilities. One of an archives' basic promotional points should be the enhanced security that it provides for the records that are transferred to it.

There are two fundamental aspects of security that are closely associated with an archives' basic preservation operation. The first is the actual physical storage areas for the archival records, which will be examined below. The other occurs in the archival program's reference function, which will

An Example of Advice to Researchers
on the Care of Archival Records

The following is from a bookmark designed for use in the Hoover Institution Archives:

To preserve the resources of the Hoover Institution Archives for present and future generations of scholars, please observe the following simple precautions:

1. Notify a member of the staff immediately if you receive material which is crumbling or brittle.
2. Handle documents carefully when returning them to their original positions in folders and/or boxes.
3. Food and drink, in addition to attracting insects, may stain documents. These substances are not allowed in the Archives.
4. Use as bookmarks only the slips of paper which the Archives will provide for you. Other objects, such as pencils and paperclips, cause considerable stress. Also, never "dog ear" paper.
5. Never mark on documents or book pages, even with a pencil. Removal of such marks can be very harmful to paper.
6. Do not use fountain pens adjacent to Archives materials because of the danger of ink leakage.
7. Do not place your own paper on top of a document or in a book when taking notes; the pressure from your writing instrument is harmful.
8. When handling photographs or film, use the white cotton gloves which are available in the audio-visual room.

Thank you.

---

be discussed more fully in the next chapter. Underlying both security aspects, however, is the fact that all individuals associated with the archival program should have a stake in the security of the records maintained by the operation. If the staff is large, one individual might be given extra responsibility as a security officer to monitor programs, assess their effectiveness, and plan for new security efforts. In most cases, however, all archival staff should be made aware of the security regulations and be trained for what to watch for and how to respond to security problems as they occur. In addition, the local police and the institution's own security force should be fully aware of the archives' security arrangements and the particularly valuable nature of the records stored in the archives.

While ensuring the preservation of archival materials is a difficult process, the institutional archivist may discover that providing security for these records is an even more difficult task. It is difficult because an archives exists to enable records to be used, and this use places the archival records in risk from theft or damage. An institutional archives might find security even more difficult than do many other kinds of archives because of the location of the archival facility within an organization's headquarters where there are a large number of people and a high degree of activity. Security may also be difficult to provide because of the freedom of access of the organization's employees to most other areas of the building (or buildings). Providing security in an archives might somehow be against the general corporate culture of the institution, a fact that is made more difficult by the general lack of understanding by many of the organization's employees about the nature of the institutional archives. The archivist will have to bear all these things in mind as he or she plans to establish a more effective security program. In all of this, as in most other areas, the archivist will have to make sure that he or she has obtained the support of the institution's top level managers.

The archivist should first make sure that the perimeters of the archival facilities are secured so that access is restricted and controlled. This result can be achieved in several ways. First, locking all access points in a manner in which break-ins would be difficult and where access to keys or combinations is restricted among staff is a logical action. Such security systems are generally, it must be remembered, for hours during which the archives is closed, hence the observations of the staff in combination with the locking devices provide the best form of security. Advice on the styles of locking devices can be obtained from external experts, although there are some written descriptions for archivists and librarians of the varieties of devices that are available and that are recommended.[6]

A second manner in which to secure the perimeter of the archival facility is to install security alarms at all key points in which access can or does occur as well as in the priority areas of the storage areas. Security alarms can be used for both after hours protection and restriction of access to certain areas during the main hours of business. Again, there are a number of variant types of security alarms, but the main guiding principle for an institutional archives should be to acquire a security alarm that is connected to the organization's main security system. In this regard, as well, the archivist should work with the organization's security staff to determine the best procedures to be used for the archives and to ascertain whether other forms of security, such as surveillance cameras, can be utilized by the archives. Sophisticated devices that require specific skills or that are labor-intensive in terms of having full-time human intervention will not be feasible for most institutional archives except those that can be built into their parent organization's larger security system.

The other perimeter security device that needs to be employed by the institutional archives is one that limits access by the nonarchives staff to a single entrance and exit area (although there will need to be additional fire escape routes for staff). Here, there is little need for sophisticated equipment except for a staff person who monitors access and checks materials being brought into and taken out of the immediate archives areas. Determining what the access and security procedures should be for the institutional archives can be a delicate manner, and the archivist should handle the matter carefully with the institution's upper-level management to make sure that no problems occur in their implementation or embarrassing situations result. Some of the specifics of this kind of security will be discussed in the chapter on reference and access, but it needs to be stated at this point that, as much as possible, nonarchives staff members entering and leaving archives areas should be restricted from carrying too much of their own materials (such as large briefcases and hand purses) in which records could be concealed and that at the exit point these items should be subjected to a brief check to ensure that no material is being taken from the archives without authorization.

Institutional archives should also seek to establish systems in which identification passes are issued and used for access to archival records. A record of all individuals given access to the records should be maintained, including information on what records they have used and for what purpose these records have been consulted. The main place where this access must be regulated is the initial point of entry to the archives facility. Individuals should be required to show their identification pass or be asked to fill out all the necessary documents and gain approval for access (as will be seen in a subsequent chapter, these records are also needed for monitoring the nature of use of the archives holdings). For these and other reasons, the archives staff must be trained to know what the access policies are and how the security system works. Most thefts or other security problems that have occurred have been committed by individuals who appear to be no threat whatsoever and who often convince unsuspecting archivists that they are what, in fact, they are not, bona fide researchers with excellent reasons for needing access to the archival records. Institutional archives should seek to develop security and access policies, have experts in the field evaluate them, make sure they are in conformity with the parent organization's policies, and hold in-house training sessions for staff and volunteers.

An essential aspect of possessing such a security system is knowing what values the records in the archives have both for the institution itself and for the outside research community that might seek permission to use them. Knowledge about these records can come through a variety of means, but in the context of preservation and security three main means will be reviewed—preservation condition surveys, the preparation of disaster preparedness plans, and the selection process for records to be microfilmed or to receive specific kinds of preservation action. There are additional means, as well, which will be discussed in other chapters.

PRESERVATION CONDITION SURVEYS

For any archives staff to be able to deal effectively with the preservation needs of its holdings, it must obviously know what those needs are in relation to the other requirements of the program. Although this statement seems obvious, it is surprising how many archives do not have adequate information about their preservation needs or stated priorities. This situation probably occurs because of the lack of staff to conduct such analyses, the press of other responsibilities, and misconceptions about what such studies require and what benefits they can return to the archives. If an archival operation, however, wishes to be able to articulate its needs to gain financial and other support for preservation and to be able to use what resources it has in an effective manner, it must conduct a survey of its holdings that can be used for analytical purposes. Since preservation can be an item that is difficult to win support for in an institutional archives, such a survey should be completed in order to provide statements of specific needs and of the precise dimensions of the preservation problems.

A preservation needs survey should be done in a manner that provides the institutional archives some very specific kinds of information. It should seek to identify the range of preservation problems, the financial resources that are necessary to deal with these problems, when and if professional conservators are required, and the types of staff training required to begin to work with the preservation problems. Ideally, this information should be written in the form of a long-range (three- to five-year) preservation plan that can be utilized to determine institutional preservation priorities, although the first priorities should always be to create environmentally sound storage conditions. Even better, the preservation needs and priorities should be incorporated into the institutional archives general, long-range plan (see chapter 2). While such a survey is a onetime snapshot of the conditions of an institution's archival holdings, it should be part of an effort to start regular evaluation of the changing conditions of the archival records. Since archival records are in a constant state of deterioration, such regular assessments should aid the institutional archives in determining what the major sources of deterioration are, so that the process can be slowed down.

There are some misconceptions about the nature of such a preservation needs survey. For one thing, such surveys do not always require the use of specially trained preservation experts, although the use of such expertise in a consulting capacity can certainly enhance the effectiveness of such an assessment. If the institution seems to respond better to the advice of outside consultants, then such an individual could be asked to help design and evaluate the results of the survey. The best use of such a consultant would be in helping the institution to interpret the survey results and to develop an effective plan that sets out to rectify the problems identified

Condition Survey

Record Series:

Date of Survey: Conducted by:

Type of Material (formats/dates):

    Unique and/or valuable items:

Use of records series:

Condition of records series:

    general appearance: discoloration:

    tears/abrasions: embrittlement:

    surface dirt and dust: evidence of mold or mildew:

    water or other stains: insect damage:

Methods of storage/storage containers:

    folders/envelopes:

    boxes/cartons:

    harmful means of attachments (pins, brads, paper clips, etc.):

    enclosures (pressed flowers, clippings, etc.):

Additional observations:

Priority ranking of record series for treatment:

Recommended treatment:

    re-foldering: deacidification

    reboxing: mending:

    removal of foreign materials: encapsulation:

    surface cleaning: preservation copying:

Adapted from SAA Basic Archival Conservation Program, Conservation Self-Study (Chicago: Society of American Archivists, January 1982).

and to determine specific types of action that are required. In most cases, however, an effective preservation needs survey can be carried out by training the staff who will conduct the survey. There are consultants and regional conservation centers that can provide such assistance either through workshops or through individual, institution-specific consultation and training. The existence of model forms that can be used to capture the information of such a survey will help any institutional archives to complete such a survey adequately.

Another misconception about preservation needs surveys is that every manuscript collection or archival record series needs to be examined in order for a survey to be completed. This belief is far from the truth. A sample of archival holdings can be worked on that will accurately reflect the range of likely preservation problems. The sample can be selected in a number of ways, partly determined by the nature, history, and previous record keeping of the institutional archives program. If the archives is just starting out or has inadequate or sketchy records about the provenance of the holdings, then a straightforward sample of 10 to 20 percent of the holdings should be thoroughly examined for the survey. If there are many adequate records of provenance and use of the holdings, then the archives might wish to develop a sample of holdings that reflects period of time maintained in the archives storage areas, degrees of usage by researchers, and originating office and original condition of the storage facilities. The specificity of this information will assist the institutional archives not only to determine the scope of present problems but to be able to foresee future problems and to plan appropriate actions to limit the occurrence of preservation problems. In the sample the operating rule of thumb should be to keep the sample as manageable as possible at the same time as achieving a representative example of the nature of preservation concerns.

The time required to conduct preservation needs surveys is another misconception about this type of effort. Time-consuming self-studies are often not undertaken by repositories whose staff already believes it is stretched to the limits to meet minimum levels of service. But these studies can be designed and carried out in ways that are not time-consuming and that do not deflect attention away from other important programmatic responsibilities. Careful planning needs to be done to ensure this goal, but it is certainly in the realm of possibility, especially when careful samples are worked out in advance and specific goals are constantly kept in view. Furthermore, the surveys can be accomplished in staff down time (evenings or week-ends) by utilizing volunteers and mobilizing every staff member, professional archivists, and others to participate. The chief institutional archivist must also convince his or her administrators about what the survey will contribute to the mission of the archives as a service agency to the parent organization so that time will not be considered as a major factor and the survey will not be perceived as a distraction from other responsibilities. This step is important not only because it may gain additional support for such analysis but because it can help direct the archives to the records holdings that it should examine. If the archives is considered to be most valuable because of certain kinds of information that it provides, the condition of these sources of information should be examined. Their loss from deterioration and lack of planning and appropriate preservation action will harm both the institutional archives and the parent organization. Finally, the survey can be helpfully viewed as an exercise that helps to get all the institutional archives staff better acquainted with the records holdings and their preservation needs. For some staff who generally work in the reference function or who perform other specialized duties, this preservation examination may be an illuminating introduction to the problems that the archivists face in making their records available for consultation.

Having considered all these issues, how should a preservation needs survey be conducted? Apart from whether a professional preservation consultant will be involved, the following steps are necessary for the completion of the survey:

1. Determination of the purposes of the survey, including what the final report will look like, how the information will be managed and likely used, the expected or desired time frame for the survey, and who will be involved in the survey.

2. Preparation of worksheets based on the nature of the purposes or adoption of model worksheets.

3. Selection of the sample of archival record groups and series to be examined, including articulation of the rationale for the sample.

4. Training and orientation of individuals conducting the survey.

5. Carrying out of the survey, including periodic assessments of progress and resolution of problems.

6. Evaluation of the survey results, that draws on advice of either the institutional archives preservation officer or an outside consultant.

7. Preparation of a final report, with assessment of preservation actions needed and projections of financial resources required for these actions, for dissemination to the institutional archives staff and the institution's upper-level management.

8. Incorporation of final results of the survey in other existing information sources regarding the institutional archives holdings.

9. Assessment of when the next survey will be required and what kinds of additional information may be required.

10. Implementation of recommendations of the final survey report.

Going through this process will strengthen the institutional archives staff's knowledge about its holdings and assist it to complete other required work for the smooth administration of the archival program. For the institutional archives (unlike the collecting historical records repository, which has collections originating from a constantly varied lot), the survey provides the opportunity for the program to identify the main sources of the preservation problems that may be stemming from conditions in the organization and enable it to take appropriate action. If the institutional archives can gain the cooperation of the organization's various records-creating offices, then many of the preservation problems may be lessened or eliminated.

The preservation needs survey should accumulate a considerable amount of data about the institutional archives holdings. This data should first include a general range of information about the institutional archives, including the types of material held by the repository, date ranges of the holdings, total volume, location of records stored, nature of storage, environmental conditions of the storage areas, nature of lighting in the storage areas, security arrangements, budgeting of funds for preservation, staff preservation activities, and similar matters. The remainder of the survey should include specific information on the condition and preservation needs of the holdings.[7]

PREPARING FOR THE UNEXPECTED:
DISASTER PLANNING

Every day institutions somewhere are struck by man-made or natural disasters. Fire, flood, earthquake, tornadoes, hurricanes, and similar events strike unexpectedly, damaging or destroying institutions, as the disastrous hurricane in Charleston, South Carolina and the earthquake in California, both in 1989, dramatically point out; in both natural events priceless and irreplaceable historic structures, art works, artifacts, and archives were lost or damaged.[8] The effective recovery by these institutions requires that it be prepared by protecting its records that are necessary for the continued operation of the organization. As was noted earlier, records managers and archivists refer to such records as "vital" and take a series of steps to protect such records, most often keeping microfilmed copies stored off-site from the main building. At least some of these vital records will be located in the archives and require the participation of the archivist in the development and management of a vital records program. But the archivist should also be involved in a disaster preparedness plan in which he or she can plan for the recovery from a calamity of the important and irreplaceable archival records held by the institutional archives.

A disaster preparedness plan is a written document, kept current, that assists the institutional archives to protect its holdings in case of natural or man-made disasters. Such a plan should include descriptions of procedures to be used to protect the archival records of greatest importance to the in-

Components of a Disaster Plan

There are many models for the structure of a disaster-preparedness plan. The following was prepared for archives and libraries by the Preservation Program of the Southeastern Library Network, Inc. (SOLINET).

* Emergency Information Sheet

* Introduction to the Plan

* Telephone Tree or Communications Plan

* Collection Priorities for the Institution/Repository

* Prevention/Protection Measures: Schedules and Checklists

* Checklist of Pre-Disaster Actions

* Instructions for Response and Recovery: Summary Version

Information for Appendices

* Collection Priorities Within Departments or Subject Areas

* Checklists for Disaster Prevention/Protection Inspections

* Detailed Instructions for Response and Recovery

* Instructions for Long-Term Rehabilitation

* Record-Keeping Forms

* Detailed Building Plans

* Resource Lists: Supplies, Services, Consultants

* Accounting Information

* Insurance Information

* Location of Keys

* Reading List

stitution or requiring special care. The plan also assigns responsibilities to the various archives staff for actions it should take in case a disaster strikes. In the case of such plans, the act of preparation is probably less difficult (although straightforward, it still requires considerable planning) than the processes of training all staff regarding assignments and keeping the plan as current as necessary to be effective. For institutional archivists, participation in the development of an organization's disaster preparedness plan may go beyond a concern with archival and vital records (both of which constitute only a small percent of the total records) to plan for the recovery of as many informational systems as possible, a somewhat different expectation than for the archivist who works in a cultural institution such as a historical society. One expert has suggested that the "disaster preparedness and recovery program" is a "supplement" to the "traditional vital records programs [that] provides for the maximum recovery of information at minimum costs following damage by natural or man-caused disasters."[9]

There are a number of models that can be used for developing an effective disaster recovery plan.[10] In general, however, the following kinds of information should always be included in the written plan:

1. Identification of the records' storage locations.
2. Responsibility of each staff member for responding to a disaster.
3. Internal institutional and external services that may be needed in an emergency situation.
4. In-house and off-site emergency equipment and supplies.
5. Description of procedures and priorities to be carried out in case of an emergency situation.
6. Records that need to be created and maintained about a disaster should one occur.

The nature of a written disaster preparedness plan need not be an elaborate one, but some issues have to be worked out carefully if the plan is to be an effective one. Putting together the plan can also be a positive activity for the institutional archivists, as the plan will require interaction with a wide range of different personnel in the organization and the setting up of a team of individuals to serve as leaders and to coordinate different responsibilities (such as recording information about the disaster, photographing damage, handling supplies and equipment, and notifying key external organizations and individuals). Handled in the right manner, the preparation of a disaster plan for the records (including the archives) of the organization is another way for the institutional archives to publicize their importance and gain internal supporters.

Several important aspects of the plan must be kept constantly in mind for it to be effective if it must be used in an actual situation. All staff members who have any responsibility for responding to an emergency must be thoroughly familiar with their responsibility and the precise nature of the actions they should take. These responsibilities will range from providing initial alerts about, and evaluation of, the disaster and its aftermath

to stabilizing conditions, packing and removing archival holdings, starting
the rehabilitation process, determining what techniques will be utilized,
and evaluating the response to the calamity. Once a plan has been prepared,
it should be widely disseminated, a training session held (repeated on a
regular basis or as staff changes occur), and practice drills held. Practice
drills are especially important to ensure that archives staff knows how to
handle certain kinds of basic equipment, such as fire extinquishers. The
dissemination of the plan should obviously go beyond just the immediate
institution archives staff and include key individuals in the organization
itself, service agencies that might provide services and supplies so that they
are aware they might be called on for assistance, and the fire and police
departments, which will undoubtedly be involved anyway if such a disaster
occurs; bringing the fire and police departments into the plan may prevent
them from unwittingly causing additional damage to the institution's archives as they respond to a fire or other catastrophe.

The preparation of an institutional archives disaster preparedness plan
probably requires several other elements. It must coordinate its activities
with the institutional records managers as well as the other staff responsible
for the maintenance and management of the building. In many cases, the
institutional archivist's main responsibility will be coordinating with these
other organizational offices in their emergency response plans. An institutional archives program must also take into consideration other unique
aspects of its organization that might affect its response to an emergency.
For example, the variety of problems that an archives in a university library
building faces will be very different from those faced by an archives in a
heavily industrialized corporation in which the potential for destruction is
much greater; in the latter case, the preparation of a disaster preparedness
plan might help the institutional archives to find the best location for its
storage of the archival records. Finally, the preparation of such a plan
should enable the archives to identify the priority importance of its archival
holdings, a process that is very essential for other work that the archives
needs to carry out, including determining what holdings should receive
what kinds of preservation action. For a disaster preparedness plan, the
reformatting of certain essential records to microforms and the storage of
duplicate copies off-site will protect the institution and preserve for the
institution and researchers the most important archival records.

The best environment for the creation, maintenance, and, when necessary, execution of disaster preparedness plans is one in which various
archives, libraries, museums, and other cultural institutions join forces to
work together. Not only does this cooperation provide the possibility of
institutions sharing the expertise of their staffs, but they can divide up the
work of contacting suppliers, vendors, and emergency services in the preparation of such plans. A number of states have, for example, recognized
this benefit and have organized disaster response teams that can take ap-

propriate action whenever a calamity strikes. Institutional archives should contact other local archives and their state archives before developing their own plan to determine whether there is already a state, regional, or local plan in existence. If there is not, there is no reason an institutional archives should not take the leadership in this matter and contact other archival repositories to ascertain their interest and ability to work together in such an area.

Another aspect of disaster preparedness that the institutional archives staff should be prepared for concerns internal problems with the institution's computer systems. There are a number of highly specialized firms that deal with such matters. Here the institutional archivist is concerned with the hardware and software down to the various diskettes that individuals maintain at their work desks and that may contain valuable information that should ultimately be transferred to the institutional archives. These disasters can have a completely different flavor from the large-scale ones that archivists normally worry about. The crash of a hard disk or the inadvertent damage of a diskette lying on a desk is a much more localized event but one that the archivist should be aware of and he or she should be involved in recovery operations. In these kinds of events, archivists will work with data processors, telecommunications experts, managers of information systems, systems analysts, and other technical people to a degree they might not in other situations.[11] The archivist should also be involved in developing procedures for backing up computer files to protect the information contained in this form.

DETERMINING PRIORITIES FOR PRESERVATION SELECTION

Selecting archival materials for preservation has recently emerged as an important topic and issue because of the finite resources for preservation and the immense quantities of archival records requiring one form of preservation action or another. Stabilizing the environmental conditions in which archival records will be stored is an important first step, as has been discussed already, but there are many records that require other forms of treatment because of their already deteriorated condition or original format or some other aspect of their origination, form, and potential use. Since resources are limited, prioritizing the institutional archives' holdings according to some scheme is an important step that can be ignored only at peril in making the wrong preservation treatment decisions.

Although selection has emerged as an important issue, the specific advice offered has been rather general. One of the Society of American Archivists' preservation leaflets offered this suggestion:

Data gathered on the physical condition of collection items must be considered in combination with the resources available for conservation activity and the relative value of the material, as the basis for setting treatment priorities. Archival material may be regarded from a number of perspectives, and values attached accordingly. In part, the assignment of values will determine which records must be maintained in their original format . . . and which records may be copied to preserve their informational content. For example, a document may have importance because it is unique. . . . Informational value must be weighed against artifactual value. Is the physical form a subject for study? Does the item have artistic or aesthetic merit? Is it useful for exhibition purposes? Age may be another criterion on the assumption that early records are scarce and thus take on added value. Some records have legal values which must be considered; other records may be of suspect authenticity, in which case it is necessary to maintain them in original format so that they may be physically examined. Records relating to the founding of an organization or institution . . . are generally seen to have high artifactual value, as do records that relate to the primary collecting focus of an institution. Use is another factor which must be considered. Collections which receive a high level of research use are likely very important to the institution; these also may be in the poorest condition because of the high degree of handling they receive. Such factors must be considered and weighed in determining—in priority order—which collections require immediate physical treatment, those which can be copied, and those which can safely await future action. Given the inherent nature of archival materials, there is no standard formula which can be applied uniformly to assess the relative values of collection material. The criteria used will vary from institution to institution, each developing its own set of factors to evaluate unique collections.[12]

Although this statement is a rather general description of the various values that need to be considered, it reflects the importance and complexity of the matter.

Institutional archivists can use their appraisal procedures and knowledge of their institution as the appropriate starting points for determining priorities for preservation treatment, whether that treatment be simple cleaning or a more drastic reformatting using micrographics. In general, institutional archivists should pay attention to three criteria levels for determining preservation priorities. Ranking the institutional archival materials according to these values will suggest rankings for preservation action that can lead to the judicious use of preservation funds. Below are a brief description of these criteria and a discussion of how they can be utilized to develop preservation priorities.[13]

The most important or primary level includes two criteria, informational content and current and projected use. Records with a high-quality informational content and significant current and projected use are excellent choices for preservation. Informational content, as already noted earlier in this volume, is the value of records for administrative use by the records creator and the research value to historians, social scientists, political scientists, local historians, and any other potential researchers. In an institutional archives, information with high value is that which, if destroyed, could hamper understanding of the development and nature of the orga-

Possible Criteria for Selecting Preservation Priorities

Primary	*Secondary*	*Tertiary*
Informational Content	Condition	Cost-Effectiveness
Current and Projected Use		

nization. This information could include records that provide important documentation essential to understanding the organization's past and present, protect the legal rights and interests of the organization and its employees and constituents, and provide information necessary to the institution's continuing operation, especially for legal and policy formulation purposes. The value of records declines if the records are supplementary to, duplicate, or are less complete than other existing information sources held by the organization.

Records with high current or projected use are those information sources that are actually used and/or requested frequently or are anticipated to have high research potential in the future. In an institutional setting these would be records that are regularly requested internally for the organization's own work and by external researchers or that possess no restrictions that retard use. Use can be accurately measured. Records that are consulted only once a year or less are probably not records that should be high priorities for preservation; the diminished use will, by itself, contribute little to the wear and tear of the documents.

A secondary criterion for determining preservation priorities is the condition of the original format of the record. Archival records that are in very poor or fragile condition always need to be considered for preservation treatment. Records in such condition, however, should not be considered as preservation priorities unless they have sufficient informational value and are currently being used or possess the possibility of future use. Archival records in extremely fragile condition are those that are in an obviously deteriorating state and that cannot be used without extreme threat to their physical format and loss of informational content. Some records will be identified as being in poor condition; that is, their information might be lost in five years or less if regularly used and untreated. Most other archival records will be identified as eventually deteriorating but are not in an immediate danger of loss.

The final criterion that institutional archivists should consider in determining preservation priorities is that of the cost-effectiveness of any suitable preservation treatment. It is a third-level criterion because, regardless of the ease of preservation, treatment will not be done unless the archival records possess a sufficient informational content and use and they are endangered or in a seriously deteriorating state. Cost effectiveness simply implies that it is not worth the cost to preserve an archival record if the cost is high, the other values low, and preservation treatment of this record or record series will lessen the possibility of treating other more important, or essential records to the institution.

There is a variety of ways that the institutional archivist can use such a set of criteria in determining preservation treatment priorities. One way, which has been suggested, is to assign weights in points according to the the criteria and the degree by which a particular records series meets these criteria. A repository could survey its holdings, weight the preservation needs of each records series or group (depending on the volume of the holdings), and use the final point totals to assist in the determination of priorities. While still a highly subjective process, this effort can add an element of objectivity to it; at the least, this process would assist the institutional archivist to make a preliminary ranking of records according to their preservation needs.[14] The archivist could also use these point assignments for a smaller portion of the archival holdings that have been identified to have serious preservation problems, and thus sort out a set of priorities within a smaller segment of the total institutional archives; the holdings not considered would be those that will benefit through general environmental controls, or simple labor-non-intensive actions or that are considered to be very stable. Finally, the archivist could eliminate the assignment of points and simply categorize the records holdings according to these criteria or another set of workable criteria. Priorities could then be set from these general categories, costs calculated, and funds sought.

Whatever selection means is used, institutional archivists must work to determine preservation priorities. Setting such priorities will help to build better arguments on behalf of organizational support for preservation and build a better sense of confidence by institutional executives that the archives is meeting its responsibilities in a sound manner. Furthermore, if the archivist does not work to establish priorities, they might be established for him or her by external individuals or through other factors and developments. For example, one division within the institution might seek to have treatment accorded its records that are, in fact, not the most important organizational records or the ones needing the most attention. As in most areas, it is better for the institutional archivist to be proactive in his or her efforts to promote and develop the archival operation.

PRESERVATION OPTIONS AND PROCEDURES

Part of the preservation selection process encompasses the selection of the appropriate preservation treatment. Treatments are, of course, de-

An Example of a Well-Planned Preservation Program
for Archival Records

One of the keys to a successful archival preservation program is applying the proper treatment to records in deteriorating condition or in poor storage conditions. The following example is from Alan Calmes, Ralph Schofer, and Keith Eberhardt, "Theory and Practice of Paper Preservation for Archives," Restaurator 9, no. 2 (1988): 108. As the title of this article suggests, the program is oriented to paper-based records.

Condition	Action
Warm/Damp Conditions	Environmental Control
Inadequate Containers	Holdings Maintenance
Random Damaged	Interception
Impermanent Copy	Replacement
Frequent Use	Distribution of Copies
Valuable/Fragile	Laboratory Conservation

As the above list suggests, the most radical and costly preservation action (conservation of individual items) occurs only when the value of the document and its condition merit; this action should be an exceptional occurrence for the institutional archivist. More normal for the institutional archivist will be working for proper environmental control, holdings maintenance, and the "interception" (selective removal for treatment) of damaged, valuable records.

---

pendent on the need of the specific records in question, as well as the institution's resources for preservation. But there is a variety of treatments that can lead both to inappropriate treatment as well as to phasing in preservation treatment as priorities, funding, and conditions merit. Above all, however, concern with such activities should occur only after the environmental storage conditions have been stabilized; investing significant resources and energies into a program where the storage areas are poor is a bad investment.

There are a number of in-house preservation procedures that can be followed simply and with little risk of damage to the archival records. All records should be stored in alkaline materials, although there are some variations due to the original format of the record; photographic records have more precise requirements for storage, best obtained through a combination of paper and plastic folders and envelopes. Metal shelving and storage cabinets should be used instead of wood materials since wood emits harmful gases. Surface dirt on paper can often be removed by using ground art gum cleaning pads. Paper records that have been folded can be loosened and flattened through use of a makeshift humidity chamber made of damp blotting paper in the bottom of a metal or plastic container that has a tight cover. Records can be easily mylar-encapsulated to prevent additional wear and tear. Cleaning of leather and other bindings can be safely done, following directions in any basic preservation handbook. Whatever in-house procedures are used, however, they should be simple and reversible; any procedure that is considered to be uncertain should not be used until professional advice can be obtained.

Reformatting the informational content of records to microforms (microfilm and microfiche) is another common preservation technique. In general, microforms are used when the original record forms are so fragile and endangered that use is no longer possible, when security copies are required for particularly valuable (either for financial or informational reasons) records, or when additional copies are desired to provide convenient reference use at different locations. Microforms also have the advantage of using very little storage space, although this is probably counterbalanced by the financial cost of producing the film and maintaining viewing equipment to read the microforms. In an institutional archives all three conditions could easily apply.

For microfilming to be successful, it must be rigorously controlled and done to meet certain standards and other specifications. Archival records need to be filmed using silver gelatin (silver-halide) film stock, which is the only archival quality film designated by the American National Standards Institute. Original negatives should be stored in environmentally sound off-site locations, intermediate (second generation) negatives made for other copying purposes, and reference copies produced on more inexpensive diazo or vesicular film. Microfilm can be stored in the same environmental conditions that satisfy the longevity of other records, although slightly lower relative humidity and temperature ranges are generally preferred (this is true for all photographic materials).[15] Institutional archives that maintain large quantities of records on microfilm should regularly inspect the film to see if any structural changes have occurred; the advantage here, of course, is that deteriorated microfilm can be replaced by producing another reference copy from the negative. There are also other standards to be adhered to for microfilm processing, targeting of microfilm, and so forth, and the institutional archivist needs to keep abreast of new research that suggests other preservation approaches or refinements in existing approaches.[16]

Preservation microfilming has long been used by archivists with significant success. Some library conservators and preservation administrators, however, have raised some valid questions about the reliance on microforms as a primary solution to the preservation of the informational content of the archival records. Dan Hazen has suggested, for example, that other technologies might provide some better alternatives to the traditional microforms and that there are certainly time and opportunity to consider such alternatives:

We know that our readers do not enjoy microfilm; we know that microformat reproductions often fail to capture even the intellectual content of original texts; we know that the book is an artifact uniquely suited to many kinds of needs. Perhaps new technologies will eventually present information in formats affording equal portability, flexibility, aesthetic pleasure, and user satisfaction. Certainly new technologies will eventually provide information that is more adaptable and manipulable than what is now available on either microfilm or computer screens.[17]

Although Hazen's comments are directed to the librarian, they will probably strike a respondent chord in many archivists. The issue for institutional archivists is to proceed cautiously in relying on any one preservation method; rather, they must consider their own institutional context and keep abreast of new preservation practices. It may be possible, for example, for the institutional archivist to preserve those records that are already being produced in microform media, such as through Computer Output Microfilm (COM), but not seek to have any new records microfilmed except those that are identified as vital records and require storage of their textual content at off-site locations for security purposes. A better set of options for institutional archivists would be to seek to stabilize the archival records in their original media. Paper-based archival records ought to be produced on alkaline paper, if such arrangements can be worked out internally. Records that are produced in electronic format ought to be preserved in a format in which the records can be accessed.[18]

STAFFING OF AN INSTITUTIONAL ARCHIVES PRESERVATION PROGRAM

There are also a number of options that can be followed in the staffing of an institutional archives preservation program. Whether such a program is staffed by a fully trained professional conservator is mainly a factor of size and institutional commitment. Few programs, however, will have such a professional since such individuals are few and hard to come by and most institutional archives programs will not be staffed to such a degree as to allow this staffing to occur. There are, however, a number of very viable options that can be followed to eliminate this problem. Existing staff can be trained in basic preservation skills, or the institutional archives can enter into contracts with service vendors.

An institutional archives can designate an existing staff member as the preservation officer and support that individual's acquisition of continuing education in the areas of preservation and conservation. This individual would have responsibility for all preservation-related decisions and activities, such as surveying holdings for preservation needs, monitoring environmental conditions, contractual relations with other conservators and micrographics vendors, and similar activities. The role of this position is not to serve as a conservator for complicated repair or other complex practices but to coordinate all preservation-related activities in the institutional archives. Obviously, the selection of such an individual must be done with care, the best individuals being those who have a solid knowledge of basic archival practices and an interest in preservation issues and techniques.

Another option for the institutional archives is to enter into an arrangement with a professional conservator or conservation center. Conservation centers provide a wide range of preservation services, from consultation to treatment, with the advantage of having knowledgeable staff, up-to-date techniques, and a full range of equipment. The Northeast Document Conservation Center, a pioneer center founded in 1973, offers services in conservation, microfilming, photographic copying, field service advice, and disaster assistance. Utilized in the proper manner, such centers can essentially replace what many institutional archives are missing—a professionally trained preservation officer. At the least, they can provide consultation services to help an institutional archives program to do initial planning for the development of a preservation management initiative.

Some institutional archives might also wish to develop relationships with commercial microfilm vendors rather than establish their own in-house programs. There are advantages and disadvantages to both methods. Internal microfilming programs can offer the institutional archives the additional advantages of better security, consistent access to records, essential control of the quality of work done, and financial savings (if there is a sufficient continuous amount of filming to be done). The main disadvantage of establishing an internal program is the initial cost of establishing an adequate microfilm operation and staffing with technical experts. Microfilm equipment is expensive, and there is a range of specialized equipment that is required for a program to be able to accommodate all varieties of microfilming. Some institutional archivists might have the opportunity to work with their organization's records management program's microforms unit. These disadvantages are directly compensated for by developing a contractual arrangement with a commercial microfilm vendor. These service bureaus have a tremendous variety of equipment and sufficient microfilm expertise and can often microfilm small quantities of records at significantly lower costs than what the institution would have to expend if attempting to do the work on its own. Entering into such a relationship, however, lessens the institution's control of the records and security, which can be a major problem if the records possess access or other restrictions.

Determining how the archives will handle its microfilming is a decision

Services of a Regional Conservation Center:
The Northeast Document Conservation Center (NEDCC)

Conservation Services

The Center's . . . experience includes conservation of books, documents, maps, photographs, parchment artifacts, architectural and other oversized drawings, wallpaper, and art on paper, collage and contemporary works. Treatment may be limited to basic stabilization, or it can include total restoration of the original bindings, or replacement of bindings too damaged to repair.

Microfilming Services

Offering a cost-effective alternative for preserving information and protecting original artifacts . . . [t]he Center is equipped to handle such hard-to-film materials as manuscripts, scrapbooks, brittle newspaper, and fragile books. Microfilming services include frame-by-frame editorial inspection, microfilm processing and duplication, and archival storage of master negatives.

Photographic Copying Services

NEDCC has extensive experience in duplicating historical photographs, especially large collections of nitrate negatives. Photographic images can be preserved by means of interpositives, microfilm, fiche, copy negatives, contact prints, and enlargements.

Field Service Office

The field service staff, NEDCC's consulting branch, emphasizes the prevention of deterioration . . . . The consultant assesses the general needs of the collections, including environmental conditions, and storage and handling techniques. A report of recommendations is submitted to the client to help develop a long-range conservation plan . . . . For individual objects or special collections, our conservators make site visits and provide detailed condition surveys and recommendations.

Disaster Assistance

. . . . Because prompt action is necessary following a flood or fire, NEDCC provides 24 hour emergency assistance on the telephone at no charge. If necessary, a representative of the Center will assist local personnel on site.

From NEDCC brochure

that must be carefully considered. The requirements of microfilm—film size, equipment needs, nature of records, condition of records, and probable use—are all factors that will have to be considered. The most important issue, however, is the cost of microfilming internally or through a service vendor. Labor, equipment, space, and supply costs all need to be factored into the equation. A basic microfilm program requires cameras, processor, duplicator, densitometer, inspection equipment, film, processing chemicals, staff, office space, lab furniture, and other elements that add up to many thousands of dollars. For institutional archives, there are a number of other factors that will also affect the decision. In large organizations, microfilming of records may already be a regular process, administered through a records management program and directed at the reduction of space requirements, security, vital records, and other such needs. In this case, the institutional archives should make an effort to develop a working relationship with the existing program in order to meet the special needs of microfilming archival records. Additionally, many organizations will have certain preconceptions of microfilm as a panacea for all records problems or as a nuisance to use. If the former, the archives program needs to work to communicate that microfilm is only one aspect of a larger archival and records management operation; if the latter, the archives program should seriously consider other alternatives than filming since it will want to have the records utilized.

PHASING-IN THE PRESERVATION PROGRAM

A couple of decades ago, George Cunha, a pioneer library and archives conservator, described a series of steps that would enable a basic preservation program to be started, starting with an examination of the environment, surveying the records conditions, and determining the range of preservation actions that were required. This scenario was an effort to enable the institution to conduct careful planning for the preservation program, as well as to phase in the major aspects of the operation. Phasing in preservation programs can be a very useful manner for institutions to proceed, requiring smaller costs at each step, enabling the program to win support for itself and prove its viability, and aiding the institutional archives to evaluate the effectiveness of every phase.

There are any number of variations possible for phasing in a preservation management program, depending on the numerous variables evident in a single institution—from size to corporate culture to leadership and interest. Securing stable environments in storage areas, along with optimal security, is probably the best place to begin. Placing archival materials in acid-free containers and folders in flat, unfolded forms is the next most important aspect. Trying to oversee the proper maintenance of records in their mode of current use, along with seeking to ensure that certain records, when

Cunha's Advice on Starting a Preservation Program

The records conservator - whether volunteer, part-time, or the director-coordinator himself - should proceed as follows:

* Examine the environment in which the records are kept, evaluating its suitability for document storage and identifying conditions causing deterioration.

* Determine and implement measures to improve the environment and prevent further damage, within potential or present budgetary limitations.

* Examine the records to determine their present physical condition and establish priorities for treatment.

* Differentiate, perhaps with two lists, those records that can be treated on the premises from those requiring professional attention.

* Establish a "work room" within your building for remedial treatment that you can do yourself, and equip it with the necessary tools, furnishings, and supplies.

* Supervise simple on-the-premises repairs and restoration.

* Establish a working arrangement with a professional conservator for the treatment of badly damaged or particularly valuable documents.

* Keep informed on new conservation theories and techniques.

From George M. Cunha, Conserving Local Archival Materials on a Limited Budget (American Association for State and Local History, Technical Leaflet 86, November 1975), 1.

---

created, use the best and most stable materials, is another excellent stage. Microfilming (or electrostatic copying on acid-free paper) is the next logical stage of developing an archival preservation program. Conservation work, including such activities as deacidification and mending, should be the last phase of development for any preservation program.[19]

NOTES

1. See, for example, James M. O'Toole, "On the Idea of Permanence," *American Archivist* 52 (Winter 1989): 10–25.

2. Larry J. Hackman, in *Invest in the American Collection: A Regional Forum on the Conservation of Cultural Property*, ed. Jane Sennett Long (Washington, DC.: National Committee to Save America's Cultural Collections, 1987), 9.

3. Carmen Crespo and Vicente Vinas, *The Preservation and Restoration of Paper Records and Books: A RAMP Study with Guidelines*, PGI–84/WS/25 (Paris: UNESCO, 1984), 23.

4. Shelley Reisman Paine, *Basic Principles for Controlling Environmental Conditions in Historical Agencies and Museums*, AASLH Technical Report 3 (1985), 1.

5. There are variations cited in the temperature and humidity ranges in different publications, but the essential point is that the lower, the better and the more regulated or stable, the better.

6. See, for example, Timothy Walch, *Archives & Manuscripts: Security*, SAA Basic Manual Series (Chicago: Society of American Archivists, 1977), 10–14.

7. SAA Basic Archival Conservation Program, *Conservation Self-Study* (Chicago: Society of American Archives, January 1982).

8. See the series of articles in the May/June 1990 issue of *Museum News* for descriptions of the effects of these occurrences and the value of disaster preparedness plans.

9. Howard P. Lowell, "Preserving Recorded Information," *Records Management Quarterly* (April 1982): 38–39.

10. See, for example, John P. Barton and Johanna G. Wellheiser, eds., *An Ounce of Prevention: A Handbook on Disaster Contingency Planning for Archives, Libraries and Records Centers* (Toronto: Toronto Area Archivists Group Education Foundation, 1985) and Sally A. Buchanan and Toby Murray, *Disaster Planning, Preparedness and Recovery for Libraries and Archives*, PGI–88/WS/6 ED 297–769 (Paris: UNESCO, 1988).

11. For a description of the kinds of operations taken on in this context, refer to Renee M. Robbins, "Taking the Disaster Out of Recovery," *Infosystems* (July 1986): 38, 40–42, 44, and Brett J. Balon and H. Wayne Gardner, "Disaster Planning for Electronic Records," *Records Management Quarterly* (July 1988): 20–22, 24–25, 30.

12. Mary Lynn Ritzenthaler, *Implementing a Conservation Program*, SAA Basic Archival Conservation Program (Chicago: Society of American Archivists, September 1982), 3–4.

13. This is based on Richard J. Cox, "Selecting Historical Records for Microfilming: Some Suggested Procedures for Repositories," *Library & Archival Security* 9, no. 2 (1989): 21–41.

14. The specific mechanism has been described in Cox, "Selecting Historical Records for Microfilming."

15. Optimum storage conditions should be as follows: relative humidity should be kept below 50 percent and is best at 35 percent, lower than is necessary for paper records. Temperature is best at about 68 degrees F, although lower temperatures are recommended, especially for color photographs.

16. For such research see, for example, James M. Reilly, et al., "Photograph Enclosures: Research and Specifications," *Restaurator* 10 (1989): 102–11, and James M. Reilly, et al., "Stability of Black-and-White Photographic Images, with Special Reference to Microfilm," *Microform Review* 17 (December 1988): 270–78.

17. Dan Hazen, "Preservation in Poverty and Plenty: Policy Issues for the 1990s," *Journal of Academic Librarianship* 15 (January 1990): 345–46.

18. It is possible, of course, that institutional archivists might need to consider placing more of their records in electronic form in order to ensure that the records are being used.

This is because the personnel of organizations are becoming increasingly accustomed to using records in this form.

19. The best description of a phased archival preservation program is Alan Calmes, Ralph Schofer, and Keith Eberhardt, "Theory and Practice of Paper Preservation for Archives," *Restaurator* 9 (1988): 96–111.

5

Arranging, Describing, and Providing Reference in Institutional Archives

USE AND THE INSTITUTIONAL ARCHIVES: DEFINITIONS

It is no secret that archival records are preserved in order to be used; otherwise, why would they be preserved in the first place? If no use of the records is made, then the energy and resources put into their care are for naught. All the potential values of archives mentioned in the preceding chapters will also never be realized. In an institutional archives, the lack of use may lead to the demise of its archival program or limit the possibility of the archives having the resources that it requires to fulfill its mission; in some cases, it could lead to the destruction (deliberate or through neglect) of the institution's valuable archival records. Use needs to be encouraged, monitored, evaluated, and reported in order to build and sustain a successful institutional archives program. For use to occur, archival records must be carefully arranged, described, and made available in a suitable reference environment.

This chapter's purpose is to describe the basics of archival arrangement, description, and reference, all of which are archival functions that have been radically transformed in the past decade, although the greatest changes are most likely yet to come. *Arrangement* is the process of organizing archival records according to elemental archival principles. A more complete definition for archival arrangement is that it is:

the process and results of organizing archives, records, and manuscripts in accordance with accepted archival principles, particularly provenance, at as many as necessary of the following levels: repository, record group or comparable control unit, subgroup, series, file unit, and document. The process usually includes packing, labeling, and shelving of archives, records, and manuscripts, and is intended to achieve physical or administrative control and basic identification of the holdings.[1]

Description is the effort to establish intellectual control over archival records so that they may be effectively used by researchers. Description and arrangrment are built on the basic archival principles of the record group, provenance, and original order, all principles that have been introduced earlier and will be described more fully here. Both functions are also essential to providing *reference* to the archival records; if arrangement and description are poorly handled, then the access to the institution's archival records will be seriously hampered. If the access to these records is hampered, then the institution's own functioning will be hurt, since the informational content of archival records is important to the institution's mission, business, activities, policies, development, corporate culture, and other aspects. In other words, use of archival records is not merely to preserve the archival program but to benefit the entire institution and society as a whole.

ARRANGEMENT AS A FUNCTION OF THE INSTITUTIONAL ARCHIVES

As an archival function, arrangement is most often linked with description and often subsumed by description and reference. But all are inexorably linked in process and implementation, the reason they are being treated together in this volume. Arrangement is a function, however, that needs to be carefully considered on its own, since problems that occur here will hamper all other basic archival work. Arrangement has tended to consume significant resources (time and money) and hindered the balanced development of archival programs. Archivists operating in institutional settings will also need to be especially mindful of the arrangement of archival records because of the organization's emphasis on current information needs and its ever-changing use of information systems, decision-making practices, and organizational structures. All of these can place pressure on purposeful rearrangement or accidental loss of arrangement of existing institutional records.

Archival arrangement has been most often concerned with levels of organization of the records. But there are other concerns that also affect all potential arrangement levels. One is the notion that records should be maintained in their original order of creation. As one archivist has described the reason for this concept:

It is recognized that records usually can be prepared for use more quickly by ascertaining and accepting their original order rather than by attempting to create a new pattern of arrangement. Moreover, it is theorized that the original arrangement had logic and meaning for the records-creating agency and may have to reveal its operating processes. It is believed, however, that original order should not be accepted uncritically. Many American archivists feel that there is justification for changing the agency-given arrangement, when it appears to be unsystematic and lessens the usability of the records. Similarly, usability becomes the principal concern of these archivists, when it seems desirable to devise another scheme of arrangement because the original one has been lost.[2]

The institutional archivist should strive to maintain the original order of traditional paper files by maintaining control of records from their time of creation until delivery to the archives, while maintaining adherence to a more important principle: "Records in an archival institution should be maintained in a state of usability, their exact arrangement being the simplest possible which assures access to the documentation."[3] Archivists, however, should also be aware that original order can be a deterrent to effective administration of archival records and some rearrangement might be required "so long as the deviations reflect the activities of the creating agency.[4] Archivists will discover a wide range of opinions and debates about arrangement practices in the archival literature; the institutional archivist must always keep in mind the needs of his or her institution, develop policies for consistent applications of arrangement, and then make sure that these fit into the present professional archival arrangement and description standards.

Archivists have generally relied upon the notion of levels of arrangement. The concept of these levels is that beyond the concern with original order and provenance, archivists will have to adhere to levels of arrangement that facilitate their management of the records and ability to provide access to them. These levels can be briefly described here, although their use can sometimes be the matter of an involved and difficult decision-making process.[5]

The *repository level* is the division of the archives' total holdings into a few major and distinct categories. These categories reflect the origination of records held by the archives. An institutional archives' repository level arrangement will depend, of course, on the specific nature of the institution and its mission. A college and university archives might be divided roughly into the actual archival records that have been created by the academic organization and the historical manuscripts that have been collected by the program because of their additional collaborative or significant documentation of the institution as well (such as the personal papers of prominent faculty, administrators, and alumni). A corporate archives might divide its holdings according to the archival records of the main business headquarters, subsidiaries, and companies that have been taken over through the

Example of Repository Level Description

The Chase Manhattan Bank, N.A.
Archives
1 Chase Manhattan Plaza
23rd Floor
New York NY 10081

(212) 552-6658

OPEN: M-F 9-5; closed weekends and holidays.
ACCESS: Researchers who are not Bank employees must submit letter detailing topic, purpose, scope of work, and institutional or professional affiliation.
COPYING FACILITIES: no.
MATERIALS SOLICITED: Records of the Bank, including executive correspondence, interoffice communications relating to policy making, financial summaries, photographs, department records, files on bank services, oral histories, and motion pictures.

HOLDINGS:
      Total volume: 650 c.f.
      Inclusive dates: 1799-
      Description: Collections relating to the history of the Chase Manhattan Bank and its predecessors in the New York City area, including the Chase National Bank, the Equitable Trust Company, and the Bank of the Manhattan Company. Some materials document the early years of the Manhattan Company (founded in 1799) and its operations as water supplier for New York City. Photographs show banking facilities, employees' work and activities, and major figures in the Bank's development.

National Historical Publications and Records Commission, *Directory of Archives and Manuscript Repositories in the United States*, 2nd ed. (Phoenix: Oryx Press, 1988), 430.

---

years. A diocesan archives might segment its holdings into the records of the diocesan administration, individual churches, and affiliated church organizations and interest groups. The repository level is not frequently used by the archivist except for inclusion in general, multi-institutional finding aids or for general efforts to promote the archives within the parent organization. The repository level is important, however, for the development or reflection of the institutional archives' mission, and provides a brief summary of the nature of the institutional archives and its potential use; this use is most often likely to be reflected in brochures and other publicity material promoting the institutional archives.

The next level is that of the *record group* and, if the institutional archives also collects related historical materials, the *manuscript collection*. The record group is a body of organizationally related records established on the basis of their provenance; a manuscript collection can be the "collected" archives of an organization or group based on the same principle or the artificially assembled manuscripts accumulated around a single theme or subject. Record groups, which should be a focus of institutional archivists, have generally been considered to follow the administrative hierarchy or structure of the institution itself. The advantages and disadvantages to this scheme will be seen in the discussion on description that follows this section, but for now it is enough to say that this arrangement scheme has been used because it is logical and easy to adapt. In an institutional archives setting it is especially important because by following the organizational structure, the archivist can fit into the ways that the organization functions and provide a fairly easy mechanism for employees and managers to follow their need for older information. Record groups in an academic institution will break down into groups ranging from boards of trustees to the president's office to the various schools and divisions within the university or college. In a business a similar kind of arrangement will be evident from its governing board to the chief executive officer through all the various main administrative levels. Religious organizations, cultural institutions, civic organizations, and other groups that establish institutional archives will reflect similar kinds of arrangements.

Institutional archivists must be careful of relying too much on the record group as the basis for arrangement. Critics of the record group concept have pointed out that it is reliant on the nineteenth-century concept of organizational hierarchy and bureaucracy, which many have concluded does not accurately capture the manner in which organizations actually work. David Bearman and Richard Lytle have captured this problem in an important essay on the topic:

In classical bureaucratic organizations, records were kept by and for the offices which used them. In the modern age of central management information systems, records retention and reporting regulations, and vigilant corporate legal staffs, these assumptions are rapidly becoming unwarranted. Offices which generate records frequently do not maintain them. When entire agencies are created or abolished, the connection with a hierarchical schema is difficult enough, but when changes take place within an agency, creating and abolishing divisions, departments, bureaus, and offices, or transferring them to other agencies, merging or dividing existing units, then a mono-hierarchical representation of these changes is impossible. Even more difficult to cope with are subtle shifts and changes over time in missions, functions, responsibilities, and reporting relationships. Yet all these changes take place within real organizations.[6]

Bearman and Lytle have urged less tinkering with the physical arrangement of the records and more creative utilization of provenance information for access points to the records; this use of provenance will be discussed later in the section of this chapter on reference. Another archivist,

Example of Record Group Description

United States.   Bureau of Insular Affairs.
Records, 1868-1945.
1,645 cubic ft.
      Founded 13 Dec. 1898, as the Division of Customs and Insular Affairs in the Office of the Secretary of War to assist in administering customs and other civil affairs in Puerto Rico, Cuba, and the Philippine Islands; designated Division of Insular Affairs, 10 Dec. 1900, and Bureau of Insular Affairs by an act of 1 July 1902; Reorganization Plan No. II of 1939 consolidated the bureau with the Division of Territories and Island Possessions, Department of the Interior.
      Record Group 350 includes general records (1898-1945, 922 ft.); other records relating to the Philippine Islands (1897-1938, 47 ft.); library records (1868-1945, 685 ft.); miscellaneous records (1898-1937, 49 ft.); and audiovisual records (1898-1939, 14,750 items).
      Forms part of: Records of the Department of the Interior.
      Described in: Guide to the National Archives of the United States. Washington, D.C.: National Archives, 1974.

      Steven L. Hensen, comp. <u>Archives, Personal Papers, and Manuscripts: A Cataloging Manual for Archival Repositories, Historical Societies, and Manuscript Libraries</u> (Chicago: Society of American Archivists, 1939), 146.

---

making the same point in a slightly different manner, has noted that the arrangement of records series within records groups leads to a confusion that such arrangements themselves accurately reflect institutional hierarchies and functions—in other words, the manner in which organizations literally work and make decisions.[7] Suffice it to say that the institutional archivist has an important role to play in the organization if he or she can expedite the use of historical information over the shifting and often confusing lines of decision making and functioning that exist in the institution.[8]

    It should be noted here, however, that the institutional archives that also acquires manuscript collections will face some additional challenges in developing an arrangement scheme. There is often little inherent order to such collections (the opposite of the institution's own records, with minor exceptions), resulting in more labor-intensive efforts by the archivist to determine how these collections will be integrated into the institutional archives, their availability advertised, and access provided. The business of deciding whether manuscript collections should be included in the institutional archives program is a tricky one that needs to be very carefully considered and determined to be done only after reflection. With the exception of institutions like colleges and universities that have special collections departments, most institutional archives should probably not become involved with the acquisition of manuscript collections. On the other hand, it is also true—and known for a long time—that "often the line between institutional archives and personal papers cannot be easily or sensibly drawn,"[9] often because of the mixing of personal papers but also because of fuzzy institutional relationships. For the institutional archivist, however, the main issue might be not to give any impression that resources are being used to preserve records that have, at best, a quasi-relationship to the institution or that fit loosely or uncomfortably into the institutional archives' mission.

The *records series* is the heart of the institutional archives' arrangement efforts. A series is the file units or documents arranged in accordance with a filing system or maintained as a unit because they relate to a particular subject or function, result from the same activity, or have a particular form or because of some other relationship determined from their creation, receipt, or use. Records series most clearly reflect the manner in which the institution creates, maintains, and uses recorded information (at least information in nonelectronic form), partly because series most often are naturally formed of transactional documents reflecting a particular institutional function (such as purchasing or licensing). Researchers, both those employed within the institution and those who come from the outside, will often seek information by inquiring about certain institutional functions that are most clearly reflected in the various records series. Regardless of the nature of the organization, records series possess great similarities, such as subject, correspondence, personnel, and various case files or the records accumulated for the preparation of a special study or report. The reasons for these similarities are, of course, that in most organizations there are extremely consistent functions, such as general administration, personnel management, accounting and finance, internal communication, and so forth. While the specific nature of the institution's business may be different, the basic functions, and hence that of the record keeping, will retain very similar characteristics. Specific series of records also often cross over institutional divisions as the organization's structure changes; the series can be intellectually maintained in the descriptive practices of the archives (indeed, many archives are maintaining a specific series physically together despite administrative changes).

The next arrangement levels are those of the specific *file* unit and the individual document or *item*. A file unit is an aggregation of documents brought together because they are transactionally related or for convenience in storage and retrieval. Examples of file units include a set of records relating to a set of transactions by the institution with a specific individual or company, documents placed together because they relate to

Example of a Records Series

Alabama. State Oyster Inspector.
   Monthly reports of oyster licenses issued and oyster tax collected,
   1891-1895.
   .33 cubic ft. (1 archives box).

   Organization: chronological.
   Summary: The major functions of the oyster inspector were
to regulate business and protect the environment by overseeing the
oyster industry. Among the activities used to accomplish this were
the registering of licenses issued to oyster fishermen's boats with
the probate judge of Mobile County, and the registering of taxes
collected on the amounts caught. This activity resulted in the
creation of this series.
   The series contains information on the licensing of oyster
fishermen: "license number, name of person to whom issued, for
whom issued, date issued, name of boat, type of rigging, number of
barrels capacity, where caught, when caught, number of catchers,
and amount of tax paid." The reports were compiled by the Probate
Judge of Mobile Co. and filed in the State Auditor's office."
Unrestricted.
Finding aids: Container listing available in repository.

Permission to use granted by the Alabama Department of Archives
and History.

---

some specific topic, or some other similar reason. The individual document
is written evidence of some specific activity of the institution. It is communication about an issue (a letter, memorandum, or report), confirmation
of an agreement (legal contract), or documentation of some fact or event
(register). Both of these levels are less used in arrangement work, except
to maintain the integrity of the records series. Most institutional archives
will develop container lists of file units fairly often, although the item level
will only occasionally be utilized for records series such as cartographic
documents that will be requested individually by researchers. If an institutional archives has to devote great attention to arranging such levels, it
can become bogged down with minutia. The energies of the institutional
archivist will be better spent in attempting to ensure that the archival
records come from their creating offices to the program with their arrangement in good order.

   The institutional archives, focused as it is on its own parent organization's
records, ought to find itself in an excellent position to control the original
arrangement of archival records from their point of creation through their

Sample Institutional Archives Container Listing

The following is a fictitious container listing of business archives. These records relate to one unit of the corporation and have been assigned record group and series numbers, as well as locations (range, stack, and shelf). The series being described here is the administrative records of the Sales Division's chief administrator. The description is essentially a list of original file folder headings (and, in one case, a heading assigned and indicated by brackets) that can be used to control the records and assist in expediting access.

Administrative Unit: Sales Division
Record Group No.:   RG 11
Series No.:   S 1

Box No.	Records Title	Dates	Location
1	*Director's Administrative Files*	*1908-13*	*22/5/1*
	Correspondence, A-C	1908-10	22/5/1
	Correspondence, D-F	1908-12	22/5/1
	Correspondence, G-N	1908-10	22/5/1
	Correspondence, O-Z	1908-13	22/5/1
	District Sales Reports, Regions 1-3	1909-13	22/5/1
2	*Director's Administrative Files*	*1908-13*	*22/5/2*
	District Sales Reports, Regions 1-3	1908-11	22/5/2
	Financial Summaries	1912-13	22/5/2
	[History of the Unit]	1913	22/5/2

use in the office to their transfer to the archives. The ideal manner in which to achieve this arrangement is by either allying the archives program with the records management operation or creating a records management structure operating as part of the institutional archives. The institution's archivist will also find it necessary to work closely with not only the records' creators but the organization's data processors, managers of information systems, and other individuals who are concerned with information creation, storage, and dissemination in electronic formats.[10] Regardless of how effective the archivist will be in having a proactive program in influencing the archival integrity of records throughout their life cycle, he or she will find it necessary to devote some resources to basic archival "processing."

THE INSTITUTIONAL ARCHIVES AND
ARCHIVAL PROCESSING

Archivists use the term *processing* to encompass the work they do to prepare archival records for use. Processing generally is meant to include arrangement, description, preservation, identification of restricted materials, and other basic functions, although the focus of processing is on the first two. While it has technically been applied only to manuscript collections that generally need significant arranging and other basic work, archival processing is also used to describe the work done on the kinds of records found in institutional archives; the difference between the processing in these situations is usually the extent of effort and resources required. Processing is essentially the linkage between arrangement and description,[11] and leads to the production of finding aids that expedite the use of archival records; as such, it is a combination of physical labor and intellectual effort, the proportion of which changes in relation to the records under review. Processing is completed "when the archivist has . . . applied the appropriate degree of arrangement, preservation, description, and screening [identifying restricted records] activities that will make that collection [or record group or series] usable for the researcher while protecting the physical well-being of the material and honoring donor and legal restrictions on the collection."[12] Processing also occurs after initial appraisal decisions, supports the identification of preservation needs, and assists the use of archival records. It falls midway in the general sequence of basic archival functions.

Processing includes a wide variety of activities. It starts with the institutional archives staff preparing to move archival records from their creating office to the archives facility. This move includes properly labeling the records so that they arrive in good order (including gathering any useful information about the records from office staff who possess useful knowledge about the records), fumigating or cleaning the records to ensure that no insects or fungus are brought inadvertently into the archives storage area, and unpacking the records.[13] In processing, the archivist then proceeds to reviewing the entire range of records to determine whether they possess an original order that can be maintained as the basis for arrangement and then description work and to identify records series and other elements of the records' original structure that can be used to determine their final arrangement scheme. Appropriate background information on the archival records, their originating office, and the office's functions and responsibilities that are available should be reviewed early in the transfer of the records in order to assist in the preparation of the records for additional descriptive work. Archivists should be especially alert for records such as administrative charts, policy and procedural statements, history sketches, and other documents that provide data about the records creators'

Some Basic Principles of Archival Processing

First, the ideal level of processing is not the same for all collections. As the intermediary between creators and users of records, the archivist should aim to do only the amount of processing that makes a collection useful to researchers . . . .

Second, more staff time should be allocated to collections with perceived research potential - those that are, or are expected to be, used more heavily - than to collections of dubious research value . . . .

Third, the processor should assume that his or her work on a collection is all that will ever be done; it is unlikely that there will be time and staff to reprocess collections . . . .

Fourth, because the processing done on any collection will vary depending on the collection's research potential, the amount of work necessary to make it usable, and the staff time available, all processing work must be decided on deliberately and must be carefully planned and coordinated . . . .

Fifth, processing is best carried out as a team project. Each processor should be supported by an assistant . . . who carries out routine tasks, freeing the processor for intellectual work . . . .

Helen W. Slotkin and Karen T. Lynch, "An Analysis of Processing Procedures: The Adaptable Approach," <u>American Archivist</u> 45 (Spring 1982): 156.

---

functioning and the nature of their information origination and use; these documents will be helpful both for the arrangement and description of the records.

Once the records have been reviewed and an arrangement scheme determined, archival processing proceeds to its next stage. The institutional archivist needs to unfold records, remove metal fasteners and other such damaging materials, and place the records in acid-free folders and boxes or supervise these tasks completed by others.[14] As the records are physically arranged, the archivist needs to relabel files that have cryptic descriptors, note when undated records are being assigned dates, and make sure that no important information is lost as wrappers and other potentially damaging packaging devices are removed. As the archivist works through the records, he or she also needs to make note of preservation needs, note important informational highlights of the records (including relationships to other records series) that will be used in preparing a final description, and remove artifacts or printed ephemera and publications while maintaining information about this material's context.[15]

If the original order of the records has been lost, the institutional archivist will face a more difficult task in archival processing. The archivist has long adhered to a belief that the original order of the records conveys important information about the records creator and the functions of the creator. Obviously, the institutional archivist should do all that is possible to ensure

Determining Archival Processing Costs

What is a standard measurement for time spent processing a collection? The most accurate is hours per cubic feet. To obtain this measure take the number of hours spent processing a collection and then divide by the number of cubic feet processed:

$$\frac{28 \text{ hours spent processing}}{4 \text{ cubic feet of archives}} = 7 \text{ hours per cubic foot}$$

By keeping an accurate count of the processing time spent on particular types of material along with the amount of material processed, an archivist can begin to project how long it will take to process a collection of 19th-century personal papers or 20th-century organizational records.

However, such raw data does not take into consideration all factors in the arrangement and description chain, nor does it give us figures on the cost of processing. To get this cost, take the basic formula used above, multiply by the cost per hour and then add the cost of supplies and shelving. This gives the cost of processing one cubic foot of archives:

$$\frac{\text{cost per hour x hours processing} + \text{cost of shelving \& supplies}}{\text{cubic feet of archives}} = \text{cost per cubic ft.}$$

Thomas Wilsted, Computing the Total Cost of Archival Processing, Technical Leaflet Series, no. 2 (n.p.: Mid-Atlantic Regional Archives Conference, 1989), 3.

---

that the order is maintained. The archivist, however, will sometimes discover that the order has been lost due to carelessness or mishap. The archivist may find that this is primarily a problem as the archival program is established and older records are transferred to the archives facility after a lengthy period of nonuse or temporary storage out of main offices. If the archivist finds that the records' order has been lost, then either the order should be reestablished if possible or another order imposed that will facilitate the use of the records. If an artificial order must be used, the archivist must be careful to explain what has been done as part of the records' description and note that there is an order other than what the records creator may have used. Providing this kind of additional information will assist the researcher to understand any difficulties he or she might face in using the records and, as well, prevent the researcher from misinterpreting what he or she sees in the records.

The institutional archivist will find that basic arrangement work is a laborious aspect of the archival operation. The work is often tedious and probably accounts for most of the effort in archival processing. Studies that have examined processing costs have indicated that the cost of processing one cubic foot of records may range from as little as $60 to as much as $1,000,[16] sums that can cripple many institutional archives in their efforts to function in other needed areas. Institutional archives should carefully consider how such processing work will be handled in the overall program's operation. Much of the work can be handled by technicians or even paraprofessionals, provided there is good professional oversight along with adequate written policies that can guide the work. Use of such technicians and paraprofessionals enables both more efficient team processing and the freeing of the well-equipped archival professionals to work on other important tasks of the archival program.[17] Institutional archivists should also keep in mind that there is no ideal level of processing that can be uniformly applied to every record group and series. The arrangement level determined appropriate to a particular set of records will depend on a variety of variables such as other processing priorities, potential research use, staff and other resources that are available, and institutional demands for information from archival records needed for its ongoing administration.

Crucial to all of this work is a sense of phasing in the work of basic processing (much as a phased preservation program was discussed in the previous chapter); by phasing, the institutional archivist can gain a workable amount of intellectual control over his or her records without getting bogged down with a small portion of records. Phasing requires a clear set of priorities at each level (that is, certain sets of records may not ever be accorded attention beyond a certain level) so that the proper selection of records for work is made. Most importantly, the archivist needs to keep in mind that arrangement work is an important step to the overall objective of gaining and maintaining control over the description of the institution's archival records.

DESCRIPTION AND INSTITUTIONAL ARCHIVES

Archival description is the final preliminary step in making records potentially available for the institution and other researchers. Nancy Sahli, an authority on archival description, has stated that "archival description is a cornerstone activity of our profession, for without adequate user access to materials there is little sense in saving them."[18] If arrangement work is the product of a considerable amount of hands-on, practical work, archival description has been tremendously modified by new theoretical and conceptual thinking and the implementation of that thinking into archival descriptive systems and networks. Less than a generation ago, the institutional archivist would have used any system—catalog cards, published finding aid, or automated catalog—that seemed appropriate to his or her organization's own internal needs and would have assumed that since archival records were unique, their intellectual control through descriptive efforts could be unique. Now the institutional archivist needs to be aware of professionwide descriptive standards and networks.

Archival description has a number of basic intentions that must always be kept in mind. Description is the final step in making sure that the informational content of archival records is readily available for research use and that the records, once used, can be accurately and reliably cited so that they can be consulted by others. To make sure that this information is available, the archivist must provide consistent data about the records and their contents that provide a suitable number of access points and that enable participation in local, statewide, and national bibliographic information networks. Providing such consistent information requires adherence to a finding aids system,[19] a goal that has been made easier by the advancement of national networks and descriptive standards. This last aspect is especially important for institutional archives and deserves a special note.

While it might not seem important for institutional archives to participate in multi-institutional networks (since these archives will always be of prime importance to the institution itself), several points need to be considered here. First, many institutions have significantly altered the manner in which they use information, a change that has, in turn, led to a very different set of expectations about how, when, where, and what information will be available to them. For example, every reasonably-sized corporation has supported a library function in which the corporation's employees have expected to be able to find information relative to their specific field in order to do research and development and marketing projections and to maintain a certain level of knowledge about developments in a variety of topical areas and disciplines. In many of these corporations, the library function has expanded from being a traditional collection of books, serials, and periodicals to supporting a partially or fully automated operation in which individuals can have access to a variety of online data bases that provide abstracts or full-text retrieval of an immense amount of literature. In some corporations, individuals have had their personal computers tied into an internal network that delivers the contents of these data bases right to their desks and even their homes. The result has been changes in information-seeking behavior. The employee expects information to be readily available in an expeditious and convenient manner. For the institutional archivist, this expectation means that information about the corporation's archives needs to be available in the same convenient manner if the archivist expects the records to be utilized as they should. It also means that the archivist should determine the most effective and cost-efficient manner in which to provide access to other institutional archives and repositories that may have archival material important to an individual's research in a particular topical area; the archivist should be able to use one or more of the available national archival data bases.

The second important aspect about participating in such networks is that it will assist the institutional archivist to make better use of one of the many automated, descriptive systems that are presently available for adoption. A number of automated systems' software have been developed that can be used on a personal computer and have a relatively modest cost.[20] Similarly, there are also software packages for records management operations that range through the entire records life cycle from creation to final disposition and generally emphasize the records retention schedule and the maintenance of records in the institutional records center. Such automated systems provide, of course, a major advantage for the overall management of the institutional archives program and enable a more efficient control of administrative actions (accessioning, preservation treatment, and exhibition) taken on archival records, as well as automating the retrieval process. They also provide the opportunity for quickly delivering information about all records (especially the archival records) to employees, managers, and executive officers of the institution.

The third major advantage of these systems is that they ensure consistency of description practices. The archival management software that is commercially available has been generally based on the standard practices of the United States MAchine Readable Catalog (MARC) Archives and Manuscripts Control (AMC) Format; in fact, an institution should not purchase such a system unless it complies with the MARC AMC Format. This standard ensures that the institutional archives will be describing its records in a manner in which the descriptions could be easily added into one of the national archival data bases. This standard and its accompanying standards also provide the foundation for continuity that is needed as staff changes occur; one of the problems that many archival programs has faced is having idiosyncratic descriptive practices that become even more of a challenge when a new individual takes over and applies yet another descriptive "system" to the records. For institutional archives, this problem is especially important because such idiosyncratic practices can lead to poor utilization by the institution of its archival records because it is hard to determine what the archives holds and how the records can be best accessed.

The institutional archives seeking involvement in national networks and/ or the use of descriptive software is taking such actions because of a concern to ensure that certain basic kinds of information are definitely included in the description products. This range of information includes basic data on the history of the records before acquisition by the archives, an accurate identification of the records, their access status, their quantity, their location, their arrangement, their basic content and date spans, their physical condition, references to any parts (such as artifacts or published items) of

Why Adopt MARC?

For several years now I have met archivists who ask me why the archival community should adopt MARC. I almost invariably give three answers which have nothing to do with sharing information . . . .

First, we should adopt MARC because it is an insurance policy for automated data. Other formats in which we store the data are non-standard . . . . If we want to be certain that we will be able to move the data we laboriously compile about our holdings from one automated environment to another, we need to be able to read it into and out of a format which allows for "migration" between hardware vendors and software systems.

Second, we should adopt MARC because the AMC format embodies standard archival practice, and as a very small profession our best chance of being able to leverage sufficient investments to get a reasonable variety of software products from which to select something which meets our needs, is to be able to provide developers of such products with a standard set of data they must address.

Third, we have an opportunity to disseminate information about our holdings through a vast array of other agencies simply by being able to output it in MARC format. If we had developed a new food product and wanted to reach the marketplace, we would adopt barcoding on our packages because the largest grocery chains would not sell our commodity unless it was barcoded. As archivists, if we want to reach the information dissemination marketplace, we need to use the facilities of the national networks and database vendors. To refuse to place MARC on our packages is akin to not recording barcodes. We will find ourselves standing on a corner with a small vending stand, wondering why we haven't reached a larger audience.

What is noteworthy about this list of arguments is that none of them hinges on any assumptions about archivists sharing, or not sharing, data with each other. None of them depends at all on the realization of national information systems. And by themselves, none of them suggests anything about the promise of MARC for cooperative documentation or cooperative collections management . . . .

David Bearman, Archival Informatics Newsletter, 1 (Spring 1987): 4-5.

---

the records series or group removed to other areas of the repository, and citations to relevant publications and studies that have made use of, or in some manner describe or reproduce, the archival records. All of these elements are essential for management of the records by the archivist and enhance the possibility of their use. It should be emphasized that if an institutional archives is just being established, it is wise to consider the early use of an automated system that uses the MARC AMC standard to avoid costly conversion at a later date.[21] Institutional archivists might also find it is easier to use the MARC AMC Format standard if they cooperate with the organization's librarian, who might be more conversant with many of the bibliographic and cataloging standards that are useful to know in starting to use the archival standards.[22]

Archivists have traditionally relied upon a variety of internal repository finding aids, what librarians would commonly refer to as catalogs. Most archives, even those that have adopted automated systems, continue to use such aids because of ease of access, the fact that experienced researchers are accustomed to these guides, and efficient management of holdings. Registers (developed at the Library of Congress for manuscript collections) and inventories (developed at the National Archives for government records) have been used by archivists for 40 years. The similarities between these two kinds of finding aids are marked, especially their emphasis on the record series.[23] Institutional archives will always use the archival inventory form, which consists of an agency history and series descriptions. Container listings, item listings, and separate indexes are very rarely used in such inventories. The agency history provides name, dates of origin and other significant events, institutional relationship, primary and other important functions, how the records reflect the agency's development and functions, and key individuals and other organizations that have a relationship to the records creator. Series descriptions consist of title, volume, span dates, records types, arrangement, and topical contents. These inventories, almost always prepared for internal use and not publication, will be of inestimable value to the institutional records creator that wishes to utilize its archival records for research, policy development, trends projection, and other essential work. Institutional archivists need to keep in mind both internal and external (by individuals not associated with the institution) research uses as they prepare such inventories.

Archival repositories have also used an array of other kinds of finding aids—such as card catalogs, repository guides, special topical guides, and online catalogs—as well as reporting their holdings through notices in scholarly journals, newsletters, and inclusion in the National Union Catalog of Manuscript Collections.[24] Now the most important variety of "other" finding aid utilizes the MARC AMC Format, a decision that the institutional archivist must carefully consider. Again, Nancy Sahli has laid out a number of issues that must be considered in the adoption of this format:

First, if the prospective user is not already involved in automation, he or she will need to decide whether the initial implementation will be manual or computerized. . . .

A second key in planning for implementation is to acquire the essential format documents. . . .

Third, the need for archivists to have a clear sense of their own descriptive needs is as important as familiarity with MARC itself. . . .

Finally, after determining the system requirements for information elements and computer hardware, it is time to start thinking about what the format is to do.

<u>A Comparison of Archival Inventories and</u>
<u>Manuscript Registers</u>

The <u>inventory</u> is the most widely used finding aid for the archives record group. Similarly, the register is the most widely used finding aid for manuscript collections . . . .

Registers and inventories differ in certain respects, but both conform to basically similar structures. The register generally incorporates sections which permit greater detail than is usually feasible in the inventory of archives records groups, but greater or lesser emphasis may be given to any element of the finding aid to accommodate the repository's requirements or the demands of an individual case.

The following table lists the elements typical of both registers and inventories:

<u>Manuscript Register</u>	<u>Archival Inventory</u>
Preface	Preface
Introduction	Introduction
Biographical Sketch	Agency History
Scope and Content Note	(Rarely Employed)
Series Description	Series Description
Container Listing	(Rarely Employed)
Item Listing (Rarely Employed)	(Rarely Employed)
and Index (Rarely Employed)	(Rarely Employed)

Committee on Finding Aids, <u>Inventories and Registers: A Handbook of Techniques and Examples</u> (Chicago: Society of American Archivists, 1976), 7.

Since it is generally not cost-effective or practical for archivists to develop their own computer programs, it will be necessary to evaluate one of the existing networks, turnkey systems, or software packages. Before reaching a decision, questions should be asked about cost, maintenance, user assistance, the layout of screens used for data entry and retrieval, and the kinds of hard copy products, such as reports, that can be generated by the system.[25]

Institutional archivists need to consider carefully the kinds of finding aids that they will use to convey descriptive information about their holdings. Their first responsibility is to their institution, and the archivist should adopt a descriptive system that will be the most usable one by institutional employees. This point is a major difference between institutional archives and collecting repositories that exist to serve scholarship and various research communities. Institutional archivists should also make sure that they have carefully cleared the use of their holdings by outside researchers before they do anything that publicizes their archival records. Finally, archivists should make sure that they work from the general to the specific and first gain general intellectual control of their holdings before developing any detailed finding aids to parts of their holdings; this work is the kind of "phasing" described in this volume in other basic archival functions. As the archivist considers the kind of descriptive system required, he or she should test out how it works. Producing a general guide to the holdings, access policies, and regulations is always a wise use of resources, although it might be possible in an institutional archives setting for automated descriptions to be the more important finding aid (especially if the institution is fully connected electronically); whether the guide is automated will depend on the nature of information technology used in the organization.

The records series description is the most important component of the institutional archives' descriptive efforts and merits some special attention here. This importance stems from the fact that the series is the most crucial manner in which records are organized as they are created. Individuals wishing access to certain information will most likely come looking for it in ways that can be easily accommodated by the series. In the institutional archives this fact is especially important since records creators will repeatedly want access to their archival records and will often seek these records in the way that they were originally arranged and visualize their records in the file cabinets or other storage containers originally used in their offices.

The basic information needing to be retained about the records series encompasses various access points. A records series description should include data about the functions of the records creator (including successor and/or predecessor agencies or organizations); title of the series; information medium constituting the series; span dates (including description of the dates that make up the bulk of records); physical characteristics of the records, including internal arrangement and volume; the intellectual contents of the records, emphasizing the functions and activities they chronicle and potential research strengths as well; and important personal, organizational, and other names that will enhance the ease of access to the records. If the institutional archives is successful in capturing such information, its arrangement and description operation will be a success and the duty of providing efficient and effective reference service will be enhanced significantly.

Finally, it is worth noting that the archival descriptive function is especially important in an institution that has a fully operational records management or information resources management program. Except for the descriptive work of the institutional archivist, there is no real records management function that is a counterpart to such work. Records managers focus on records inventories, retention and disposition schedules, and the administration of records in a records center, all of these activities requiring a less complete description of the records. Records retention and disposition schedules, the backbone of the organizational records management program, focus on the values of the records for the institution and less on the means for promoting appropriate access to the records. It is assumed that the records creators will know the files and documents that they require. Preparing more detailed descriptions, relating the informational content of archival records to the informational needs of the institution, and stimulating the use of organizational records are all tasks that are generally unique to the archivist and that institutional archivists should aggressively promote as they provide reference to their holdings. The removal of archival records by a records management program to a protected area for storage, without any real commitment to administering such records, is not only an important gap in an institution's information resources management but a responsibility that archivists should meet in ways that communicate the relevance of their holdings to the current business of the organization. Arrangement and description must be effectively done to ensure that this result may happen; an adequate reference operation must then be in existence to ensure that the archival records can be used by the institution.

THE PURPOSE OF ARCHIVES:
USE AND THE REFERENCE FUNCTION

Archival records are preserved to be used. This thought is hardly new; it is, in fact, the principle that has guided the work of archivists since the beginning of this discipline. Archival *reference*—the activities undertaken to provide information about archival records or, in some cases, from these records—is, for archivists and their clientele, the raison d'être for archival programs. It can also become an issue for researchers. In 1989, the National Coordinating Committee for the Promotion of History released a report that was addressed to the National Archives administrators, federal government, and archival profession because of concern for access to the archival records held by this institution. This report was built on the principle that "in the final analysis it is the use of records that makes archives valuable."[26]

Despite this guiding principle, however, use of archival records can operate in different fashions in different settings. For the institutional archivist, two basic issues will always be at hand. First, how can the archivst ensure that the institution's management and employees draw upon the holdings of the archives in ways that are meaningful to the institution? In the first chapter of this book a variety of potential values of archival records was enumerated. The establishment of an institutional archives does not mean, however, that these values will be evident. The institutional archivist, by virtue of a sufficient institutional profile and adequate descriptive and reference systems, must constantly work to demonstrate that the archival program is serving an important function. Second, the institutional archivist will face the matter of who will be able to use the archival records. This is the issue of access—making archival records available for use because of legal and other authority. An institutional archives, as it has been stated many times, primarily exists to preserve and administer these valuable records for the benefit of the organization. For many institutions and their archivists, this purpose raises the issue of whether outside scholars and researchers will have access to the records and what records they will be able to use. For outsiders, a lack of access or a severely restricted access completely undermines the merit of having an institutional archives exist in the first place.

As an archival function, reference has undergone significant change in activity and perception over the past decade or two. During the early years of the formation of the archival profession, archivists seemed to operate solely on the notion that the assembling of archival records would bring researchers to their doors and that the researchers would be sufficiently well versed in their own fields to know what they want and to require little in the way of finding aids and descriptive apparatus. Archival reference was generally an intellectually vacuous function. It was not always well related to other archival functions, such as appraisal and preservation, nor was it clearly defined or always well maintained. Archivists were often rotated through the reference room to perform "more important" responsibilities, or archivists junior in experience were put into the reference room for "seasoning" or to allow the more experienced professionals to carry out "higher priority" activities. Archivists also generally maintained very low-level information on what reference activities were being carried out and saw little need to do research themselves about how individuals used their materials and whether they were able to complete satisfactory research at all. This situation is why researchers have sometimes found it necessary to complain, as in the 1989 report to the National Archives, about the quality of reference services and the degree of access. Use as a reason for existence of archives was often given only vocal expression and support, not support in terms of resources or priorities.

For institutional archivists, such problems have been even more evident. For many institutional archives, there is only one or two professional staff members, and the concern becomes how reference service and access will be provided along with the other important functions needed to maintain and to nurture an archival program. In this environment, research requests can often become, ironically, nuisances or distractions. This situation is additionally complicated by the fact that internal use within an institutional

Reference in a Business Archives

Reference service in the Chase [Manhattan Bank] archives is one of its most important functions, and is certainly the most time-consuming and the most consequential to those outside the department. At least 50% of all staff time is spent on reference work . . . . An average of 35 requests per week are answered. Nearly 60% of all requests are from within the bank and the remainder come from outside the institution.

Internal requests come from every area of the bank. Offices that have records on deposit in the archives frequently need to have information from their own records. Legal department researchers often need to use past records regarding bank policy, procedures or personnel. Corporate communications staff heavily use past speeches, clippings, photographs and publications. The percentage of internal requests often increases as a result of archives' outreach activities such as an exhibit for employees, a presentation at a large meeting, or an article within an internal publication.

External requests are extremely varied. Users range from photo researchers for textbooks to scholarly researchers. Urban archaeologists have used records from the early water company to document the early Manhattan water system. Economic historians have done significant research in several areas of U.S. economic development.

Requests are most frequently received over the telephone or by personal visit, and a modest number of external requests are made by mail. How a research request is completed depends on the nature of the inquiry. If the request is placed in person or over the phone, the archivist must interview the requestor to try to determine specific information requirements. Few researchers know the best approach to an archives . . . .

. . . . the interview method is clearly an important step in meeting the requestor's need efficiently and effectively.

Anne Van Camp, "The Paper Chase: Reference Service in the Bank's Archives," in Reference Services in Archives ed. Lucille Whalen (New York: Haworth Press, 1986), 109-10.

---

setting can bring with it a different set of problems, such as the desire by records creators to remove back to their offices their archival records for convenience of use and the specific, knowledgeable requests that institutional staff can make that seem to ease the need to have structured reference programs. In addition, the specter of external requests for sensitive institutional records and the difficulty of balancing external with internal research requests can make reference and access in the institutional archives a function with serious problems to be resolved. Institutional archivists not only will need to win support for the fuller development of their programs but will have to work hard to ensure that the organization's management understands the importance of their archival records to the broader research community. This test is difficult and complicated.

Fortunately, archival reference and access are an area that has begun to be rethought and restudied by the archival profession in recent years. Archivists have realized that they actually know little about research use within their reference rooms. For decades, archivists tended to evaluate and assess research use by numbers (how many, when, and patterns in heavy and light use) and types of researchers (scholars, genealogists, local historians, amateur historians, and institutional staff) rather than by the nature, success, and significance of their research. One archivist has recently suggested, for example, that the archival community had generally failed to answer the question, "What difference does research in archives make—in terms of individual enlightenment, solution of practical problems, benefits to the public good, scholarly advances, or additions to the sum total of human knowledge?"[27] Another archivist proposed a research agenda on the matter of use of archival records for a number of reasons: "If archivists wish to understand the *how* of archival practices and the *why* of principles or theory, [they] must shift [their] attention from the physical record to the uses of records," and "without this data archivists lack a baseline of information against which to measure and compare access and retrieval, reference services, acquisitions, management, even appraisal guidelines and documentation strategies."[28] New tools such as the US MARC AMC Format, greater awareness of ergonomic factors such as the design of reference rooms, experimentation in user studies, and reevaluation of traditional finding aids have supported changes in the archivist's administration of reference services. For institutional archivists, these kinds of concerns suggest that they need to understand the nature of use in their own organizations and the implications of that use, as well as how to promote new uses.

THE BASIC ELEMENTS OF AN INSTITUTIONAL ARCHIVES REFERENCE SERVICE

To provide adequate reference services, the institutional archivist needs to have seven basic elements in place. Supporting all of these basic functions should be a set of consistent policies and procedures, a staff that is aware of these policies and procedures as well as knowledgeable about the archival holdings, and an apparatus that enables analysis and measurement of the reference services to ascertain how effective they have been and what changes, if any, should be made.

The most important and basic aspect that the institutional archivist must consider in providing adequate reference services is the maintenance of a suitable research facility. The best-run institutional archives program can be undermined by the lack of a facility that encourages research. Such a facility must have regular hours (times that are well known to the organization's staff and other researchers), comfortable chairs and tables, satisfactory lighting, and easy access to the archives' finding aids and other important reference materials such as dictionaries, encyclopedias, and the finding aids to related archival repositories or to specialized topics generally represented in the archives' own holdings. Essential to this facility, as well, is security. Researchers should never be left unattended, and the facility needs to have a location that is both accessible to researchers and easily administered by the archives' personnel.

For the institutional archivist, several challenges are present in achieving such a facility. Since the archives usually will be in the organization's headquarters, space may be a problem, and having the reference room located in easy proximity to the archival storage areas may be difficult. The institutional archivist may have to decide between placing the reference facility in a high-visibility space that encourages use through easy accessibility and being conveniently located near storage of the archival records. Institutionwide visibility should always be given precedence over convenience; an archival program that is well known and well used will have a better chance, in the long run, of securing support for resolving problems. The institutional archivist might also have a difficult time in acquiring other reference resources because of an attitude that the program is only to provide access to records created by the institution itself and to provide services to institutional employees. Here user studies about information sought and other needs in making use of the archival records and demonstrating the need for a wider range of assistance asked for should be carried out and reported to the organization's managers and resource allocators. Alliances with the organization's library and other information agencies will assist the institutional archivist to support such arguments. The matter of external access to the organization's records is a more problematic matter that will be considered later in this chapter and in this volume.

Second, the institutional archives should possess a clearly written set of researcher rules and regulations. Most well-maintained archival programs have forms that researchers must read and sign, agreeing to the regulations, before being allowed access to the archival materials. These written policies and guidelines should provide certain basic information to the researcher that facilitates his or her access to the records and aids the archivist to allow usage of records without their damage or loss. These policies should indicate to the researcher that he or she is working with unique archival records. They should specify that smoking, eating, and the use of fountain or other ink pens are prohibited to prevent damage to the records. How archival records will be retrieved (such as a limit on the number of boxes or folders), procedures for making photocopies of archival records, and the restricted use of records in a specified reading room are the kinds of things that the researcher should understand and with which the archival reference staff should be familiar so as to implement and explain them to researchers. These policies should also let researchers know that they may

Typical Reading Room Rules for an Institutional Archives

Material Brought to the Reading Room

The researcher may bring only those materials needed for research and a pencil to Reading Room tables. All coats, books, briefcases and other items should be placed in lockers.

Materials Provided to Researchers

The researcher is responsible for safeguarding any material made available to him/her in the Reading Room. Researchers may not remove materials from the Reading Room for any purpose or rearrange the order in which they are delivered.

Pens

The use of any kind of pen is prohibited in the Reading Room. Pencils alone should be used.

Use of Materials

Manuscripts and books may not be leaned on, written on, folded, traced from or handled in any way likely to damage them. In certain cases, researchers may be required to use microfilm or printed copies of manuscripts or books when such copies are available.

Eating and Smoking

Eating and smoking are prohibited in the Reading Room.

Photoduplication Services

The Archives will consider requests for the photoduplication of material when such duplication can be done without injury to the material, and does not violate copyright restrictions. Single copies will be provided for the researcher's personal reference use. The photocopy must be further reproduced. Supplying a photocopy is not authorization to publish. Photocopies are usually ten cents per page.

Telephones

Researchers are asked not to use Archives' telephones. A telephone for inside calls may be found on the second floor landing of the south wing of the library. A telephone for outside calls may be found at the entrance to the Science Library.

Recommended Citation

For citations in published or in unpublished papers, the repository should be listed as the Institute Archives and Special Collections, M.I. T. Libraries, Cambridge, Massachusetts . . . .

From Archival Forms Manual (Chicago: Society of American Archivists, 1982), 80.

face certain restrictions when seeking use of the archival records. An unprocessed series of records might not be accessible, or the records might
be temporarily restricted because of proprietary information or other privacy issues. Finally, these guidelines and policies should specify how researchers should properly cite the records and that the researcher assumes
full responsibility for the use of the records.

From this description of the researcher rules and regulations, it should
be obvious that the administration of a reference function within an institutional archives program will face some unique kinds of challenges. For
many archives and historical records programs, their reason for existence
is to serve certain very specific research clienteles. A historical society
manuscripts program, as just one example, exists to enable research by
scholars, local historians, and the general public on the history of the
locality or other broad topics. While researchers may have to meet certain
qualifications to use the manuscripts, the purpose of this kind of repository
is to allow wide and equal access (within, of course, the parameters that
allow secure and safe use of the records). The institutional archives, such
as the corporate archives or the university archives, exists to allow research
primarily by the employees of the records creators; external researchers
are a secondary objective, and, as well, many of the holdings of the institutional archives may be closed to outside researchers due to privacy or
proprietary or other sensitive information. In this setting, careful statements of research policies must be drawn up to regulate the research use
within this variety of archives. In addition, the institutional archivist will
need to determine carefully how institutional employees will be able to
use archival records. Ideally, the institutional archivist should be able to
control the use of records within the archival facility and ensure that the
records will be protected and available for other researchers, but the extent
of restrictions and regulations in this environment must be carefully thought
through, managerial approval and support sought and obtained, and these
restrictions and regulations adhered to in order to safeguard that there are
no inconsistencies in implementation.

Third, some of the nuances of providing reference in an institutional
archives can be seen in the management of researcher applications. Researcher applications, completed by the researcher on his or her initial
visit, gather information such as personal data on name and residence,
institutional affiliation, the purpose of the research (for article or book,
dissertation or thesis, personal curiosity, and so forth), the research topic,
and whether there are objections to sharing the research. There are many
reasons for using such applications. In an institutional archives, they will
enable the archivist to determine whether there are any potential problems
in allowing the individual to have access to the records. In all archival
settings, these forms can assist the archivist to keep track of the nature of
research being conducted in his or her holdings, the kinds of questions

that are being asked by researchers both about their topic of interest and about how research is carried out in the archives, and the collections or series that are being used. Accurate records on these matters will help enhance security of the reference area as well as enable the archivist to provide profiles of research use in the institution as needed. In an institutional archives, a firm record of research topics and interests will help the archivist to provide additional information from time to time as it becomes available through other accessions or the processing of additional holdings. This record of research topics and interests will assist the institutional archivist to become a valuable supplier of information for the operations of the organization; in this regard the archivist can serve an important role in overcoming some of the limitations that individuals working in the organization might have when it comes to using effectively the archival records of the institution.[29]

Fourth, the entrance and exit interviews of researchers should also be used by the institutional archivist. The entrance interview is intended to ascertain a researcher's needs beyond what is indicated on a research application form. This process is also an effort to determine the researcher's degree of experience in archival research. In an institutional archives, especially one that might house records of a sensitive or proprietary nature, this interview should be the time when the archivist can determine if the researcher should be granted access to the records, whether any additional clearance is required, and what records should be provided. The exit interview is intended to enable the archivist to determine the degree of success that the researcher had in using the records. It provides an opportunity for the archivist to identify additional records that the researcher might need to examine, as well as to identify any problems in the reference process, finding aids, or other aspects of the archival operation. The institutional archivist should always seek to obtain an exit interview with researchers both to ensure that the archives is being properly used (in the case of outside researchers) and to determine whether to follow up in providing additional information from the archival records (in the case of researchers from the organization). The latter is especially important since the existence of the institutional archives is dependent upon its ability to provide information to the organization in a timely fashion. Furthermore, the institutional archivist has the advantage of having the institutional researchers nearby; he or she can conduct exit interviews after the researcher has left and provide additional information in a ready fashion. The institutional archivist should develop a working relationship with the organization's staff in such a way as to be able to encourage the use of the archival records and to supply certain limited amounts of research on important issues that can be gleaned from the archival records.

The use of such devices as entrance and exit interviews and researcher applications must have a basis in the attitude that archives exist for the

Example of Institutional Archives Researcher Form

WALT DISNEY ARCHIVES

Date _____

Last Name _____ First Name _____ Initial ____

Address _____

(___) _____
City, State, Zip Code _____ Phone

Permanent Address (if different) _____

I hereby request permission from Walt Disney Productions to view its Archives files or other materials listed below relating to the history, activities and productions of Walt Disney Productions and its subsidiaries for purposes of:

_____

_____

Listed below are the titles of the files or descriptions of other materials which I wish to view:

Title/Description   Date of Access

_____

_____

_____

If I am permitted viewing access for the above stated purpose, I agree not to copy, publish, exploit or otherwise use any materials viewed as a result of such permission being granted unless by separate written authorization from an officer of Walt Disney Productions.

Signature _____ Date _____

Institution, Organization or Affiliation _____

Address of Institution _____

Title or Position _____

If a student, indicate degree sought and faculty member directing research.

References: (Below are the names and addresses of two persons acquainted with my work.)

_____

From Archival Forms Manual (Chicago: Society of American Archivists, 1982), 77.

Evaluating Researchers' Use of Archives

The [archival] profession needs more and better tools for monitoring research use. The forms, procedures, and approaches should gather information needed to thoroughly understand researchers' purposes and the significance of the information derived from the archival material. Of course, the gathering of such information would require cooperation on the part of researchers. These key questions would need answering:

* What was the exact subject and purpose of the research?

* How did the researcher find out about the repository and the materials? What are the implications for the repository's finding aids and public relations efforts?

* What records were used?

* What was the researcher's information need? What were the questions that he or she needed to answer?

* Did the researcher find the information sought, anticipated, or needed?

* How rich and extensive was the information gleaned from the records? How significant was the information for the researcher's purposes?

* Did the information cast new light on or lead to a new interpretation of the subject being researched?

* Did study of the material suggest or open important new lines of inquiry for the researcher?

* Did study of the material uncover or suggest other sources for the researcher to pursue?

From Bruce W. Dearstyne, "What Is the Use of Archives? A Challenge for the Profession," American Archivist 50 (Winter 1987): 79-80.

---

user. Elsie Freeman, one of the leading advocates for greater outreach in the archival profession, has written most eloquently about this issue:

[T]he identity and the research habits of our users—who they are, how they think, how they learn, how they assemble information, to what uses they put it—must become as familiar a part of our thinking as the rules of order and practice . . . that now govern the acquisition, processing, description, and servicing of records. We must begin to learn systematically, not impressionistically as is our present tendency, who our users are; what kinds of projects they pursue, in what time frames, and under what sponsorship; and, most importantly, how they approach records.

Put another way, we must begin to think of archives administration as client-centered, not materials-centered.[30]

Freeman, in considering how to move to this "client-centered" approach, has suggested that archivists study who users are and how they do research, reach out to attract users of their records, make the use of archival records easier and more attractive to actual and potential researchers, and so forth. Others, such as Bruce Dearstyne, have suggested that improved understanding of the use of archives can assist archivists to promote additional and new kinds of use, acquire additional support for programs, and build alliances with certain user groups that can assist in the resolution of difficult archival problems.[31]

These points are particularly important for the institutional archivist, who must work to ensure that holdings are being effectively used by the organization. In both for-profit and nonprofit organizations, underutilized resources are likely to be viewed as financial liabilities. The institutional archives must be client-centered in order to survive. This attitude must be carried over even to the policies, like those dictating the administering of research requests, that relate to the reference function. Mary Jo Pugh, one of the leading authorities on archival reference, has written an important critique of the manner in which archivists perform the basic reference function, a critique that all institutional archivists should read. She noted that the repositories have tended to rely on the knowledge of researchers, their own memory of the records, rather than studying and understanding how researchers ask for information and incorporating this behavior into suitable systems that can expedite research.[32]

At least one other archivist, Paul Conway, has proposed a model for analyzing research use intended to benefit the repository and, ultimately, the researcher through improved services. Conway has suggested: "[I]n an archives, information transfer occurs in many different ways, but most typically when a researcher with a specific information need interacts with archivists and finding aids and in the process acquires archival information of use in meeting some part of the need. For archivists, the three important parts of this equation are users, information need, and use."[33] For analyzing research use that an institutional archivist could adapt for his or her own needs, Conway has used these parts to construct a framework and accompanying forms for collecting data.

Fifth, every archives, especially, however, the institutional archives, should also have a policy for the manner in which it will handle other than in-person research visits. The archives should set a policy for what kinds of letters it will respond to, how it will evaluate these letters, and what degree of detail and time and resources it will devote to answering letters. The archives should have a mechanism for assigning letters to be answered and consider developing form replies for commonly asked questions. The archives should consider doing the same for telephone requests. The institutional archivist will have a different twist on this matter, of course. Unless the institutional archivist is part of a multilocation organization, he or she will mostly be handling requests for information in in-person requests. In organizations that have adopted a heavy use of electronic telecommunications, archivists might need to devise ways of responding to information requests via electronic mail and other such systems. The institutional archivist, however, will have to develop a policy for responding to outside research requests, many of which will come via mail or telephone. This will require careful coordination by the archivist with the organization's management to make sure that there is no uneasiness about the archives' priorities and how it is being utilized.

Sixth, the archives also must support a reprographic service. Any archives needs to be able to provide adequate reference reproductions, through electrostatic photocopying or sometimes microfilm, as researchers require them. Service costs should be reasonable, primarily seeking to recover the labor and technical costs. Providing this kind of service requires that the archives restrict copying to records that are in good condition and can withstand the copying. The institutional archivist must also have a good understanding of copyright and other issues that might restrict copying. For many institutional archives, whether copies will be provided is often dictated by whether the requester is an organizational employee or not, rather than specific contents of the records. It is a matter of broader access concerns.

Finally, the institutional archivist, concerned with the viability of his or her program in the everyday functioning of the parent organization, should view the reference area as a means to study the organization's use of information and, as a result, the potential role of the archives. There have been many recent calls for such studies by archivists, such as those by Elsie Freeman, referred to earlier. Lawrence Dowler has suggested that the study of the use of archives will both aid the archivist establish programmatic priorities and test the effectiveness of services, as well as provide a "better conceptual basis for archival practices and principles."[34] For the institutional archivist a thorough knowledge of user patterns and the success of research in the holdings can be both offensive and defensive devices. The archivist can use this knowledge to argue for an increased role for the archival operation or, as is sometimes necessary, defend the program against excessive budget cuts. Dowler, for example, has noted that a study of the "attributes of various groups or categories of users based on the nature and methods of their inquiry" can help "archivists . . . begin to gauge the possible impact of use on archives and, even more, the availability of archival material that could satisfy a particular user group."[35] This knowledge can be powerful for an institutional archives and enable the archivist to supply more efficiently and readily the needed information for the institutional researcher and to understand the needs of the external re-searcher. These data can be used to help institutional archivists devise ways of effectively automating their finding aids as well and lead to more in-formed revisions of these finding aids based on actual patterns of successful use rather than the guesswork of the archivist about what seems to work. As Dowler has also suggested, archivists should recognize that researchers often "care very little about the form of the information they need to use or where they find it."[36] This may mean more in an organizational setting, where the archives should be viewed as another source of information for the institution's operations rather than a museum of old records and ar-tifacts. In the modern electronic information age, museums of obsolete information forms may themselves become obsolete, harming the institu-tion's effectiveness as well as robbing society of the chance to understand that institution and the broader culture supporting it.

REFERENCE AND THE ISSUE OF ACCESS IN THE INSTITUTIONAL ARCHIVES

The question of who will have access to the institutional archives is an important issue to be resolved. The American archival community has long adhered to the notion that equal and broad access is important. As Sue Holbert has written, many private and institutional archives set restrictions to access, "but in keeping with the American belief in access to information, openness and equality of access should be goals."[37] The Society of Amer-ican Archivists' guidelines, in need of updating and revision, are based upon the premise that archivists should grant access to their holdings except for records that have been specifically restricted due to legal or donor-imposed restrictions.[38] The institutional archivist will face many decisions to make in this regard, but he or she must start by knowing existing legal concerns and then seek to apply these to his or her own repository.

For most archivists, legal issues are quickly translated to mean a concern with copyright. The Copyright Revision Act of 1976 has considerably mud-died the waters for archivists and manuscript curators in this area, placing a burden on the researcher to determine whether a particular document, records series, or collection is under copyright restriction or not, and leav-ing many of the resolutions to difficult problems to the courts and legal precedents; unfortunately, the courts in recent years have tended to be making decisions that work against the interests of both researchers and archivists. The decision in the case involving the J. D. Salinger biography ruling is a dangerous precedent for the archival community; this case ruled that the "biographer has no inherent right to copy the 'accuracy' or the 'vividness' of the letter writer's expression. Indeed, 'vividness of descrip-tion' is precisely the attribute of the author's expression that he is entitled to protect."[39] While such copyright concerns have numerous implications

for archivists working in collecting repositories for such matters as nego-
tiations with donors, the use of the records, publication of research based
on the records, and the duplication and publication of the records, the
institutional archivist has a number of other, similarly sticky issues.

Most importantly, many institutional archivists will need to determine
the degree of access to their organization's records. Generally, an archivist
will need to set restrictions for any of five basic reasons, including when
personal or institutional privacy might be violated, when proprietary business information might be revealed, when personnel information could be
seen by others, when investigative information is inadvertently released,
and when statutory restrictions are breached. For most institutional archivists, proprietary business information and personal privacy will be the
most important matters. But many such archivists will also need to pay
heed to federal and related state and local laws as well. For example, the
archivist of a college or university will need to pay attention to the Family
Educational Rights and Privacy Act of 1974, which stipulates that parents
of students under 18 years of age have the right to view a student's records
and students beyond this age have the right to view their own records,
excluding records on parents' financial conditions and certain letters of
recommendation.[40] Archivists of institutions that conduct business with
federal agencies might also need to be aware that what they believe to be
the records of their own organization may fall under some of the laws that
define and regulate federal records, such as the Freedom of Information
Act (1966, amended 1974) and its revisions and the Privacy Act of 1974.
Records generated by grants from, and contracts with, federal agencies
may specify, for example, how long the records should be kept, how they
should be maintained, and even whether they are federal records or not.
For example, the Freedom of Information Act specifies that a number of
records should be restricted, including those identified by executive order
to be kept closed; personnel and medical records; records closed by statute;
trade secrets and commercial or financial information having a privileged
or confidential status; and legal investigatory files. Institutional archivists
obviously should be aware that, depending on the nature of business of
their organization, some of their records may be affected by these
restrictions.

When at all possible, the institutional archivist should seek to make
available as many records as possible. This goal is responsible and achievable because of various professional standards and ethics statements and
because making such records available to the research community can be
an important public relations tool for the organization.[41] This can be a
difficult and sensitive task, however. The difficulty is not only in achieving
approval to release records to outsiders and in convincing executives and
upper-level staff that the use of these records in other research can benefit
the institutional creator of these records; but also a result of the past decade

which has been a time of tightening rein on the control of information. In the mid–1980s, for example, Congress passed amendments to the Freedom of Information Act (FOIA) that gave federal agencies broader discretionary powers in setting and waiving fees for access to certain records. This action reflects an information policy environment in which there are increasing confusion about the definition of a federal record and a hostile attitude to the increasing demand for FOIA requests by researchers, journalists, and concerned citizens.[42]

The role of the institutional archivist always ought to be achieving the archival information needs of his or her organization, but the archivist also has a responsibility to make as many records as possible available to outside researchers (including both organizational employees outside of the immediate records-creating unit and external researchers). The increasing hiring by institutions of historians to prepare histories or to do historical research on certain more specific topics relating to the organization's business without restrictions on producing an official past is an indication that the archivist has a chance to make these records more widely available. This may help to solidify the organization's reputation in its local community, provide the organization insights it might not have received through any other fashion, and place a different set of responsibilities on the archivist's requirements to arrange, describe, and provide reference to his or her records holdings. The greater the external usage, the greater the need for the archives' linkage to the archival and research communities through bibliographic utilities and the like. Archival records, however, are preserved to be used, and the greater the use, the more vital role that the institutional archives plays in the organization and society. Unfortunately, however, there is a wide range of opinion regarding preferred degree of access, much of that opinion tinged by conservative legal advisers or inappropriate fears.

NOTES

1. Quoted in David B. Gracy II, *Archives & Manuscripts: Arrangement & Description*, Basic Manual Series (Chicago: Society of American Archivists, 1977), 4.

2. Harold T. Pinkett, "American Archival Theory: The State of the Art," *American Archivist* 44 (Summer 1981): 220.

3. Frank Boles, "Disrespecting Original Order," *American Archivist* 45 (Winter 1982): 31. This article is an excellent treatment of the pros and cons of adhering to this concept of original order.

4. Uli Haller, "Processing for Access," *American Archivist* 48 (Fall 1985): 412.

5. A fuller description of these levels can be found in Gracy, *Archives & Manuscripts*, 4–15. The classic description remains Oliver W. Holmes, "Archival Arrangement—Five Different Operations at Five Different Levels," *American Archivist* 27 (January 1964): 21–41. There is another level, the subgroup, which is not as consistently applied in

general archival practice, although some archivists see it as a crucial aspect of arrangement; see Haller, "Processing for Access."

6. David Bearman and Richard Lytle, "The Power of the Principle of Provenance," *Archivaria* 21 (Winter 1985–1986): 19.

7. Max J. Evans, "Authority Control: An Alternative to the Record Group Concept," *American Archivist* 49 (Summer 1986): 249–61.

8. Institutional archivists will first deal with such problems when they carry out appraisal to document the institution. See chapter 3 for similar discussion of such problems and challenges.

9. Lester J. Cappon, "Historical Manuscripts as Archives: Some Definitions and Their Application," *American Archivist* 19 (April 1956): 105.

10. See Richard M. Kesner, *Information Systems: A Strategic Approach to Planning and Implementation* (Chicago: American Library Association, 1988). Kesner, in this book, adheres to four basic assumptions about institutional information systems. First, general management approaches provide the essential context for deciding about and managing information systems. Second, the management of information systems can be properly achieved only by teams that include records managers, archivists, librarians, data processors, telecommunications experts, and general administrators united by a common mission of efficiently and effectively managing information for the institution. Third, each of the different information specialists who make up such teams brings unique and needed skills and perspectives to the management of information. Fourth, the creation, use, and administration of information are undergoing rapid change and transforming many of the basic notions presently held by the various information professionals.

11. Gracy, *Archives & Manuscripts: Arrangement & Description*, 38–40.

12. Megan Floyd Desnoyers, "When Is a Collection Processed?" *Midwestern Archivist* 7, no. 1 (1982): 23. For a brief description of the rudiments of processing, refer to Gracy, *Archives & Manuscripts*, 15–19.

13. For some straightforward, practical advice about this issue, refer to Arthur J. Breton, "The Critical First Step: In Situ Handling of Large Collections," *American Archivist* 49 (Fall 1986): 455–58.

14. Under the best of circumstances, such tasks should be completed by paraprofessionals or technicians.

15. For some guidance about when and how this work should be done, see Richard C. Berner and M. Gary Bettis, "Disposition of Nonmanuscript Items Found Among Manuscripts," *American Archivist* 33 (July 1970): 275–81.

16. Terry Abraham, Stephen E. Balzarini, and Ann Frantilla, "What Is Backlog Is Prologue: A Measurement of Archival Processing," *American Archivist* 48 (Winter 1985): 31–44; William Maher, "Measurement and Analysis of Processing Costs in Academic Archives," *College & Research Libraries* 43 (1982): 59–67; and Uli Haller, "Variations in the Processing Rates on the Magnuson and Jackson Senatorial Papers," *American Archivist* 50 (Winter 1987): 100–09.

17. Richard M. Kesner et al., "Collection Processing as a Team Effort," *American Archivist* 44 (Fall 1981): 356–58.

18. Nancy Sahli, "Finding Aids: A Multi-Media, Systems Perspective," *American Archivist* 44 (Winter 1981): 16.

19. Lydia Lucas, "Efficient Finding Aids: Developing a System for Control of Archives and Manuscripts," *American Archivist* 44 (Winter 1981): 21–26.

20. For the range of such software that is available, refer to Lynn Cox and David

Bearman, comps., *Directory of Software for Archives & Museums, Archival Informatics Technical Report* (Pittsburgh: Archives & Museum Informatics, 1990) and read the quarterly newsletter *Archives & Museum Informatics*.

21. Patricia Cloud, "RLIN, AMC, and Retrospective Conversion: A Case Study," *Midwestern Archivist* 11, no. 2 (1986): 125–34. Cloud estimates that it costs (in 1986 dollars) about $21 per record entry into RLIN, requiring 2.7 hours of professional time.

22. For a description of some of the issues involved here, refer to Steven L. Hensen, "The Use of Standards in the Application of the AMC Format," *American Archivist* 49 (Winter 1986): 31–40.

23. SAA Committee on Finding Aids, *Inventories and Registers: A Handbook of Techniques and Examples* (Chicago: Society of American Archivists, 1976) is the best introduction to the nature of these finding aids. See also, Gracy, *Archives & Manuscripts*, 19–30.

24. Gracy, *Archives & Manuscripts*, 34–37.

25. Nancy Sahli, "Interpretation and Application of the AMC Format," *American Archivist* 49 (Winter 1986): 12–18. For additional advice about acquiring automated systems, see David Bearman, *Automated Systems for Archives and Museums: Acquisition and Implementation Issues*, Archival Informatics Newsletter & Technical Report (Pittsburgh: Archives & Museum Informatics, Winter 1987/1988). While the MARC AMC Format can be used in a nonautomated system, the nature of decision making involved is still similar to what must be considered in acquiring an automated system. Even those archival programs that begin to use the MARC AMC Format in a nonautomated form are most often looking forward to installing an automated system.

26. Page Putnam Miller, *Developing a Premier National Institution: A Report from the User Community to the National Archives* (Washington, DC: National Coordinating Committee for the Promotion of History, 1989), 8.

27. Bruce W. Dearstyne, "What Is the *Use* of Archives? A Challenge for the Profession," *American Archivist* 50 (Winter 1987): 77.

28. Lawrence Dowler, "The Role of Use in Defining Archival Practice and Principles: A Research Agenda for the Availability and Use of Records," *American Archivist* 51 (Winter/Spring 1988): 75.

29. For example, historians—a group that would be expected to possess good research skills—often have exhibited severe limitations in their knowledge of basic bibliographic tools and other research aids; see Margaret F. Stieg, "The Information Needs of Historians," *College & Research Libraries* 42 (November 1981): 549–60. If this group has this problem, individuals working in an institution who have not been trained in the use of basic research guides or the use of archival records will likely face greater obstacles to overcome. The institutional archivist will need to devise as many user-friendly approaches as possible.

30. Elsie Freeman, "In the Eye of the Beholder: Archives Administration from the User's Point of View," *American Archivist* 47 (Spring 1984): 112.

31. Bruce W. Dearstyne, "What Is the Use of Archives? A Challenge for the Profession," *American Archivist* 50 (Winter 1987): 76–87.

32. Mary Jo Pugh, "The Illusion of Omniscience: Subject Access and the Reference Archivist," *American Archivist* 45 (Winter 1982): 33–44.

33. Paul Conway, "Facts and Frameworks: An Approach to Studying the Users of Archives," *American Archivist* 49 (Fall 1986): 395.

34. Lawrence Dowler, "The Role of Use in Defining Archival Practice and Principles:

A Research Agenda for the Availability and Use of Records," *American Archivist* 51 (Winter/Spring 1988): 77.

35. Dowler, "The Role of Use," 78.

36. Dowler, "The Role of Use," 84.

37. Sue Holbert, *Archives & Manuscripts: Reference & Access*, Basic Manual Series (Chicago: Society of American Archivists, 1977), pp. 2–3.

38. SAA Committee on Reference, Access, and Photoduplication, "Standards for Access to Research Materials in Archival and Manuscript Repositories," *American Archivist* 37 (January 1974): 153–54.

39. See David Margolick, "Whose Words Are They, Anyway?" *New York Times Book Review* (November 7, 1987), 1, 44–45.

40. See, for example, Charles B. Elston, "University Student Records: Research Use, Privacy Rights, and the Buckley Law," *Midwestern Archivist* 1 (Spring 1976): 16–32.

41. Elena S. Danielson, "The Ethics of Access," *American Archivist* 52 (Winter 1989): 52–62 is a good review of the complexities of these problems, although there is no explicit reference to the problems and issues faced by institutional archivists.

42. The changing environment can be seen through the creation of organizations such as the National Security Archive, a private organization created by two lawyers to obtain federal records through FOIA requests to assist the research in controversial federal government matters. See Frankie Pelzman, "The National Security Archive: Keeping the Government Honest," *Wilson Library Bulletin* 64 (May 1990): 31–32, 35–36, 132.

6

Building Internal and External Support for Institutional Archives Programs

GAINING SUPPORT FOR A FUNCTIONAL INSTITUTIONAL ARCHIVES

The previous four chapters have described the basics of administering any institutional archives program. Key to the success of these functions and the overall mission of the archival operation is, however, strong internal and, to some degree, external support for the archives.[1] Achieving any degree of support is a difficult task, but it can be even more cumbersome in an institutional archives. In this environment the archival program often exists primarily, almost exclusively, for the benefit of the organization. Concepts of the public benefits of institutional archives are often malformed and become obstacles to overcome in the program's gaining the necessary support that it requires. For some institutions, however, their archival records have a significance beyond themselves and provide crucial information for individuals, families, communities, causes, and the like. In these instances, the individual responsible for managing the institutional archives must work to gain increased internal support for, and public recognition of, the program and its important holdings.

There are two general ways for the institutional archives to acquire the needed administrative and financial resources that it requires for operation. The primary means must always be seeking the support of the institution itself. This support is especially important for an institutional archives since a program of this type is meant primarily to serve the organization; it is natural to expect the organization to fund something that supports its work. All through this volume there has been discussion about ways that the institutional archivist can gain additional support, ranging from providing crucial information from the archival records for special and ongoing activities to providing a kind of corporate memory of the organization. This chapter will reemphasize some of these kinds of activities.

The other means of gaining support is through the creation and development of outreach or public programs. This idea is new in this volume, and it reflects, as well, relatively new thinking in the archival profession. Although the concept of public programs must be carefully reconsidered when used by institutional archives, these activities can be crucial for the success of the institutional archives. In fact, any archives that does not work to some degree in this arena is bound to suffer in its degree of support and development for its mission and mandates.

THE CONCEPT OF PUBLIC OR OUTREACH PROGRAMS AND THE INSTITUTIONAL ARCHIVES

While the concept of public programs is one of the more recent developments in the archival profession, these kinds of activities have been well defined and described.

Public programs are tools that support and enhance other archival functions, including research, reference, preservation, and collecting. They can be highly educational, both for planners and participants; they can foster a greater appreciation for history and archival records; and they help ensure firm and continuing support for future archival endeavors.

Perhaps most important of all, they encourage greater communication between archivists and the various institutional, social, and professional communities to which they belong. Archivists who plan and take part in public programs gain new insights into client needs and interests—insights that can help them do a better job of serving all archival constituents, from first-time visitors to experienced researchers.[2]

To this definition can be added the aspect of fund-raising and grantsmanship; acquiring external funding is a process that is often dependent on the archival program's perception and the ability of the archivist and his or her administrators to convince others of the importance of the basic archival functions.

Despite the seemingly logical importance in building and supporting archival institutions, public programs have only recently come into prominence in practical ways and, for many archivists, still remain a secondary function. Many professional, experienced archivists consider public programs a task that takes time and resources away from the more essential requirements of appraisal, preservation, arrangement and description, and reference, while others see the kinds of activities that constitute public programs as essential for acquiring the necessary support for these other functions. For most archivists, however, the continuing malformed nature of the public's image of the archivist, archival programs, and the archival mission has made public outreach an important and primary task. One archivist noted, for example, that even the steady users of archives suffer from "archivaphobia" because of misinformed opinions of essential archival work.[3] Each and every archivist must, nevertheless, ascertain whether his or her own program merits a focus on this kind of activity and the degree of the focus.

Several aspects of the definition of public programs should be of interest to the institutional archivist. Public programs can gain increased support for the basic archival functions. They can impart understanding about the nature of archival records and the programs that administer them. They can strengthen communication within an institution or institutions about the archives. Finally, public programs can increase insight by the institutional archivist about how his or her program is perceived and how those perceptions can be improved or expanded. All of these aspects will be discussed below.

The nature of public programs might be a deterrent for some institutional archivists because of their emphasis on the "public." The degree to which these kinds of programs can be utilized depends, at least partly, on the scope of the archival operation's constituency. An institutional archives, like a college or university or religious archives, will probably have a sizable external public and wish to develop this public even further. An institutional archives, like that of a business or a professional association, might wish to have a more limited public because of the confidential and/or proprietary nature of the records. Many of the forms of public programs discussed below, however, such as exhibitions and publications, can be equally effective for building internal support in these latter types of institutional archives. What the institutional archivist must keep in mind is the audience that he or she wants to reach with these activities, since one of the ultimate aims is to increase interest in the institutional archives.

All of the basic archival functions—appraisal, preservation, arrangement and description, and reference—require financial resources to be properly carried out. For most institutional archives, this requirement means winning support from the parent organization to provide these resources and from some portion of the public or external users of the archival records. But using public programs also provides an opportunity for the institutional archivist to probe more deeply into the nature and effectiveness of his or her program's ability to administer these crucial functions. For example, the effectiveness of a program's descriptive systems can be partly measured by the archival staff's ability to locate certain kinds of records for use in an exhibition or publication. Likewise, the identification of certain kinds of records that could be used in an exhibition or as an illustrative item in a publication might lead to a reevaluation of criteria used to select records needing to be maintained in original forms (possessing intrinsic value). Determination of audiences to reach in lecture series or other special events might also require some reflection on current groups reached by the archives' reference operation; whether the program's reference records can adequately reveal the nature of use and users can be determined through the planning process used in such an outreach effort. It should be obvious, therefore, that incorporating an outreach component into an archival program can lead to more serious assessment of the main archival functions.

Outreach programs are also mainly educational in purpose. One of the pioneering advocates of outreach programs by archivists has defined this relationship between education and outreach in how the archivist conceives of his or her audience.

Our first job, then, is to recognize that we have many publics, ranging from institutionally connected researchers to general users, and across a spectrum that includes, among others, teachers at all levels of the educational system; elementary, secondary school, college and university students; genealogists, avocational historians, government employees, publicists, media professionals, and the merely curious. Next we determine those potential publics in relation to our own mandates, depending on whether we represent, for example, a state archives, a county historical society, a state university, or a private institution. Finally, we must think in terms of providing service to the largest number of people within any one of these publics in ways which fit the intellectual and logistical needs of its members. Only then can we begin to conceive of educational activities as programs rather than as scattershot episodes or events.[4]

For the institutional archivist, the educational implications of public programs means that these public programs can be used to develop a higher level of understanding by individuals and groups both within and without the institution. For example, a newsletter describing recent activities and accessions of the archives can be developed effectively for both internal and external audiences. News of innovative research or of the acquisition of records that can lead to such research can help institutional managers responsible for the creation of such records and other potential institutional and outside researchers understand more fully the nature and importance of the institutional archives. A special exhibition on a historic anniversary of the institution, utilizing archival records, can be used not only to develop a stronger internal sense of the organization's corporate culture, with a strong dose of the value of the historical perspective, but also to reach out to the institution's local community to convey the significance of that institution in the community and vice versa. If such an exhibition is done properly, the importance and values of the institutional archives should also be conveyed.

Developing effective internal communication about the institutional archives can be a difficult process. Since individuals, especially middle managers responsible for much of the crucial work of the organization, are generally awash in information, more information about the institutional archives is often likely to get lost. This difficulty is often the challenge of catching the attention of the organization's managers, diverted by the urgency of important daily matters, in order to make a case that the archival program ought to be accorded the status of a priority activity. Public programs provide such an opportunity. An interesting film, arresting publication, or timely lecture sponsored by the archives can be a different enough activity to capture the attention of the institutional staff. Once that attention is captured, the archivist can use this time to provide information about the archives, its services, and its values to the organization. Capturing the attention of outside individuals, the actual and potential researchers, might be more difficult from a logistical point of view (determining what the archives should encourage use of and what the institution wants to communicate regarding its public image) but it is easier once the programs are decided upon and offered. A corporate or similar institutional archives might be an unusual archival program in the community to be offering public-oriented activities, attracting interest for this reason. The institutional archivist should take advantage of any interest of this variety.

Public programs can also be used to ascertain the perceptions, again both internal and external, of the archival operation. Activities that attract various groups to an archives can be used not just to communicate to these groups what the archives does or its importance, but to determine what perceptions are already held about the archives. Determining these perceptions can be done both directly and indirectly. The direct method is through asking attenders at public programs to fill out forms with pertinent questions or to ask for formal and informal vocal impressions. A more indirect method is observing the success of various kinds of activities and products that are offered and listening to the kinds of comments that are made about the institutional archives. The archivist should also realize that he or she can learn a considerable amount by evaluating what programs work or do not work. A seemingly good activity can fail because of the public perception of the archives, and the archivist needs to be on the alert to be able to determine this possibility. A certain amount of risk taking or experimentation in the variety of public programs can help the archivist to gain a good sense of how the archives is perceived. With this knowledge, he or she can develop activities to change the image (if a change is desirable). Ascertaining such perceptions is also extremely important for gaining additional external funds, an issue that will be a major focus of the second part of this chapter.

THE FIRST PRIORITY: INSTITUTIONAL SUPPORT
FOR THE INSTITUTIONAL ARCHIVES

There should be little question that a successful public outreach effort can improve the prospects for the organization's support of its own archives. Indeed, the institutional archivist should not engage in many extra activities that do not lead to a strengthening of its role and image within the organization, nor should he or she seek external funding if the organization itself is not providing adequate support or does not seem interested in providing such support. If it can be accepted that any organization is never quite standing still but is either moving forward in a growth phase or declining, then the importance of the archives' keeping the primary institutional mission in mind should not have to be questioned. But it is also important to realize that the institutional archivist should not forget that the primary responsibility for his or her own archives rests with that organization. Public programs and outreach can help the cause, but they should never be viewed as a mechanism for getting some individuals or groups other than the organization's managers and owners to have financial and other responsibility for the archival operation. What does such support mean? How is this support gained and nurtured by the institutional archivist?[5]

Every organization that wishes to have an archives program ought to expect to support it fully. This point was discussed to some extent in the second chapter of this volume, but it is worth reiterating here in this slightly different context. Such support means the hiring of a professional staff (its size dependent upon the size and other characteristics of the organization), possessing an adequate facility that is environmentally sound and physically secure, providing the necessary equipment for a successful archival operation, providing financial resources ensuring that all the archival functions can be performed (at least to a basic level), allowing a records management program to be administered in coordination with, or as part of, the archival program, and endorsing the archival program's authority to identify and preserve institutional records with continuing value. This level of support should be a goal for every organization that seeks to have an effective archival program. Of course, any institution will probably have to consider phasing in such an archival program, but it is important, nevertheless, that there be a clear vision for what the organization owes in the way of support for its archives. Furthermore, to what degree an organization should seek additional external support depends on its nature; a nonprofit organization, like a museum or religious denomination, might be expected to find some funds on the outside from federal agencies or foundations while for-profit corporations should be expected to provide their own financial and other support. Ways to seek financial support from the outside will be considered later in this chapter.

Since many institutions will make at least (and sometimes little more than) the initial step of hiring a professional archivist or supporting the reequipping of an existing staff member for archival work, the burden of building an effective archival program might depend solely on the skill of the archivist. Some archivists seem to accept without question the role of the lone archivist in the institution and determine their responsibility as identifyng, arranging and describing, and providing reference to the organization's archival records. While these responsibilities are important, the archivist must decide whether they will be met by his or her own efforts or by efforts to win additional support for the program. There is no right or wrong answer here, the approach followed depending completely on the institution, the actual resources provided, the potential resources, and the scale of the archival program. In most cases, however, the archivist must set aside some portion of his or her time to work on building the program.

Building an institutional archives program requires the archivist to do a number of things. The main attention of the archivist should be to determine what the institution's notion of the program is and the quantity and nature of resources that are intended to be available for the archives' development. The archivist must have this information in planning for his or her activities and selecting the first activities to undertake. Without question, the archivist must make sure that the program lives up to its initial, internal expectations. The archivist should also, however, identify where there are weaknesses in these expectations and take, at the appropriate time, actions to correct such assumptions. For example, if there seems to be a perception that the archival program is mainly intended to assist public relations initiatives or to serve as a museum of record relics, then the archivist should work hard to demonstrate that the archival records have other values to the organization. This work will require the archivist to understand the ongoing work of the institution and the major current issues being handled by it; the archivist should make every effort to reveal how the archival records might provide insights into these activities and issues. In the same manner, if the archivist discovers that the institution's level of funding is weak, due to misconceptions about the nature and scope of archives, then the archivist might want to seek external funding for special projects that rectify the internal perceptions and wins additional, ongoing, internal financial support. Additional comments about building effective public programming as a means of supporting the overall development of the archival operation will be made later in this chapter.

The institutional archivist needs, then, to have a proactive perspective on his or her work. The archivist should be out of the records stacks and in the organization, especially in the early period of the program's development. The archivist needs to communicate to management and other employees of the institution what the program is there for and what values it can have for the organization's work. The archivist needs to promote the program so that it has a high visibility and so that its records are effectively used. Without such effort, the archival program's chances for adequate development are significantly reduced; moreover, when the organization faces changes such as reductions in force or reorganization, the institutional archives that does not have a sufficient profile might be prone to be eliminated or severely reduced in its scope of activities. While the institution has a responsibility to support its archives, the archivist has a responsibility to ensure that the program is meeting its responsibilities and has secured a place in the organization's work. Here is where public programs can play an important role in promoting understanding of the archives' importance and its use.

THE VARIETIES OF PUBLIC OR OUTREACH PROGRAMS

There are several main forms of outreach efforts that the institutional archivist can utilize. One form is the publication promoting and explaining the archival program. Another type is the workshop or class that instructs individuals about certain aspects of the archives. Special events can also be used to promote the archives. Institutional archivists should also use press releases and other publicity approaches to inform the organization's employees and broader public about the work of the archives. All of these efforts can be effectively utilized by the institutional archivist to build support for, and recognition of, the archival program. All of these must be going on, with some beneficial results, if the archivist wishes to seek additional external funds through public granting agencies and private foundations.

Publications by and about an institutional archives program can take many forms. Every archival program should have, at the least, a general brochure describing the archives' mission, mandates, activities, holdings, acquisition policy, access policies, address, and hours of operation. Such a brochure should be attractively published and provide the basic needed information without a heavy text that discourages individuals from reading it. The message should be clearly conveyed, and if it is well done, the brochure can be used for general publicity, answering requests about the nature of the program, and building a profile for the program both within and without the parent organization.

Newsletters are also very popular and useful forms of archival publications for institutional archives. These publications can be used to build interest within the organization, attract external public interest, or target specific clientele that should make greater use of the archival records. Institutional archives should probably use newsletters primarily to build support within the organization. These newsletters do not have to be issued in a fancy, expensive manner (in fact, they could be dispatched over the electronic mail system), but they should contain up-to-date news about new archival holdings and, as well, describe interesting uses of the current archival holdings in a manner that encourages greater and more varied research in the records. However the archivist decides to use a newsletter, this kind of publication should always be evaluated regularly and its purpose kept in mind and reassessed from time to time; such evaluation can often be done by putting into the newsletter a reader response survey on specific issues or on the matter of the newsletter itself.

Archival programs should also issue special publications to mark special events or anniversaries or on topics of sustained interest by both the researchers using the archival records and the general public, which may or not have any interest in the archival operation. Institutional archivists might want to develop special brochures, pamphlets, or finding aids on topics for which records are consistently sought. A university archivist who is often asked by various faculty for materials on past curricular proposals and revisions might produce a brochure that identifies the major records holdings on these topics, available finding aids, and how researchers can get access to these records. A religious archivist who is sought after by genealogists for the archival records of births, deaths, and marriages might consider producing a similar guide or brochure oriented to this kind of research. Special anniversaries and events can also lead to onetime publications by archival programs. The New York State Archives and Records Administration, for example, issued a pamphlet on how to research the histories of schools as a way of celebrating the bicentennial of the Board of Regents and the University of the State of New York.[6]

A final form of publication (aside from finding aids discussed in chapter 5 or publications accompanying exhibitions discussed below) is the audiovisual production. Archivists have become increasingly enamored with these productions as means of communicating the importance of their programs and archival records in general. These are very expensive enterprises for most archival programs, however, and require professional help in script writing and illustration as well as requiring cost-consuming production preparation.[7] If the institutional archives can find the resources (or if the organization has a media production unit that can assist it) to produce an audiovisual show about itself, these productions offer many advantages. They can provide dynamic introductions to archival programs, as they are more memorable than written materials and can capture the attention of busy institutional employees. These productions can also be used over and over for both internal and external presentations about the archival program and used both with archivists present and, on other occasions, without archivists there. Even if the archival program cannot afford the development of a full-fledged audiovisual show, it should at least look into the possibility of developing a good stock set of photographic slides

Producing A Good Slide-Tape Show

The primary ingredients in a successful slide show are a story worth telling and an imaginative and technically competent way of telling it. Incorporating these ingredients into a production is unquestionably a challenge. But with receptive visitors, a wealth of historical resources, experience, and high standards, any historical institution can make effective shows.

Institutions that can undertake audio-visual productions will reap benefits in excess of the resources committed. The commitment will prove worthwhile when the board of directors applauds after seeing the show for the first time, a school system wants to purchase a copy for the audio-visual library, visitors keep their seats for a second showing, a newspaper mentions it in the "About Town" section, or a civic group asks to screen the show at its monthly meeting. Any one of these indicates that your institution's efforts to educate the public have been successful. And education is a large part of what historical agencies and museums are all about.

Nancy E. Malan, Producing Professional Quality Slide Shows: A Systematic Approach, Technical Report 2 (Nashville: American Association for State and Local History, 1985), 17.

---

about the archival program that can be used for lectures and other public presentations.

The next major category of public or outreach programs is the workshop or instructional class. Institutional archivists will need to think of these activities in two ways. First, the archivist can develop and present brief workshops within the organization that will provide an orientation to the organization's employees about the archives. Such workshops can concentrate on a general overview of the archival program, the nature of the archival records and their potential use in the organization, how to conduct research in the archives, and the kinds of records that should be transferred to the program. The latter workshop would be most effective if the archives is connected to a records management program; if this is the case, workshops on files maintenance, the scheduling and disposition process, and other records management topics should also be offered. When and how these workshops should be offered and how long they should be depend on many variables, most notably the common means by which the organization supports such internal training opportunities. The archivist should adapt to how the organization handles continuing education and make sure that the important issues are being dealt with that provide the archival program its important role within the organization.

The second form of workshop that the institutional archivist should consider is the variety that reaches out beyond the organization's boundaries. Whether the archivist uses this form or not is dependent upon the nature of the organization that the archives serves and the desirable amount of access to the records that the public should or could be provided. Since, however, in nearly any organization some records will be open, the archivist should make every effort to offer workshops in this area. The topics described above—orientation, basics in research, and potential uses of the archival records—can all be offered, probably with some modification, to the general public. The institutional archivist will want to tailor these workshops to the prevailing interests shown by the external researchers, and for many institutional archives selecting these topics will not be extremely difficult. The diocesan archives will, for example, undoubtedly have records of tremendous interest to genealogists and family historians. Building on such existing interests can lead to opportunities to promote other types of research as well.

Institutional archivists should also look for additional opportunities for reaching different audiences about their programs and the valuable records they administer. One group that has become of greater interest to the archival profession is students of all levels, and, depending on the nature of the institutional archives, these programs should seek to reach these groups. The students of today represent future users and supporters of archives, a fact that archivists have begun to take more seriously over the past decade or so. Archivists have created user packets that provide facsimiles of historical documents usually built about a particular event or theme. Such packets have usually been done in coordination with local history requirements in the public school curriculum, the packets being designed specifically for these age groups and curricular uses. Their creation has been justified as helping students to think critically by aiding them to weigh and interpret evidence, developing social skills by providing students varied opinions and information, and assisting them to consider alternative solutions to problems, understand the process of historical research, and place themselves in their social and historical context. There is no reason that institutional archives should not help in reaching out to students, although most of these archival programs will probably be able to do so only in cooperation with other archival programs, school boards, and other groups. Some institutional archives might have some interesting opportunities, however. A diocesan archives could develop for its own parochial schools special curricular packets that concentrate on the church's history, development, and present issues. A business archives could work with an undergraduate or graduate business program to develop case study material in business problems. At the least, the institutional archivist should be aware of the possibilities of working in this arena.

Special events will provide another rationale for public or outreach programs. Special events are essentially onetime affairs that focus on some specific event such as an anniversary or starting of a new initiative by the organization. The kinds of programs that accompany these special events

Business Records and Student Document Packets

One of the advantages of a capitalistic society is that it generates a massive array of private business records, many of which survive for later educational uses . . . . They reflect the economic conditions of an era, the methods of production, and the living conditions of the working force.

Advertisements for merchandise provide many clues to how people lived. There are word-mysteries to untangle regarding the nature of various products, and advertising styles provide a great deal of social commentary . . . .

Ledgers and account books from stores show a different method of purchase and payment from what is commonly encountered. Students can see how people kept running accounts with a store and that they bought in large quantities, in contrast to current afternoon trips to the supermarket. These facts provide insight into the influence of transportation on shopping patterns, the need for storage systems for large amounts of materials, or the lack of ready cash in agricultural areas.

Records relating to employees show such things as wages, job requirements, and practices of hiring and firing . . . .

Bills for goods indicate both the variety of goods sold and the cost of merchandise. Since many include the address of the business, they can be used to study development of business districts and uses of buildings. They also are often imprinted with detailed drawings of the type of merchandise sold or of the building where the store is located, thereby providing useful visual information as well.

Business records lend themselves to studies of economic conditions at any given time, providing information students can compile and correlate on wages and prices. In addition, they are an excellent resource for studies of the nature of working life for all levels of society, as well as the growth and development of our economic system.

Kathleen Roe, Teaching with Historical Records (Albany: New York State Archives, 1981), 20-21.

---

are exhibitions, open houses and tours, lectures and film series, ceremonies or commemorative observances, and the like. For the informed and imaginative archivist, these kinds of activities will provide many opportunities; identifying when they can be utilized requires that the archivist is well informed about the institution's past and current activities. Determining how to mark these events will depend, however, on the resources available to the archivist.

Exhibitions can be a particularly troublesome area for any archivists who wish to make full use of all public programming techniques, and they deserve a little more consideration. The main key to successful exhibitions is finding topics that capture interest, and institutional archivists should rest assured that their records reflect such topics. For example, one of the more successful exhibitions at the National Archives concerned baseball:

Researchers coming to the [National] Archives expect to find documentation dealing with battles, congressional legislation, land policy, and Indian relations. They don't expect to find documents relating to baseball, an activity not usually associated with the federal government. Yet such documents are here, and their presence indicates that the records in the National Archives in fact cover the broad spectrum of American life. The baseball documents chosen for our exhibit reflect the workings of the federal government just as thoroughly and intimately as their more conventional documentary counterparts do, and therefore properly qualify as legitimate archival holdings.[8]

Nearly every institutional archives will be able to discover such topics reflected in their records. All that is required is a little imagination and sensitivity to the major issues of the day.

Yet, exhibitions are very difficult to do well, requiring careful planning, considerable advance preparation (meaning it is difficult to do them at the last minute), and significant knowledge about both exhibition technique and the care of archival records in exhibitions. In a fine manual laying out the basics of archival exhibitions, the author described the various issues and problems in these efforts:

There is every reason to believe that archives can prepare *good* exhibits without overextending their resources. . . . The subject of the exhibit, its placement, and the quality of its design and execution are more important than size in determining its effectiveness. . . .

But exhibits do require time, skill, and money; they pose certain risks in the areas of security and conservation; and they are usually temporary, making both the costs and risks difficult to justify. Archivists must carefully evaluate their objectives in light of their overall needs and capabilities before embarking on an exhibit program, or when considering whether to continue an existing one.[9]

For the archival program connected to an organization with a museum function or with considerable resources (so that professional exhibit designers can give assistance), exhibitions might be a good expenditure of time and resources. For most institutional archives, exhibitions will be less frequently used, and, if they are used, they should be done in a manner that allows them to be used to the greatest possible extent (so, for example, that they could be made portable and reused). Several cases of pertinent documents can be changed on a regular basis (provided there are adequate security and environmental conditions in the exhibition area) as an alternative to the more substantial efforts, but the archivist must be prepared to determine whether these more modest endeavors do any real good in promoting the program; even a few cases of documents can require the expenditure of enormous amounts of time in selection and research.

A better use of time than exhibitions for institutional archivists might be conferences on issues or themes intimately connected to the institution.

Where to Go For Additional Help
In Developing Exhibition Programs

1. Become an active exhibitgoer. Take along a camera and a notebook and study the techniques used.
2. Get acquainted with staff members at local museums. They are usually more than willing to offer constructive criticism and provide the names of suppliers, designers, and fabricators.
3. Inventory the skills and hobbies of staff members. Are there any amateur photographers or art majors? Any carpenters or seamstresses? Manual dexterity is an important skill in exhibiting.
4. Explore the possibilities of using volunteers and student interns.
5. Talk to your building superintendent about local building codes, contractors and suppliers in your community, and what can be done to upgrade the quality of the lighting, security, and maintenance of the exhibit area.
6. Test your ideas on friends and colleagues to determine how well the exhibit will be accepted by different audiences.
7. Consult subject-area specialists on specific questions related to the exhibit's content. If the consultation becomes than an informal discussion, you should offer an honorarium.
8. Contact colleges and museums that offer training programs in museology. Art schools and college art departments sometime conduct mini-seminars for students preparing works for exhibition that include demonstrations of matting and framing techniques and the procedures for wet and dry mounting.
9. Attend sessions on exhibits at meetings of archival, library, and museum associations.

Gail Farr Casterline, Archives & Manuscripts: Exhibits, Basic Manual Series (Chicago: Society of American Archivists, 1980), 56.

Like exhibitions, these public programs can be oriented to special commemorations of significant milestones in the organization. The centennial celebration of a major university could lead to a conference on the history of higher education showcasing the particular institution. The anniversary of the founding of a high-technology company could lead to a meeting on the history of these businesses with predictions for future trends and with use of the particular institution as a case study. It should be obvious that these kinds of meetings can not only provide opportunities to promote specific institutional archives but lead to explorations in the importance of these historical records and provide information—such as on research trends and what aspects of the topic are not being adequately documented—that the archivist can use for improving the performance of his or her own archival operation.

For conferences and meetings, as with most other forms of public programs, the institutional archivist must ask some basic questions about purposes and benefits. Since such events will draw attention to the archives' holdings, the degree of access to these records will determine whether conferences involving academic scholars and other researchers will be a good idea or not. If an archives intends to try to attract a wider portion of the public, well-known popular speakers will need to be involved to attract attention; the public will not be enchanted by scholars presenting formal papers with musty-sounding or cryptic titles. The institutional archives will also have to weigh the potential benefit for such a conference against the resources necessary to sponsor it. Although there are ample supplies of public and foundation monies around that can support such activities, these events still require considerable advance planning and legwork to be effective.

The final form of public programming to be considered here concerns publicity programs using press releases and media contacts to publicize the institutional archives. The first consideration in developing such an outreach activity should be to determine whether the organization already has a publicity or public affairs office. If the institution has this kind of unit, the archivist should make every effort to work with such individuals for a number of reasons. These individuals may already possess well-established contacts with media representatives. The publicity personnel generally have specific professional expertise in the art of writing press releases and working with the media. Finally, the organization might require all publicity to be funneled through this office; if the organization has such an office, this requirement is a great likelihood. In this kind of environment, the archivist's role becomes trying to educate the publicity personnel about the mission, activities, and importance of the archival program to ensure that it gets adequate coverage.

If the institution lacks a public affairs office, the archivist faces a different challenge. The main responsibility then becomes determining what kind of press coverage is desirable and what kinds of hooks or angles the archival program might have to attract media coverage. The archivist should also seek some professional counsel in writing press releases and in developing contacts with the media. Archivists, like many other professional specialists, tend to write press releases that please themselves but that no newspaper or television news division will usually ever express interest in using. The tendency is to write releases on professional issues or to use professional jargon, both occurrences that will diminish the chances of attracting the desired attention. The archivist needs to work with experienced publicity people and to have patience. Developing a good publicity program requires sustained effort and the long view.

BUILDING AN EFFECTIVE PUBLIC
OUTREACH PROGRAM

As the above comments should suggest, effective public outreach programs take time, resources, trial and error, and patience to build. An
effective public outreach program can identify groups to reach with news
about the archival program, communicate with those groups, and see and
monitor changes in the individuals who are using the archival records and
who are aware of the archival program. To develop these kinds of programs, institutional archivists need to keep in mind at least three matters.

The archivist must first assess the general attitudes held toward the
archives by the organization's management and other employees and by
the general public that constitutes the program's legitimate research community. The archivist needs to gather data that will help him or her to
answer the following kinds of questions:

- How well known is the archival program in the organization and research
  community?
- Has the archival program identified the major audiences and groups that it should
  be serving? What efforts has it made in the past to reach these groups? How can
  it target these and other groups for future outreach?
- Is the institution willing to make the financial and staff resource commitments
  to support an adequate outreach program? Is the institution willing to make the
  necessary commitments to meet expectations that outreach might generate?
- Has the archival program considered the needs for public outreach in light of its
  other mandates, commitments, and priorities? Does the program understand how
  outreach activities will be used to support the development of other archival
  functions?

Once the archivist has answered such basic questions as these, then he or
she is ready to start planning specifically for a public outreach effort.

Second, the archivist must also have in place the means to evaluate his
or her outreach activities. Knowing what is effective requires, of course,
that the archivist have a clear sense of the program's mission and the desired
impact of any outreach activities. Additionally, however, the archivist must
have in place mechanisms to evaluate whether the activities are attracting
new people, causing unused records to be used, and transforming weaknesses in the program's image to strengths. Spot surveys, follow-up interviews, precise charting of research trends, and other similar activities all
must be done to ensure that outreach programs are worthwhile investments
of resources and energies. The archivist might wish to look at the museum
administrators' and curators' evaluations of exhibitions and other educational activities. As one recent museum administrator wrote: "Whatever
the goals of a museum exhibit—imparting information, stimulating interest

An Example of an Archives Audiovisual

"Let the Record Show: Practical Uses for Historical Documentation" is the title of SARA's [New York State Archives and Records Administration] new AV show about the importance of historical records to society.   The 16-minute show highlights vignettes that demonstrate the benefits New Yorkers derive from using historical records: a research botanist using century-old botanical journals to document ecological changes at Goat Island, Niagara Falls; a member of a homeowner's organization near Syracuse studying the plans and blueprints of an old bridge to help determine if it is still safe; a Saratoga Springs teacher whose students study century-old community records for a better understanding of how people lived in the past; and a dance company in New York City that uses videotapes of its own performances and other records to plan future presentations.   The basic message is: historical records are crucial to meet a variety of important, practical needs.

The show includes a discussion on how historical records are selected, cared for, and made available in repositories across New York. It introduces the idea that well-developed, adequately supported programs are needed to administer these invaluable resources.

. . . . "Let the Record Show" is designed to appeal to a variety of audiences, including trustees of historical institutions, professional organizations, civic and cultural groups, and teachers and students.   It can serve as an excellent device to stimulate discussion about the location, accessibility, and condition of historical records in one's own community.

For the Record, 7 (Summer 1989), 7.

---

in a subject, changing or reinforcing opinions, providing aesthetic experiences—you must be aware of the public's response to know if the exhibit is achieving its goals. Learning what visitors like, learn, and feel about exhibits can guide decisions about what to keep and what to change, what works and what needs improvement."[10]

Finally, the archivist must determine whether he or she is making good use of the existing resources that are available for outreach activities. If a program wants to make some dramatic point about preservation dangers to archival and library materials, then it might wish to make use of existing audiovisual programs like *Slow Fires*.[11] To explain the mission and nature of the institutional mission, it could also use a brochure published by the Society of American Archivists on what archives are and what archivists do. It might inquire into the possibility of renting exhibitions produced by other museums and archival agencies that communicate issues that are important to the institutional archives. With the reuse of all of these materials, the archivist could produce, at much less cost and time, accompanying materials that promote the archives. Many state archives have

produced brochures, publications, and audiovisual presentations specifically for reuse by other archival programs; the New York State Archives
and Records Administration has, for example, produced a self-study guide
for historical records programs, a brochure summation of the guide, and
a film on the nature and uses of historical records (all of these are described
in the final chapter of this book). Institutional archivists must always be
on the lookout for such existing materials that will enhance their own
activities and that they can use to evaluate for their own activities.

FUND-RAISING AND THE
INSTITUTIONAL ARCHIVES

Archivists need to understand that the problems in image and funding
that they and their programs face are challenges needing to be faced with
imagination, hard work, and devotion to tasks not normally associated with
archival administration. Their focus needs to be shifted to capturing the
attention of those within their own institutions and from external sources,
in a way that will gain the support necessary to build a solid program
enabling the effective management, preservation, and use of the archival
records. The archivist, to accomplish this goal, adopts a holistic view in
which functions such as public programming, outreach, advocacy (to be
discussed in the next chapter on cooperation), and fund-raising—the latter
activity being dependent on the effectiveness of the former functions—are
properly connected to the more basic archival endeavors of appraisal,
arrangement, description, preservation, and reference. Most importantly,
perhaps, the archivist—especially the institutional archivist—views the acquisition of outside funding as always secondary to winning financial support from within the institution. Archivists should not seek to substitute
raising funds externally for winning internal support, and, in fact, programs
that fail to have strong internal support will likely fail at external fund-
raising.[12]

The archival profession has already begun to address its lack of success
at building numerous first-rate, well-funded archival programs, primarily
by acknowledging that activities such as publicity and fund-raising are
crucial and need to be fitted into an overall archival program design. SAA's
report on archival goals and priorities stated that "few archivists receive
any training in administration, planning, fundraising, or public relations.
If there are to be enlarged public support and financial resources, the
training and skill of archivists as managers must be improved."[13] Such
awareness has led to increasing attention on archival image and societal
worth,[14] efforts to define and track the values and significance of use of
historical records,[15] and some descriptions of means by which to acquire
additional financial resources through grant writing (a topic to be discussed
below). The institutional archivist needs to stay abreast of these trends in

the wider archival profession, while realizing that such attention by archivists is in a nascent stage, and that the profession needs more tools, analysis, and guidance, especially in fund-raising, both in conceiving and carrying out this function.

Archivists' misconceptions have influenced, often adversely, their acquisition of funding. The archival profession's primary focus on raising funds has been in the public sector, mainly (in the United States, at least) the National Historical Publications and Records Commission (NHPRC) and the various programs of the National Endowment for the Humanities (NEH). *Preoccupation* may be a better term than *focus*, since many archivists seem to think only about these sources when seeking external funding, despite their limited availability, duration of support, restricted uses of funds, and the intense national competition for the awarding of grants. The few million dollars available for records grants from the NHPRC will often barely begin to meet the needs of one state's repositories, let alone the thousands of other repositories scattered across the nation. The problem of limited funds significantly weakens the potential value of the public sector grants and, thereby, the opportunity for professional staff to contribute to the financial base of their programs to gain funds that provide a catalyst for continued program development. The point is very simple: archivists must correct some common misconceptions they have had about the nature of fund-raising and tap private sector sources of funding to ensure that their archival records are adequately maintained. Some of these misconceptions can be especially troublesome for institutional archivists.

In addition to conceiving of fund-raising primarily as writing grants to public funding agencies, what are the other major misconceptions by archivists about fund-raising? First, archivists tend to approach fund-raising as another research-oriented activity, rather than an advocacy effort. Archivists seem to want to do research in foundation indexes or study how-to books rather than do what needs to be done, communicating to, and winning over, a large portion of the public about the values of archival records and the programs that care for them. This should strike a respondent chord for the institutional archivist who must be constantly seeking internal support as well as pursuing possibilities for external funds. Research is very important for fund-raising, but presentations on fund-raising at conferences and meetings often are little more than lessons in public agency grant writing or introductions to references such as published foundation indexes, valuable for those who have had no exposure to such activities and references, yet barely scratching the surface of the dynamic nature of effective fund-raising.[16]

Second, archivists often take it for granted that what they do is important and assume that all society should think the same way. The need for institutional archivists to work to develop recognition of their program's importance has been emphasized, of course, throughout this chapter and volume. It is doubly important to consider this need when planning for fund-raising. Successful fund-raising is dependent on the public's understanding something about the archival mission and why historical records are worth preserving. Achieving this understanding requires significant planning, effort, and patience. Historical and archival records repositories likely to have the most success in fund-raising are those well known in their community with clear missions and publicity and other materials demonstrating that these missions are being taken seriously. Institutions that do not possess a community profile and the instruments necessary for building such a profile will face a lot of work in readying for fund-raising initiatives.

The third misconception is that there are "magic" formulas for fund-raising, rather than hard work and commitment to the resource development function that will bring in funding. Resource development is just as serious a responsibility as any other aspect of archival management. Archival administrators who contend that they do not have the time for such work because of processing backlogs or reference demands will need to reevaluate their priorities. Investing in public outreach and in developing a stronger profile of the historical records program within its larger institutional setting, with an aim toward enlarging the program's base of support, seems the better investment over the long haul. Although there may be temporary frustrations because of shortfalls in efforts to keep pace with the more traditional archival activities, historical and archival records programs may eventually gain the resources necessary to resolve many of these constant backlogs of work and the expensive efforts to preserve and manage their fragile holdings. One archival manager has predicted that the need in this area will be addressed and resolved in the future:

There will be a gradual diminution in the perception that there is a conflict between being a professional archivist and being a manager or program developer, or that becoming an effective program developer implies leaving the archival community. Building program development skills [program planning, advocacy, communication, basic management, and leadership skills], and thereby stronger archival programs, can lead to the more tangible rewards that will retain competent archivists in archival programs.[17]

For institutional archivists, the skills of the program developer may be, in the long run, the most important skills to have.

Finally, archivists seem to have ignored the largest source of prospective funds, the private sector. The private sector encompasses individuals, businesses and corporations, and foundations on local, state, and national levels and accounts for billions of dollars in contributions to worthy causes. These individuals and institutions only remain to be convinced that historical records are worthy of support. Doing this convincing may require a re-configuration of how many archivists spend their time, but no archivists would suggest that their records are not worthy of such support. Institutional archivists, at least those in corporations and businesses, might have an advantage in learning about fund-raising since their parent organizations may often have foundations of their own. While their own program will not be eligible, the institutional archivists can discuss issues of fund-raising with their own foundation administrators. Archivists in institutions of higher education and related fields can discuss these matters with the fund-raising counsel that their organizations likely will have employed.

Although convincing individuals and other funding sources that they should part with their money for the benefit of historical and archival records requires hard work and excellent interpersonal skills, there are some basic principles for fund-raising that largely determine whether an archival program will be successful in this area. What follows has been gleaned from a variety of manuals by fund-raising experts, advice from a fund-raising consultant, and experience in adapting this information for use in fund-raising workshops for historical records programs held in New York State.[18]

1. The archival program should understand its own business and needs before ever seeking monies from the outside. Successful fund-raising is dependent on the archival program's governing board and staff's knowing the program's mission, long-term goals and objectives, and needs. Funds should be raised to meet priorities; priorities should not be dictated by funding opportunities. Letting this occur can produce a malformed and weak program, with much activity (some of it even good activity) that is not directed to any specific purpose or with any measurable result. Seemingly prosperous programs can exist that are seriously neglecting, or at least not gaining the necessary resources for, the management and preservation of their historical records holdings.[19] In institutional archives, in fact, this kind of activity can result in undermining the institution's support for the program.

2. An archival records program must have support from its governing board and/or parent agency before embarking on a fund-raising effort. Governing board members, resource allocators, and key administrative staff must always take responsibility to start and aid a continuing fund-raising initiative. Successful fund-raising is dependent upon strong support from governing boards, especially in terms of both financial support and seeking such support. Fund-raising experts consistently suggest that the chances of successful fund-raising are severely diminished when there is no financial giving from governing board members and when board members do not take the active lead in seeking out and nurturing financial donors.[20] Archival staff is there to promote interest in raising additional resources for the management of holdings, to provide information about the repository and its activities and needs for a well-developed and effective program for the management of archival records, and to assist governing board and other fund-raisers in their effort to increase the financial resources of the repository.

Institutional archives will especially have to demonstrate that there is some solid organizational support for the program and, perhaps, that the fund-raising is being done for some special project or projects and not basic support.

3. Archival programs should carefully consider their funding possibilities. After determining their financial needs, archival programs' governing boards and staff should identify prospective donors, from individuals to local corporations and businesses to local, state, and, if appropriate, national foundations.[21] Armed with such a list, the governing board members and chief repository staff should selectively interview prospective funding sources to ascertain the public perception of the program and degree of knowledge about the program's mission, activities, and needs. This interviewing should also provide the archival program with a general idea of the level of financial support that might be available to it, determine the strengths and weaknesses of the repository as perceived by this select public, and indicate what a donor might want to know before contributing money. For institutional archivists, this should also help them determine what restrictions they might have for access to these additional financial resources; corporations with archival records that are primarily closed to outside researchers, for example, will probably not have much chance of acquiring funds from public agencies unless they make changes regarding access. No matter what this process tells the archival program, even if it indicates it might not be prudent to embark on a fund-raising effort at this time, the repository will have built some additional public support by informing more individuals about its mission and activities.

4. An archival program should have a "case statement" to facilitate its fund-raising efforts. A case statement is a formal, written (it can also be orally presented) presentation by a program addressed to prospective private sector sources to raise money. It is equivalent to the formal grant proposal submitted to public sector funding programs and, as such, is crucial to any fund-raising effort. Case statements can vary in length (largely depending on whether their audience is the general public, corporations and businesses, or foundations) and appearance (they can be attractively published or neatly typed on repository letterhead).[22] They generally include a brief summary of the program's mission, a concise history of the repository, descriptions of the strengths and needs of the program, potential of the program and the use of the solicited funds, and a description of a vision for the program's future, including what the new funds can help the program accomplish and the difference the new monies will make. The content of case statements must be endorsed by the repository's governing board or parent agency, since these individuals will often be the ones primarily soliciting the funds; in addition, an institutional archives might often have the opportunity (and the responsibility) of working with its own organization's development and publicity offices. Case statements must also be accurate and clear since they will help guide the fund-raising efforts by the governing board members and perhaps other interested volunteers, most of whom will not be professionally trained archivists.[23]

5. The archival records program should tie its funding priorities to its best and most logical sources of funds. Although this principle seems fairly obvious, it is nevertheless an extremely important one to keep in mind and reinforces how

important it is that the program first determine its own needs and priorities. If a program's main funding objective is short-term and primarily encompasses the actions of professional archivists, such as producing a finding aid or reducing a backlog of unprocessed holdings, then a public sector funding source might be most appropriate for an initial effort. If a program is after funding for a specific project, it might be able to match corporate donor prospects with the need: a desired exhibition on the history of banking and its archival sources just might interest a local bank or a financial institution; a paper preservation project might attract a local paper manufacturer; or the need for renovating or constructing historical records storage facilities could be discussed with a local construction company. These kinds of examples might be inappropriate for many institutional archives because of their focus on their own organization's records. The point here, however, which remains an appropriate one, is the careful matching of aim with funding or other support source.

Although an archival program is wise to seek additional funds from public granting agencies and private sector foundations and corporations, the program should always put an emphasis on a broad-based fund-raising effort that seeks to build continuing support for the program and goes after the largest pool of outside resources—individuals. Individuals not only represent the largest pool of funds donated to worthy causes by the private sector, but they are often more flexible and potentially better able to support everything and anything that an archival program does or is interested in doing. Institutional archives can have friends groups and regular external research clientele, so that individuals would be a logical and proper place for these archival programs to embark on fund-raising efforts.

GRANTSMANSHIP AND THE INSTITUTIONAL ARCHIVES

Although it is impossible to lay out a precise or perfect set of steps that will guarantee success in the desired objective or that will not require some modification because of circumstances peculiar to the institution, a series of basic steps is a useful blueprint to have in mind. What is really being considered is a solid fund-raising and grantsmanship (each applied appropriately to provide mutual support) for the institutional archives. Institutional archives can modify these steps according to their own needs and peculiar situations. The process described below also rearranges the foregoing basic principles for fund-raising and adds elements essential for grant writing to form a convenient and logical sequence of actions that archival programs can experiment with and adapt as necessary.

1. Know what the historical records program's mission is and what it is that the repository hopes to accomplish, in both the short and the long-term. Make sure that the institutional archives' governing board or parent agency supports the

mission, the repository's plan, and the effort to raise additional funds from outside the organization. For the institutional archives, it is especially important to make sure that there is nothing in the proposed fund-raising initiative that subordinates (or hints at such subordination) the archives' services to the institution.

2. Identify prospective funding sources (in both the public and private sector) and their potential levels of support. Match these sources against the priority needs of the institutional archives. For the institutional archives, it is especially important that there is nothing in the requirements of the funding sources that compromises the institution's access regulations or, if there is, that these issues are resolved before a proposal for funding is prepared and funds actually sought.

3. Inform and involve potential funding sources so that they learn more about the institutional archives and its activities. For the public sector this step includes phone calls and letters seeking the appropriate information, and, in many cases, there are convenient opportunities for face-to-face meetings with representatives of these agencies. For the private sector this step means the preparation of a case statement, whether for a general campaign for an endowment or a fund-raising initiative for a specific project, and the mobilization of governing board members and other volunteers for the asking of funds. This kind of effort provides the means for the institutional archives to convey to the prospective funding agencies how its program serves more than merely the institution; if the institutional archives does not have any services beyond its own institutional environment, it should not be involved in a fund-raising effort to begin with, except with people that have somehow been involved with the organization.

4. Ask for the money. For the public sector, this step requires preparing the grant proposal and submitting it according to the funding source's guidelines. For the private sector, this step means writing letters, making phone calls, making oral presentations, personal solicitation, and involving in all of these activities the governing board and volunteers. There are no special circumstances here for most institutional archives.

5. Acknowledge the contribution. For public sector grants this step means publicity about the grant and recognition of its source in publications and in other ways; guidelines for such agencies are usually fairly explicit about what should be done. For the private sector this step means a thank-you letter, press release, events such as repository open houses and tours, and token gifts such as plaques and publications. With private sector donors it is important to honor their wishes about recognition (some prefer to remain anonymous) and to keep them informed and involved in the archival program (the repository may go back to these sources again in the future).

6. Evaluate the funding effort. At some time evaluation should occur to determine the effectiveness of the fund-raising effort and to begin to prepare for follow-up work for the next effort. Except for projects that have specific starting and ending points, fund-raising and grant writing will be an ongoing function for the archival program. Public sector granting agencies usually provide guidelines that enable or require some evaluation. Evaluation of private sector efforts should enable the repository to consider the time and other resources expended in comparison to the financial gain to the institution.

7. Plan for the next fund-raising and or grant-writing effort. Archival programs
   will need to start the process again, continually trying to raise their level of
   financial support to the point that they can responsibly care for their valuable
   holdings. Each successful fund-raising or grant-writing initiative should lay the
   groundwork for a more effective effort the next time.

While the above steps need to be kept in mind for both fund-raising and
grant writing, a few extra issues need to be considered when institutional
archives consider writing grants to government agencies. Institutional archives need to remember that such public funding sources have their own
specific requirements, priorities, and funding trends. Institutional archivists
need to consider whether these patterns have any relationship to the institutional archives' needs and mandates. An institutional archives' own
priorities should not necessarily be changed to be able to acquire such
funds, unless specific grant-funded projects can enhance and support the
programs' larger aims. These issues can be worked out by contacting the
grant-funding agency and discussing these matters and concerns.

Institutional archivists, when considering getting involved in writing a
grant, should contact similar archival programs that have experience in
grants. Discussion with other programs will often provide valuable information about how to prepare such proposals. Institutional archivists should
also seek to determine the level of impact that such grants have had or
might have on their programs overall.

Since preparing grant proposals to public funding agencies often requires
significant time of the professional staff of any institution, it is important
for the institutional archivist to have carefully planned how the intended
project relates to the program and its value to fulfilling the program's
mission. Institutions lacking professional staff or generally adequate resources will be at a disadvantage not only in preparing the proposal but
in competing for the funds. Public granting agencies have specific requirements, which usually include showing that the institution has made some
substantial commitment to an archives operation. Sometimes the institution
will be able to acquire a challenge grant or some kind of grant that will
allow the organization to get a good archival program started. These and
other considerations need to be kept in focus when the institution considers
preparing a grant to a public funding agency.

Finally, the institutional archives might need to consider the use of fund-
raising and grant-writing consultants. Since effective, ongoing fund-raising
and grant writing are a function that has not become incorporated into the
normal management of most institutional archives programs, a logical question to ask regards the use of fund-raising consultants. Although most
archival programs are very accustomed to having consultants advise on
archival functions,[24] the use of external advisers from other disciplines,

such as fund-raising and resource development, is a less common experience and needs to be addressed briefly.

Fund-raising and grant-writing consultants should not be necessary for most repositories, provided they have followed the kinds of actions described above. Consultants can be reassuring to program governing board members and staff, however, who have no experience in this area. Such consultants can be very valuable assets under these circumstances. They can help the repository consider whether it is ready to undertake a fund-raising or grant-writing effort; train governing board members, staff, and volunteers to be involved in such efforts; direct the actual fund-raising campaign or grant-writing effort; and provide information on, and needed products for, specific aspects of resource development. This kind of assistance might be more possible for some institutional archives since they may be part of organizations that regularly utilize consultants.

ARCHIEVING THE PRIMARY OBJECTIVE: THE HIGH-PROFILE AND UNDERSTOOD INSTITUTIONAL ARCHIVES

How public programming, outreach, and resource development will be utilized by an institutional archives depends on both the nature of the archives and its parent organization. While all these activities are ongoing, it is also true that how these functions are being carried out should also be changing. Institutional archivists should not be in the business of constantly explaining what their mission is, but they should be seeing their program become better known and be able to find themselves in the position of elaborating their purposes. Increased and better use, more constant and adequate financial resources, and more intelligent discussion of the institutional archives should all be obvious results of the public programming and related activities of the archives. These are all measures of success that the institutional archivist can use in his or her work.

NOTES

1. The appropriate degree of external support depends on the nature of the institutional archives. Institutional archives, as in colleges and universities, that serve a wide variety of constituencies will have a wider range of options for building external support. Institutional archives, as in corporations and businesses, that serve primarily or exclusively their parent organizations will not have nearly as many options.

2. Ann E. Pederson and Gail Farr Casterline, *Archives & Manuscripts: Public Programs*, Basic Manual Series (Chicago: Society of American Archivists, 1982), 8.

3. Virginia C. Purdy, "Archivaphobia: Its Causes and Cure," *Prologue* 15 (Summer 1983): 115–19. Purdy described the causes of this phobia as being the quantity of records confronting the researcher, the nature of archival finding aids, and the manner in which the records are arranged for use.

4. Elsie Freeman Frievogel, "Education Programs: Outreach as an Administrative Function," *American Archivist* 41 (April 1978): 148.

5. Of course, the organization might well make the decision to end the archives program and so raise a whole new set of issues and concerns. Should the organization work to find a home for its institutional archives in another archival repository? What sort of responsibilities does the organization have for finding such a home and for providing some kind of ongoing financial support? These and other questions have not been adequately studied by the archival community, nor have adequate models for such scenarios been worked out.

6. *Researching the History of Your Schools: Suggestions for Students and Teachers* (Albany: New York State Archives, 1985).

7. An excellent description of producing such programs is Nancy E. Malan, *Producing Professional Quality Slide Shows: A Systematic Approach*, Technical Report 2 (Nashville: American Association for State and Local History, 1985). This publication describes the initial planning, defining objectives, script writing, preparing slides, producing the sound track, and packaging it into a coherent show.

8. John Vernon and Richard E. Wood, "Baseball, Bubble Gum, and Business: The Making of an Archives Exhibit," *Prologue* 17 (Summer 1985): 79.

9. Gail Farr Casterline, *Archives & Manuscripts: Exhibits*, Basic Manual Series (Chicago: Society of American Archivists, 1980), 8.

10. Minda Borun, "Assessing the Impact," *Museum News* 68 (May/June 1989), 36.

11. Archivists have produced a number of useful audiovisuals. Although outdated, Timothy L. Ericson and Linda J. Ebben, comps., *Audiovisuals for Archivists* (Chicago: Society of American Archivists, 1985) provides a good directory to the range of such materials that are available.

12. The reason is that fund-raising is dependent on strong governing board support and effort in the process that ranges from self-study that leads to plans that identify funding priorities to soliciting the necessary funds from private sector sources. For an interesting recent essay on working to gain increased internal support, see Harley P. Holden, "Athens and Sparta: The Archivist and Resource Allocators," *Provenance* 5 (Fall 1987): 37–46.

13. *Planning for the Archival Profession: A Report of the SAA Task Force on Goals and Priorities* (Chicago: Society of American Archivists, 1986), 18.

14. David B. Gracy II, "Our Future Is Now," *American Archivist* 48 (Winter 1985): 12–21; and Gracy, "What's Your Totem? Archival Images in the Public Mind," *Midwestern Archivist* 10 (1985): 17–23.

15. Elsie T. Freeman, "In the Eye of the Beholder: Archives Administration from the User's Point of View," *American Archivist* 47 (Spring 1984): 111–23; William L. Joyce, "Archivists and Research Use," *American Archivist* 47 (Spring 1984): 124–33; Paul Conway, "Facts and Frameworks: An Approach to Studying the Users of Archives," *American Archivist* 49 (Fall 1986): 393–407; Bruce W. Dearstyne, "What is the *Use* of Archives? A Challenge for the Profession," *American Archivist* 50 (Winter 1987): 76–87; and David B. Gracy II, "Is There a Future in the Use of Archives?" *Archivaria* 24 (Summer 1987): 3–9.

16. Research in such indexes is even more problematic since such sources generally describe only larger foundations and funding sources that are generally unavailable to the majority of archival programs and are not easily indexed for effective use by archivists since there are so few grants for archival work.

17. Larry J. Hackman, "Toward the Year 2000," *Public Historian* 8 (Summer 1986): 95.

18. There is a vast literature on this subject, but the following publications will provide a good start: Thomas E. Broce, *Fund-raising: The Guide to Raising Money from Private Sources* (Norman: University of Oklahoma Press, 1979); Joan Flanagan, *The Grass Roots Fund-Raising Book* (Chicago: Contemporary Books, 1984); Mellon Bank Corporation, *Discover Total Resources* (Pittsburgh: Mellon Bank Corporation, 1986); Frank Setterberg and Kary Schulman, *Beyond Profit: The Complete Guide to Managing the Nonprofit Organization* (New York: Harper and Row, 1985); and Paul Schneiter, *The Art of Asking* (Amber, PA: Fund-Raising Institute, 1985). Individuals interested in additional publications on fund-raising should contact the Foundation Center, a nationwide organization headquartered in New York City, which also has many branch libraries throughout the country.

19. The necessity of carefully using the financial resources available to a historical records program is partly a factor of the immense resources needed for managing and preserving the materials of the documentary heritage. For a disturbing assessment of this fact, see Howard Lowell, *Preservation Needs in State Archives* (Albany: National Association of Government Archives and Records Administrators, February 1986).

20. For example, fund-raising experts note that individuals should be contacted for financial donations by individuals, governing board members, or persons associated with the repository who have made donations of amounts comparable to that being solicited. Such a principle rules out staff solicitation since staff will likely not have made such contributions and since their positions may be dependent on the outcome of the fund-raising campaign. The concept to be followed here is for peer-to-peer solicitation.

21. National foundations will be out of reach for the vast majority of archival programs except for those that might have archival holdings of national or international importance. Most repositories should concentrate on the potential financial resources within their community, resources that can considerably improve their operations since these monies have largely been untapped by the archival programs.

22. Case statements should always be prepared after initial contact with the targeted donor audience, although the repository should have identified its funding priorities and the purpose of its fund-raising effort. For example, if a repository is seeking funds from a number of businesses in its community, it might be surprised to learn how different are their requirements. Some may require only a simple letter, while others will expect some background information and detail about the expected use of the funds. Nevertheless, the structure of the case statement can be followed usefully in meeting these different needs.

23. This fact certainly indicates the importance of involvement by archival staff in the determination of the priorities of the fund-raising campaign and the content of the case statement.

24. See Virginia Stewart, "Transactions in Archival Consulting," *Midwestern Archivist* 10, no. 2 (1985): 107–15.

7

Cooperation and the Institutional Archives

In the first chapter of this volume the variegated landscape that characterizes the community of institutional archives was described. As was mentioned there, the common mission of these programs can sometimes be partly obscured by their diversity in structure, resources, conditions, and administrative placements. Their commonality in mission, however, as well as in their use of basic archival techniques and involvement in a variety of other matters (such as professional organizations and telecommunications networks), provides an opportunity for cooperation and coordination in a number of basic functions and activities. This opportunity is especially true for institutional archives serving similar kinds of organizations (such as corporate archives for high-technology firms or archival programs serving hospitals) and/or located in relatively close geographic proximity. Businesses, museums, religious organizations, or medical complexes, to name only a few institutional types, could find many ways in which to work together to develop institutional archives. The opportunities to work together are made even more possible since all of these kinds of organizations often concentrate in certain geographic areas (such as cities, suburbs surrounding cities, and industrial parks).

Cooperation offers some alternative prospects for institutional archives. Chapter 2 described in detail a number of essential elements that need to be in place for the reliable functioning, or—at the least—the starting point for the development of an institutional archives. As originally defined in

A View of Archival Cooperation

To the cynic, cooperation means getting everyone else to do what you want them to do. To the librarian, cooperation means sharing resources to avoid duplication of effort. To the archivist, cooperation means joining with others to figure out what to do next.

Archivists are raised professionally in the tradition of uniqueness. We invoke uniqueness as both rational for action and excuse for inaction, but we have made the mistake of extending the concept of the uniqueness of our records to a uniqueness in the techniques of managing them. We look on related disciplines . . . with xenophobic disdain, blinding ourselves to the possibilities of friendly assistance. Even worse, we often look with similar disdain on our colleagues in other archival institutions and object to the minor differences that separate us, rather than seeing possibilities in the major similarities that we share. The truth is that archivists face problems shared by many different institutions, from libraries to mail-order houses; and there is much that we could learn and use to our advantage.

Frank G. Burke, "Archival Cooperation," American Archivist 46 (Summer 1983): 294.

---

the second chapter, archival cooperation in this book is meant to include the involvement of two or more archival programs working together to achieve an improvement in the performance of their basic functions, either through consortia, cooperatives, and regional systems or through networks (multitype or other varieties) that are essentially telecommunications linkages enabling such things as descriptive data bases and communications systems.[1] Cooperative efforts are intended to lower costs, allow more effective use of existing resources, and improve services, although, as many librarians have commented upon, there are many stated reasons for, and opinions about, the nature of cooperation and networking.[2]

Without the basic support that the existence of such elements suggests, institutions would be better off seeking alternatives to the establishment of internal archival operations (such as entering into an agreement for another archival or historical records program to serve as repository for the institutional archives). That is, poorly supported and badly structured archival programs are not necessarily any better than not having archival programs at all. Cooperation is not merely a device that is situated halfway between running an internal program and entering into an agreement whereby an archival collecting program takes custody of the institution's records. Cooperation has tremendous potential for ensuring the protection of significant institutional archives, and, as well, every institutional archives should seek to be involved in some form of cooperative endeavors; these efforts are, or should be, the marks of well-managed archival operations. Institutional archivists must be aware, however, of cooperative ventures' strengths and weaknesses and be able to decide when their program should seek participation in such cooperative efforts.

Cooperation can start anywhere, but it is probably best commenced with after determining the institutional archives' mission. Chapter 2 provided a concise description of a mission statement, which sets forth a written expression of the nature, scope, functions, and rationale for existence. While the mission statement might not explicitly mention where cooperation should or could occur, it is true that a carefully thought through and crafted mission statement should provide implicit clues where cooperation might enhance the archives' operation. Along with other basic administrative documents, such as a strategic, long-range plan and an acquisition policy, cooperative activities need to be incorporated into the basic thinking about the effective administration of institutional archives. Indeed, a separate policy on cooperation might be a useful exercise for staff of an institutional archives to prepare and to utilize as a basis for discussion with its governing body and the administration of its parent agency. Possibilities for program enhancement may result, and a stronger institutional archives might be possible.

Even apart from such deliberate efforts to determine the prospects for cooperative endeavors, any institutional archives naturally—and by necessity—looks for efforts that are fundamentally collaborative. In the preparation of written procedures, for example, it has been noted that the archivist seeks to adopt and adapt existing archival standards and guidelines and remind the institutional archivist of his or her program's connection to the archival profession and community. This chapter describes the range of cooperative possibilities for the institutional archives, draws on the potential inherent in each major component of such a program, and considers (at certain key points) cooperative efforts in the related field of librarianship, a profession that has had some notable successes in cooperation and a much longer history of cooperative work.[3] Archivists' drawing on the library profession's notions of, and experience with, cooperation is not a new idea, this perspective being the cornerstone of one of the earliest classic essays on archival cooperation.[4]

The aspects considered for cooperation in this chapter are divided into two major components, the general management of institutional archives programs and the basic archival functions that constitute these programs. Cooperation in general administration (at least as described here) includes financial resources sharing (including the more creative use of shared facilities and the organizational merger of institutional archives as a "cooperative" device of last resort), staffing and the education and training of existing staff, the management of, and cooperation with, the parent agencies of institutional archives in a cooperative environment, the use of telecommunications systems for networking, and the potential of change wrought by cooperative efforts. Cooperation in the basic archival functions

A Rationale for Archival Cooperation:
A View from New York State

Despite notable exceptions, historical records programs overall in New York operate independently and in isolation from each other. Virtually all historical records programs are part of larger institutions - State government, local governments, libraries, historical agencies, or, in the case of institutional archives - churches, businesses, colleges and universities, and other organizations. Records programs, therefore, usually have developed primarily to serve only the immediate purposes of their parent institutions. Because of this narrowly conceived purpose and focus, and because of the absence of statewide leadership and coordination, historical records programs have developed with little concern for how their efforts relate and contribute to the broad purpose of preserving New York's documentary heritage. No systematic means have been developed for managers of historical records programs to meet and discuss common problems or to explore common solutions. Only a few cooperative programs have been developed, and these only on an *ad hoc* basis; formal networking arrangements have not received serious consideration. There also has been little discussion about how New York's relatively new State archival program and local government archival activities should relate to the thousands of nongovernmental historical records programs in the State. This continuing process of separate and independent development of historical records programs has been detrimental in several ways:

> A. . . . . historical records programs sometimes compete with or duplicate each other's efforts, while, at the same time, important topics are underdocumented because relatively few repositories happen to collect on those subjects.

> B. There has been a failure to recognize common historical records programming needs and to develop common approaches or solutions.

> C. There has been little recognition of the advantages to be gained by pooling and sharing resources to promote program development and accomplish goals that individual programs cannot achieve by themselves.

> D. Because of the plethora of programs, researchers may overlook documentation important for their work, or it may be difficult and confusing to pursue source material on a given topic or geographic area.

New York State Historical Records Advisory Board, Toward A Usable Past: Historical Records in the Empire State (Albany: The Board, January 1984), 58-59.

considered here is in archival appraisal, preservation, arrangement and description, reference and use, and public programs and outreach. These basic archival functions provide the most logical, and perhaps best, opportunities for cooperative endeavors among institutional archives. They lay, at the least, a suitable foundation for effective cooperation for institutional archives.

COOPERATION AND GENERAL ADMINISTRATION

Although the archivist's mission, in whatever institutional setting, has remained generally unchanged since the inception of the archival profession, ideas about how to meet that mission, as well as impediments to its successful completion, have been noticeably transformed. Prior to the 1960s, the archivist focused on his or her own institution, its mission, and its activities. In the 1960s and especially in the subsequent decade, many archivists became interested in cooperation between archival programs, primarily through the establishment and development of state or regional networks dedicated mainly to the collaborative acquisition of archival records.[5] During the 1980s, some archivists devoted considerable energy to pondering the potential for cooperation, such as state and national networks and consortia and even cooperation with other disciplines.[6] There has been, then, a progression of broadening interest and focus by the archivist from the institutional to multi-institutional to interdisciplinary and to state, national, and international arenas.

One fact is very clear, however: the archivist has not satisfactorily connected his or her ongoing and primary organizational interests, responsibilities, needs, and activities to the broader and more creative thinking that has characterized the discussion and much of the writing of the archival profession in the past decade. Although there have been perceptive essays on archival cooperation and likewise some stimulating banter about this at professional archival gatherings, there is little evidence that such a connection is commonly practiced, except in fairly limited ways, even though archivists have not been immune to the "necessity and goodness of cooperation."[7] Most archival administrators continue to manage their programs today much the same as they did in the 1940s or 1960s; word processors and online catalogs instead of typewriters and traditional card catalogs indicate that the archival operations are in the 1990s, but the malformed nature of cooperative activities suggests there is a long way to go—despite more optimistic predictions of one or two decades ago. This situation is especially true for institutional archivists, for whom cooperation has been less developed than in other segments of the archival community. In fact, whereas librarians' notions of cooperation have been transformed partly because they have been involved in such work for such a long time, the archivists' cooperative endeavors still are generally on the primitive

External Influences on Archival Cooperation

There are . . . a number of external forces that are generating a countervailing pressure. The first of these is the current economic crisis, which has diminished funding to such an extent that archivists, like many others, have been forced to reexamine both the basic hypotheses and the methods under which they operate. Indeed, archivists must begin to justify their very existence in the face of assertions that neither public nor private funding should be devoted to activities that do not produce an immediate economic return. They also confront a different kind of intellectual threat from those who would prefer to see only certain acceptable portions of our history documented, while at the same time they must meet the challenge of the new history and its omnivorous appetite for documentation. Finally, technological advances have confronted them with the terrifying challenge of shaping the record of our society by deliberate and conscious choices rather than leaving it to chance.

Any of these challenges should be enough to prompt a thorough reexamination of archival goals and priorities as well as methodology. Such a reexamination, however, will be successful only if archivists develop a different mind set and begin to think within a broader context than they have done heretofore. They need to be more analytical about the sources of the assumptions on which they operate and to understand better the nature of the conflict between the internal and external forces that drive them first in one direction and then in another. Moreover, they cannot do this in isolation. They must, therefore, begin consciously to forge links to other groups, disciplines, and professions in order to learn from them, to allow the others to participate in the process of redefinition upon which they are embarked, and to gain allies in confronting some of the challenges they face.

Margaret S. Child, "Reflections on Cooperation Among Professions," American Archivist 46 (Summer 1983): 287-88.

---

side. The potential for beneficial cooperation, however, even among institutional archives with responsibility primarily owed to their parent organizations, is very great. Engaging in cooperative endeavors is also essential to the well-being and viability of the institutional archives and the archival profession in the twenty-first century.

Cooperative Financial Resources Sharing

One of the most commonly cited rationales for cooperative ventures in the library and information professions is that these endeavors enable more to be done with less, although there continues to be heated debate about whether such activities reduce or increase costs to institutions. This debate has been especially evident in librarianship, a field increasingly seeking to reevaluate the costs benefits of library cooperation and re-examining the foundation of networks and other collaborative efforts. One librarian has stated that the reasons for participating in such efforts are to "enhance the quality of services," to support the notion that "sharing is good and working together seems to be the professionally right thing to do," and to "reduce their libraries' costs," while realizing that some types of cooperation may actually increase costs.[8] Another librarian has stated that cooperation in this profession is based upon beliefs that "(1) no library has the resources to satisfy all its patrons' needs, (2) library cooperative efforts will fill the gap between patron needs and resources, (3) a national library network built from the bottom up is a self evident good, and (4) libraries have a democratic responsibility to minimize the gap between the information rich and the information poor."[9] Similar statements could have easily been expressed by archivists.

Archivists have not, however, developed (in comparison to librarianship) an articulated set of premises supporting cooperative financial resources sharing, but there seem to be many opportunities for formulating such a set of premises. John Fleckner's 1976 seminal essay revealed the promise of cooperation evident in those years:

Cooperative arrangements at present engage but a small portion of the energies of American archivists. Yet the promises archivists face and the forces shaping their responses suggest that this situation will change. The problems are familiar: lack of storage space for ever larger collections, badly deteriorating holdings, constantly changing technologies, escalating user demands, inadequate budgets, and, above all, the responsibility not merely to accession the accidental accretions of time but thoughtfully to select from the universe of original documentation materials for permanent preservation.[10]

An institutional archives program may not operate effectively without adhering to good management principles that include cooperative efforts to make efficient use of financial and other resources. Financial benefits can range from relatively simple efforts, such as joint purchasing of supplies and equipment, to more complex initiatives, such as the temporary exchanging of staff between institutions for needed training, the completion of projects that necessitate specialized expertise, and the joint hiring of consultants for certain defined projects. Considering such efforts requires careful planning, experimentation, and learning, but the potential return from the efforts appears to be great. All of these activities can lead to improvements in the quality, not just speed of delivery, of some of the basic services of institutional archives, an observation similar to the sentiments revealed by some librarians.[11]

Institutional archivists, contemplating the prospects of cooperating with other archival programs or participating in existing library or related consortia and networks, need to consider a number of factors that possess financial implications. First, of course, the archivists should investigate matters such as the prospects for reliable, efficient, effective, and qualitative services that could be gained through cooperation. If a new cooperative venture or joining an existing group does not promise such services, costs become an inconsequential matter. Second, the archivist should carefully consider the actual costs involved and compare these costs to the present financial obligations of the archival program.[12] Some librarians have argued that the networks' shared cataloging actually adds costs, although other benefits might override any increased financial obligations.[13]

Institutional archivists should be especially alert for possibilities for reducing costs or using existing financial resources through multi-institutional and other forms of cooperation. Some of these possibilities include the following:

- Jointly hiring a consultant (or persuading one program to coordinate joint hiring) to help a group of institutional archives in a geographic area identify areas and plan for cooperative activity to lower costs, enable costs avoidance, and expend funds more efficiently and effectively

- Creating or working with already established, local consortia or networks that will allow the reduction of unit costs for standard archival supplies and materials

- Identifying major equipment, such as for microphotography or preservation work, that could be jointly purchased or leased and made more affordable to the archival community

- Identifying short-term projects, such as for the production of publicity materials or for the sharing of expertise for appraisal and other similar work, which could be effectively afforded only through cooperative efforts

There are, as well, two other more drastic cooperative devices for effective sharing of financial resources. Sharing facilities for storage, preservation, and access to archival and manuscript records is another important way in which to make better use of financial resources. It is also an old concept that has had some limited, but notable success. A half-century ago one pioneering archivist recommended that the federal and state governments should construct and manage together joint archival repositories, a proposal that has not been followed, and suggested a plan for regional centers for the placement of corporate and business records, another idea that has found few adherents.[14] Regional historical manuscript and archives collecting networks, already alluded to above, also have focused on the notion of shared storage facilities.

There is no reason (except for organizational resistance and lack of consensus) institutional archives in close geographic proximity to each other could not share facilities for the storage of, access to, and general administration of some or all of their archival records. Such sharing could reduce costs in the construction or renovation of such storage facilities, assist the institutions to gain optimal space for their archival programs, eliminate the problem of being forced to use less than adequate space within the organizational facilities, lessen dependence on commercial records storage space (except for such things as the storage of master negatives of microfilmed records), and create a higher public profile for the institutional archives. Problems such as staffing and the physical separation of the different archival records are within the realm of possibility of resolution, and the potential benefits should provide extra incentive for the resolution of any obstacles.

The organizational merger of certain institutional archives might seem to be a rather drastic, as well as administratively difficult, form of cooperative effort. Indeed, it has already been referred to as a cooperative effort of last resort in this chapter. The extreme use of merger might be appropriate when one archival program simply cannot be adequately sustained; as one archivist noted in the early 1980s, "For those archives that cannot afford an archivist, or any of the elements that would constitute a program, professional accountability requires all of us to urge that institution either to improve its care of its records or to deposit them in a repository that can appropriately manage them."[15] Following this kind of action in the realm of institutional archives, of course, suggests that the parent organizations may have ceased operation. There are, however, some precedents for other kinds of organizational mergers, as when a variety of adjoining local governments enter into mutually administered archival programs.[16] If this sort of cooperation can occur in the government realm, it should be able to be replicated in academic and other organizational settings.

Cooperative Staffing and Staff Education and Training in Institutional Archives

Archival experience and expertise are very important, even essential, to the success of any archival program. Institutional archives have at least two basic options open to them for acquiring such experience and expertise, besides the hiring of their own staffs. First, they could jointly hire professional staff. This option will work, of course, only if the archival programs are similar in scope and purpose and if they are located in the same geographic area. Library networks have done such joint hiring, in effect, through the staffing of network headquarters for such services as retrospective conversion of library collections and the quality control of original cataloging submitted by member libraries to local and national bibliographic utilities. Admittedly, this staffing role of library networks is easier to achieve than it would be for archival programs because of the more rigidly standardized nature of library cataloging. Institutional archives that are responsible for records possessing proprietary information or that administer documents with restricted access might, however, find it extremely difficult to achieve cooperative hiring for such purposes.

Second, and a better option for institutional archives, is the combining of the resources of a number of archival programs to support staff training in certain identified priority areas or to convince universities and colleges to offer needed courses on archival, records management, and related topics. Institutional archives could cosponsor workshops and institutes. They could also work with existing professional associations, such as local chapters of the Association of Records Managers and Administrators and local and regional professional archival associations, to develop viable continuing education programs for both professional and paraprofessional staff and volunteers. One primary focus of these educational efforts should be to enable institutional archivists and their staffs to remain current with professional archival standards and guidelines that will strengthen their work. Institutional archives searching for models to emulate in this regard would do well to consider local library consortia or regional library networks. These consortia often are the result of a number of libraries in a tightly defined geographic area banding together to create an opportunity for the library staffs to seek mutual exchanges of ideas and advice, as well as to conduct more formal continuing education opportunities.

Institutional archives, like other archival programs, can take advantage of a rich array of continuing education programs already offered by professional associations and universities and colleges. At the same time, institutional archives need to work to persuade these associations and organizations to be more creative in the ways in which they make available such education. For example, corporate archives might be able to utilize "distance learning" techniques (techniques that have been so far ignored in the archival community) to offer important education on matters such as access issues, appraisal of related records, and criteria for personnel in these kinds of programs.[17] Library cooperative efforts have even been shown to have had the greatest impact on training support staff in nonprofessional positions, and institutional archivists should keep such potential problems and challenges in mind.[18]

The Management of Institutional Archives, Cooperative Efforts, and Archival Parent Agencies

John Fleckner, in his perceptive and early description of archival cooperation, noted that "planning for cooperation must recognize that cooperative activity creates a new entity which, in various ways, changes the original cooperators."[19] Making this kind of cooperation among institutional archives potentially even more difficult (unless the organization is using the cooperative effort to foster internal change or is not afraid of change) is the fact that change is a possibility in organizations in which archivists often operate with different premises and in different cultures from those of their parent organizations. The difficulty of fostering a cooperative spirit in organizations in which there are different corporate cultures has been hinted at in the writings on library cooperation. Susan Martin noted, for example, that "there is a major cultural gap between the library world and the business world. Librarians . . . tend to operate by consensus, on a low-risk, lengthy time-frame basis. The business world, on the other hand, leaves decision making in the hands of a few, who are expected to take risks and who operate within a limited time frame. The former stresses a nearly perfect product, the other stresses the bottom line."[20]

Patricia Glass Schuman, looking at library networks, also suggested that these networks "create new and different workloads."[21] Michael Gorman, examining academic libraries in automated networks, has suggested that such networks will be successful in institutions that allow traditional hierarchical staffing patterns to be replaced by "an open structure of clusters of staff interacting with each other in a multidimensional and innovative manner."[22] Institutional archivists contemplating persuading their parent organizations to allow them to participate in external arrangements and activities with other archival programs or archival support groups must be aware of these kinds of consequences. Humanities-trained archivists laboring in a for-profit business environment might have some serious marketing of their own to do in persuading their organizations to allow the archival operations to participate in such cooperative activities.

Institutional archivists will also need to be able to explain to their parent organizations about the benefits of cooperative work. Librarians writing about library cooperation and networking have articulated a number of criteria needed to be considered before entering into such library activity. The possibilities for organizational independence, levels of support, decision-making processes, institutional influence on the network, representation on the governing board, and similar concerns all must be satisfactorily addressed.[23] Institutional archivists must also be able to explain the nature of archival cooperation as well as the specific provisions of each prospective venture.

Institutional archivists must also be sensitive to the organizational nature of their own institutions. Some librarians have tried to consider the insights of organization theorists and have noted how institutions react to change, innovation, external pressures, and the like.[24] This activity is, of course, worthwhile for each institutional archivist. Additionally, institutional archivists must work within organizations with diverse information and records management systems and, as well, with a diverse group of staff ranging from executive personnel to filing clerks, security staff, and housekeeping services. Consideration of cooperative efforts must take into account the impact of these efforts on each of these groups.

Telecommunications, Networking, and the Cooperation of Institutional Archives

Much of what happens in library cooperation has been established by the development and enhancement of telecommunications systems supporting the sharing of information about the holdings of libraries.[25] Archival programs have followed suit with similar bibliographic networks as well. This development has opened up the possibility, of course, for the participation of institutional archives in these networks (the benefits of which have been alluded to in chapter 4). Limiting this potential participation are both the notion of the internal limitations imposed by the archives' parent agency (such as restricted access to proprietary or confidential information found in the archival records) and the fact that the existing bibliographic networks have been dominated by organizations that share few characteristics with certain types of the institutional archives.[26]

It is especially important for institutional archivists to determine initially whether the demands on the archives merit their involvement in more sophisticated telecommunications services. Some librarians have questioned some of the assumptions of their profession in the benefits of developing and using more elaborate and speedy telecommunications networks to facilitate such basic services as interlibrary loan. Thomas Ballard has stated, for example, that "the world has 100,000 or 200,000 scientific periodicals, and no library can possibly have all of them. The only way to gain access to them is to arrange to borrow from some library that already owns them. Quite true, but first it is necessary to establish there is a demand for all of them." Ballard posited, instead, that other factors have a more significant impact on use and, as well, that interlibrary loan places an unfair burden on a small number of libraries.[27] Whether Ballard is right or not is not the point here, but the kinds of questions and issues that he posed ought to be considered by institutional archivists.

Institutional archivists should be in an excellent position to take advantage of cooperation offered because of advances in computerized telecommunications. Academic and corporate institutions are, for example, notoriously well connected to electronic communication and networking. Archivists tied to college and university libraries that are often already part of cooperative networks, for example, could take advantage of these relationships in a variety of ways; this fact is especially true since archivists have adopted a standard record format for bibliographic description. Even those archivists administering the records of other kinds of organizations and not already connected to networks and consortia could seek either to join existing groups or to form their own. After all, those networks that have been successful are those that have been able to subordinate differences to common interests and to "accommodate" the "diversity" of the various institutions involved.[28]

COOPERATION, BASIC ARCHIVAL FUNCTIONS, AND INSTITUTIONAL ARCHIVES

In the mid–1980s, the American Association for State and Local History completed a disturbing analysis of the condition of American historical institutions: "Historical agencies and museums [archival programs as well were included in this assessment] occupy a crucial position in American society. They are in the vanguard of collecting and preserving our cultural heritage, yet the majority are doing so without the money, people, and technical know-how they need. Because they lack adequate resources, the physical remains of America's past—documents and artifacts alike—are in peril."[29]

Institutional cooperation discussed in the initial part of this chapter was primarily focused on the financial sharing and staffing solutions to the money and people problems. The remainder of this chapter is concerned with the technical know-how that can be gathered by examining cooperative efforts in the basic archival functions. The various basic archival functions—appraisal, preservation, arrangement and description, reference and access, and public programs and outreach—are all susceptible to being enhanced by cooperative approaches. Indeed, over the past two decades or more, each archival function has been transformed (from its theoretical principles to practical applications) by holding it under the scrutiny of potential cooperation.

Cooperative Archival Appraisal

If limited financial and other resources have had an impact on the primary missions of librarians and archivists, the increasing complexity and quantity of information sources have had an equally significant impact on these professionals' attitudes and outlooks. There are some fundamental differences, of course, in the process of information selection as practiced by librarians (generally selecting publications available in multiple copies) and archivists (generally selecting from transactional documents that are usually unique) due to the nature of the materials they are responsible for analyzing and managing. Surprisingly, however, the cooperative principles enunciated by librarians (usually referred to as coordinated collection development) can provide some valuable insights for archivists and have been at least partially appropriated by archivists in "cooperative" appraisal concepts such as documentation strategies (introduced and described in chapter 4 of this volume). Institutional archivists, despite their necessary focus on their parent organizations, still have much to be gained from cooperative approaches to appraisal.

There is a vast literature on coordinated collection development in the library field. Coordinated collection development is the notion that two or more libraries can meet their collection needs and provide services to their users by agreeing to share in the definition, selection, and management of their holdings. As Paul Mosher, who has written extensively about this concept, has described it:

The goal is *collaboration*—working, laboring, together in new communities of enterprise which leap the walls of our local libraries—or [*sic*] even our large campus library complexes. Collaborative collection development requires communities of librarians who know their patrons and their programs well. It requires librarians who are active rather than static, less clerical and more professional than in the past. It requires librarians who are change agents rather than reagents—the agents of proactive change rather than the effects of it. It requires librarians who will manage library collections that are more program and client centered and less collection centered than in the past.[30]

Adherence to this notion has led to a number of initiatives, most notably (at least in terms of the amount of attention in the library literature) the Research Libraries Group's Conspectus, "a collection evaluation instrument to facilitate coordinated collecting activity," providing a "breakdown of subject fields in such a way as to allow distributed collection responsibilities for as many fields as possible."[31] The Conspectus tool consists of subject areas (based on the Library of Congress subject headings) and codes for six levels of subject strengths ranging from "out of scope" (not collecting at all) to "comprehensive" and language coverage.

Although library coordinated collection development, at least as typified by the decade-old conspectus effort and older multi-institutional collection development plans, has not been thoroughly analyzed for its effectiveness, a number of benefits have been cited that indicate a better selection process is at work because there is closer scrutiny of the collections, more careful planning, enhanced communication with subject experts and users, and improved tools for cooperative, multilibrary efforts.[32] The key to all of this is, of course, the cooperative perspective on collection management.

Archivists have been influenced in their appraisal work by some of the library cooperative collection concepts, both in appropriation of, and reaction to, these concepts. A decade ago, Jutta Reed-Scott introduced library coordinated collection management concepts directly to archivists and called for archivists to see if these approaches were applicable to this profession.[33] Other archivists, such as F. Gerald Ham, have incorporated these concepts into appraisal principles, suggested that "inter-institutional cooperation is an essential feature of a complex and interdependent technological society" as "our library allies know," and proceeded to consider a number of potential cooperative efforts, including "coordinated acquisition programs."[34] Other archivists have remained more skeptical. Max J. Evans has noted, for example, that he believed that it was impossible to develop a "single set of appraisal standards . . . generalized to fit the multifarious

The Nature of the Documentation of Science and Technology: A Role for Institutional Archives

To appraise effectively, archivists need to understand that the nature of the scientific and technological process and the complex patterns of communication and funding affect the existence and location of records. Scientists and engineers do not work in isolation; they rely on and communicate with networks of peers and administrators. They have internal communication with team members, staff, students, colleagues, administrators, and grants office personnel. They have external communication with colleagues, granting agencies or contractors, professional societies, and institutions hiring consultants. For archivists this complex environment of internal and external associations requires comprehension of a universe of interconnected documentation. Archivists need to realize that records received from individuals or found in laboratories are only part of the records documenting the individual, project, or laboratory. An awareness of the complexities of communication patterns, and administrative and funding activities, will enable archivists to understand the records they are appraising, the location of records that should be sought in other locations and added to the collection, and the location of records that need to be considered in the appraisal process but are not to be added to the collection.

Joan K. Haas, Helen Willa Samuels, and Barbara Trippel Simmons, Appraising the Records of Modern Science and Technology: A Guide (Cambridge: Massachusetts Institute of Technology, 1985), 23.

---

needs of hundreds of archival institutions," but it was nevertheless important to share information (and to develop mechanisms for exchanging such information) about appraisal decisions regarding similar or related records.[35] Others have seen the basic merits of cooperative efforts. Sometimes cooperative appraisal and documentation work has been described as being as simple as two or more institutions' deciding to work together because of mutual concerns and interests. An interest in documenting Dallas political history brought two Dallas-based archival programs together for an oral history project because they "decided that through joint participation more people could be interviewed, more tapes and transcripts could be processed, and Dallas history could be explored in greater depth."[36] The involvement of Dallas institutional archival programs, representing important players in this city's political events and development, could also have been a logical step in achieving such documentation.

Obviously, there are a number of potential cooperative appraisal activities for institutional archivists. Such archivists must attend first, of course, to their own organization's requirements. Archivist Evans was also generally correct when he stated that "each institution must develop its own appraisal methods and standards based on its own corporate culture."[37]

What should be added to this statement is that each institution must be fully aware of archival appraisal theory and when to seek involvement in cooperative appraisal activities. The institutional archivist could seek to cooperate in appraisal in at least two ways. First, this archivist should be involved in sharing appraisal decisions, reports, and related materials with other institutional archives that may possess similar or related kinds of records. Second, the institutional archivist should be working with other archival programs, historians and other researchers, and other records-creating institutions to develop appraisal strategies in topical or geographic areas related to the institutional archives. The end result of such work should be the improved appraisal knowledge of the institutional archivist and, consequently, better appraisal decisions regarding the institution's records and strengthened documentation of the institution.[38]

Cooperative Archival Preservation

The preservation of library materials is an area that has recently (in comparison to other cooperative efforts) motivated librarians to unite to seek solutions through new methodologies as well as political advocacy and collaboration with other disciplines. As Dan C. Hazen has recently written, "Preservation is in style," revealing its status as a "growth sector" in the library profession.[39] More than any other area, in fact, preservation has stimulated solutions to be developed that are appropriate and even necessary for multi-institutional, regional, and national collaboration.[40] This cooperative role in the preservation function at least partly emanates from the fact that even within a single institution the individual responsible for this must have authority across institutional boundaries.[41] Moreover, there has been a longer interest in cooperative solutions to conservation and preservation problems. Such cooperative efforts, starting with coop-erative preservation microfilming projects, have been in existence for half a century.[42] Ross Atkinson, for example, has argued that preservation decisions must not only be made in "consultation" with collection staff but, in certain areas, be coordinated among many libraries.[43] Some existing library networks have incorporated preservation into their operations as essential aspects of service to their libraries and, in some cases, have even extended their operations to archival and museum programs.[44] If anything, the nature of the national, cooperative focus on the preservation of library materials has led to a tension between local and national preservation problems; one commentator on this issue has written:

As the national brittle book program evolves, libraries and their primary users will have to balance local and national priorities. If the program is to succeed, libraries with significant subject collections will be obligated to preserve those materials for the rest of the library community. Since full funding is unlikely to be available for national program participants, library staff will need to work hard to convince local users and budget administrators of the long-term local benefit of this approach.[45]

Still, there is a strong consensus that the preservation issue is a matter that must be tackled by libraries working together.

The archival profession has adopted, as well, a broad perspective in dealing with preservation problems. Some of the assumptions adopted by the Canadian Council of Archives reflect his approach: "Archivists and conservators must jointly come to understand the physical state and environment of the collection as a whole, and both must be less dogmatic"; "the setting of priorities, and solutions to other similar problems, should be arrived at consensually, based on archival appraisal criteria"; and "conservation problems have a commonality across large and small archives."[46]

After two or more decades of struggling to establish viable mechanisms for providing effective preservation actions, archivists have linked themselves into library networks, consortia, and other cooperative efforts for this purpose. One of the "operating principles" of the New York State conservation/preservation program emphasized this kind of perspective:

Within New York, preservation programs should be developed on a regional basis. Preservation services and conservation facilities in New York should be located convenient to repositories in all regions of the State and widely shared, thereby encouraging the use of existing regional service systems, promoting effective cooperation among institutions, and building programs and services that are close to those served and responsive to their needs.[47]

Such a regionally oriented, cooperative approach is intended to provide services to a wide range of archival and research materials repositories, including institutional archives.

The institutional archivist will realize, of course, that he or she has the opportunity to resolve some of the institution's preservation problems through cooperation. Some of the preservation approaches recommended for the use of the institutional archivist in chapter 4 of this volume are naturally cooperative. The use of established regional conservation centers, like the Northeast Document Conservation Center, or micrographics service vendors, like the Mid-Atlantic Preservation Service, is an essential step that every institutional archives needs to take in protecting its holdings. Preparing viable disaster preparedness plans is even more fundamentally cooperative. The preparation and execution of such a plan require the participation and coordination of a variety of archives, libraries, and mu-

An Example of Institutional Cooperation in
Archival Preservation

The local history archival collections of both the Baldwinsville Public Library and the Museum at the Shacksboro Schoolhouse will be receiving professional attention this year [1988].

Under the terms of a grant from the N[ew] Y[ork] S[tate] Conservation/Preservation Discretionary Grant Program, the institutions have hired recognized paper conservator Ellen Riggs Tillapaugh from Cooperstown. Tillapaugh has reviewed the organization's collections and is preparing a recommended program for storage, use, and conservation of the materials.

A graduate of Skidmore College, Tillapaugh has received specialized training in museum studies at the Cooperstown Graduate Program, State University at Buffalo, and the State University at Albany. Tillapaugh resides in Cooperstown where she has established a private conservation practice which specializes in paper and textiles. Her clients include private individuals as well as museums throughout the Northeast.

Local items included in Tillapaugh's survey included photographs, rare local history books, a sketchbook by Dr. Beauchamp, and handwritten documents, including a collection of early Baldwinsville deeds and bills of sale. The materials included in the survey were all deemed to be locally significant. Most of the items were also unique, or one of a very limited number of copies.

The Baldwinsville grant is one of only 47 awarded under this program for 1988/89. This program is designed to encourage the conservation and preservation of unique archival materials throughout the state. Consideration is given to the significance of the materials, the accessibility of the materials to the public and the level of the institution's commitment to preservation. Baldwinsville's application was ranked in the top 30% of all the applications which were received.

From Baldwinsville Messenger, Summer 1988, quoted in The New York State Program for the Conservation and Preservation of Library Research Materials: Selected Press Clippings About Projects Funded by the Discretionary Grant Program 1988/89 and 1989/90 (Albany: New York State Library, 1990), 3.

---

seums as well as service agencies, the fire and police departments, materials suppliers, and industries.

Institutional archivists could also take other cooperative actions for the preservation of their records. They could work with other archivists and archival programs to hire jointly a conservator or a preservation management consultant, develop state-of-the-art archival storage facilities, cooperatively buy archival storage supplies, and cooperatively buy or lease equipment for certain kinds of preservation work (such as microfilming). The extent to which an institutional archives will participate in such cooperative preservation activities depends on the extent of the institution's preservation needs, resources for preservation, and availability of other archives and preservation programs in the same geographic vicinity for mutual support.

Archival Arrangement, Description, and Reference and the Cooperative Perspective

Automated library cataloging and the increasing capability of telecommunications systems technology have been the primary catalysts for library cooperation and networking. In fact it has been pointed out that "utmost in the minds of the pioneers of the cooperative movement was bibliographical description," with "resource sharing" being an "offshoot" of this objective.[48] Even though the development of computer technology has promised the return to less centralized, local library systems, the increasingly more sophisticated online and commercial systems are altering the ways in which libraries supply information to their patrons.[49] Just as nationally and regionally focused library preservation schemes have presented some major issues for local needs and decisions, cataloging and online information networks have posed dilemmas for the local libraries.[50] The resolution of these issues, however, may only lead to different kinds of networks and improved access by patrons to library resources.

Automated bibliographic systems have also had a significant impact on the archival community in terms of its cooperative efforts. It has provided an opportunity for archivists to support improved access to researchers. The New York State Archives and Records Administration's efforts to create a statewide data base to archival records were commenced because "there is a burgeoning need for efficient and effective access to a wide range of information contained in New York's historically valuable records as well as in certain current records administered by its governments."[51] As the state archives' brochure on the statewide network pointed out, achieving such a data base and seeing that it is effectively used require the cooperation of many institutions and professions. The increasing emphasis by archivists on automated systems for description has led to a new interest in standards and, as well, a greater understanding of the need for cooperation since cooperation is at the heart of the standards process. This interest has come, partly at least, from failures by archivists initially to incorporate agreements on standards in their early automated efforts.[52] As the Working Group on Archival Descriptive Standards has stated, descriptive work requires standards, the "successful development and implementation of standards require cooperation and collaboration among all affected parties," and "cooperative efforts usually require consensus on standard practices or procedures."[53]

There are, of course, some fundamental differences between what libraries and archives can do and what they want to do in providing reference to their holdings. "Libraries must depend significantly," it has been noted, "upon effective access to a large universe of resources."[54] Archives are

Cooperation and Archival User Studies

A general framework for understanding users can serve as an agenda for talking about the archival profession's progress toward the goal of user responsive programs and services. But at some point the talk must take a back seat to cooperative study projects. Perhaps the classroom is an appropriate place to begin building a research tradition. Elsie Freeman has suggested that archival education should include training in survey research techniques. Archival educators might consider transforming the practicum portion of a two-course sequence into a laboratory for teams of students to design, carry out, and evaluate archival research projects, including user studies.

Knowledge from user studies will have value beyond single repositories only if widely shared. Mechanisms for a cooperative effort need to be developed and supported. At the very least, an archival clearinghouse . . . should be prepared to actively gather, evaluate, and disseminate the results of user studies. A proactive clearinghouse can serve the same broad functions for archives that the perceptive critics of user studies served for libraries - to discover patterns in isolated studies, encourage further research, and develop strategies for integrating research findings into standards of practice.

Paul Conway, "Facts and Frameworks: An Approach to Studying the Users of Archives," American Archivist 49 (Fall 1986): 409.

---

fundamentally distinct, providing access to holdings that are unique in nature. Nevertheless, the interrelatedness of even "unique" archival records has become more evident to archivists in recent years, mostly in appraisal work but also in how archivists have come to change their perspective about the manner in which researchers want access to archival sources. Archivist Avra Michelson has pointed out some of these basic differences well:

First, archival records describe heterogeneous collections that require many more index terms than those used to describe monographs. The average number of index terms assigned to records by the [archival] survey respondents was thirteen; the average number assigned to books by the Library of Congress is 3. . . . Second, archival material is complicated by less adequate authority control and the tendency toward less convergence of terms because archival cataloging is primarily original and seldom derivative. . . . Third, the expectations of library and archival users differ, which creates conflicting demands on the system. The retrieval of *some* relevant citations . . . normally satisfies most library patrons. Scholars using primary source materials, however, are more likely to expect an exhaustive listing of the relevant collections.[55]

Despite these differences, however, the adoption and adaption of library bibliographic practices and standards have proven useful to the archivist.[56]

Even historians have been forced to appreciate the necessity of library science approaches, used in tandem with the way other disciplines conduct research, for being able to support automated retrieval of the records.[57]

Institutional archivists will find many opportunities to cooperate in arrangement, description, and reference functions. In chapter 5, institutional archivists were advised about the merits of participating in national bibliographic organizations such as the Research Libraries Group (RLG) and the Online Computer Library Catalog (OCLC), but there are a number of other, easier ways to carry out such cooperative arrangement and descriptive activities. Institutional archives could exchange existing finding aids to their holdings with other institutional archives and archival repositories either in the same geographic region or with programs that have similar purposes and research clientele. Institutional archives could jointly prepare and publish finding aids, hold workshops and public programs for potential researchers, and even hire professional staff for undertaking special and needed arrangement and description projects. Institutional archivists could also work with other archivists to study researcher trends and to exchange examples of significant internal uses of institutional archives in order to build general arguments for the benefits of the archival programs. Such relatively simple actions could lead to more complex cooperative agreements later on.

Public Programs, Outreach, and Advocacy and the Cooperation of Institutional Archives

H. G. Jones, in reviewing past efforts to build archival programs, once remarked that "your greatest contribution as an archivist may not be the quantity and quality of the work that you accomplish in the archives; rather, it may be the degree to which you are successful in persuading the public— and particularly public officials—of the essentiality of your work in a civilized society."[58] Jones's statement concerns the archivist's involvement with both public programs (reaching out to communicate about the nature and importance of archives with the general public or specifically defined aspects of the public) and advocacy (working to effect change and win support for archives from policy setting bodies). This concept is not foreign to librarianship.

Librarians have developed a strong appreciation for public programs and advocacy efforts. This profession's concept of public programs is very similar to that practiced by archivists and ranges from the production of publicity materials such as newsletters and brochures through efforts such as public forums and lectures.[59] Not surprisingly, there have been a number of statements regarding the value of cooperative action in library programming, suggesting activity from the local to the national levels.[60] More impressive have been the library profession's concerted efforts to advocate greater public support in terms of both financial aid and policy. Most impressive has been the history of the Library Services and Construction Act (LSCA), a federally funded program that has supplied billions of dollars to library services and dramatically changed the nature of the profession and its institutions.[61] The success of this program has been the ability of the library profession to lobby effectively on its behalf.

Like the other basic functions described in this chapter, institutional archives have much to gain from working together in public programming and advocacy. In terms of public programs, institutional archives can work with other archival programs to develop and offer exhibitions, publications, publicity efforts, lecture series, audiovisual productions, and other products that convey to the public why it should be interested in archival programs. Since all archival programs share certain common elements in their operation and purpose, such cooperative efforts make considerable sense. Advocacy, even more than public programs, is most effective as a cooperative effort. A group of archival programs, united in common cause, can monitor legislation that might affect the documentary heritage, lobby for legislation that better supports this, unite in letter-writing campaigns to policymakers and government leaders, and pool resources to support such advocacy. Archival programs that are united will have a much more pronounced profile than if they operate unilaterally. One of the reasons the movement to gain political independence for the National Archives succeeded is the "diversity" of the coalition that formed to work for it.[62]

CONCLUSION

One of the issues that makes interinstitutional cooperation and networking difficult is that the nature and concepts of institutions are changing. Susan Martin, looking at this concern in library networking, described networking's context as a "chaotic and anarchistic information society," which means that "library networks are being embedded and overlooked in a confusion of options, possibilities, and developments."[63] Or, as has also been hinted at in this chapter, the "political and technological factors have militated for a more decentralized mode of networking," indicating that societal and other factors are having an impact on the very notion of library cooperation.[64] All of these trends have not been foreseen by librarians (or, for that matter, archivists). Harold Billings summarized this problem when he wrote the following: "The initial efforts of libraries and librarians in network development were very much ones of organization building. Large amounts of individual effort, institutional resources, and personal pride and commitment went into the work of getting library networks created. Little attention, however, was given to providing for the inevitable changing of organizations or for their eventual dissolution."[65]

As has been already suggested, cooperation itself brings change to the institution.

The archival mission at the end of the twentieth century remains the same as it was in the early years of the century and the profession. What is changing, however, is what the archival programs look like—how they fit together, how they work together, how many there are, how archivists evaluate them, how their futures are assessed, what they do and so forth. The reasons that archivists articulate for wanting to strengthen their institutions need to be transformed as well because the society and institutions they serve and document are rapidly changing, presenting new challenges, and exhibiting new needs. These challenges are the topic of the next chapter.

NOTES

1. The concepts of cooperatives and networks are based on library cooperation. See, for example, R. T. Sweeney, "Financial Impacts of Networking and Resource Sharing," *Public Library Quarterly* 2 (Fall/Winter 1981): 91.

2. S. T. Dowd, "Library Cooperation: Methods, Models to Aid Information Access," *Journal of Library Administration* 12, no. 3 (1990): 63–81 has suggested there are four types of cooperation: the expansion of the range of scholarly resources, reduction of material costs, improvement of library clients' access to information sources, and the decrease in costs of collection maintenance. Many of the other library writings on cooperation cited in this chapter pose different forms, explanations, and definitions of library cooperation.

3. For some essays on the evolution of library cooperation, refer to Robert R. McClarren, "Public Library Cooperation and Cooperatives: An Historical Overview," *Public Library Quarterly* 2 (Fall/Winter 1981): 5–16; Henriette D. Avram, "Current Issues in Networking," *Journal of Academic Librarianship* 12 (September 1986): 205–9; and David C. Weber, "A Century of Cooperative Programs Among Academic Libraries," *College & Research Libraries* 37 (May 1976): 205–21.

4. John A. Fleckner, "Cooperation as a Strategy for Archival Institutions," *American Archivist* 39 (October 1976): 447–59. The first five pages of this essay summarize and evaluate the library profession's experience with cooperation to the mid–1970s, concluding with the following assessment:

Archivists, laboring in a closely related field, often with strong institutional ties to libraries, have much to learn from this experience [with cooperation]. The fundamental fact, of course, is that cooperation can succeed; that through cooperative means institutional barriers to achieving mutual goals can be breeched; that existing institutional structures, so much the accidents of history, need not entirely shape our professional world. A second lesson from the library experience is that cooperation develops at its own pace, building on previous successful endeavors, on changing technologies, on changed perceptions of the way one's professional world might be ordered, and on capable leadership and skillful management. Third, we can learn something of the limits of cooperation, which is neither an end in itself nor a substitute for strong basic programs underwritten with adequate funds. Finally, library experiences provide us with a wealth of practical information, much of it in published form (450–51).

See also Frank G. Burke, "Archival Cooperation," *American Archivist* 46 (Summer 1983): 293–305 for another important assessment of archival cooperation.

5. Fleckner, "Cooperation as a Strategy," 452–55; James E. Fogerty, "Four New Regional Networks: A Progress Report," *Midwestern Archivist* 1, no. 1 (1976): 43–52; and Richard A. Cameron, Timothy Ericson, and Anne R. Kenney, "Archival Cooperation: A Critical Look at Statewide Archival Networks," *American Archivist* 46 (Fall 1983): 414–32 provide a good introduction to the nature and development of these archival networks.

6. For a description of the archival profession's development in the 1980s, refer to Richard J. Cox's *American Archival Analysis: The Recent Development of the Archival Profession in the United States* (Metuchen, NJ: Scarecrow Press, 1990).

7. Fleckner, "Cooperation as a Strategy," 451.

8. D. B. Simpson, "Library Consortia and Access to Information: Costs and Cost Justification," *Journal of Library Administration* 12, no. 3 (1990): 86–87.

9. C. B. Lowry, "Resource-Sharing or Cost Shifting?—The Unequal Burden of Cooperative Cataloging and ILL in Network," *College & Research Libraries* 51 (January 1990): 13.

10. Fleckner, "Cooperation as a Strategy," 457.

11. Linda G. Bills, "Cost and Benefits of OCLC Use in Small and Medium Size Public Libraries," *Resource Sharing and Information Networks* 3 (Spring/Summer 1986): 9-34. As Bills concluded, "Access to additional [information] resources was generally valued more than speed in acquiring those resources" (33).

12. James G. Williams, "Performance Criteria and Evaluation for a Library Resource Sharing Network," in *Library Resource Sharing*, ed. Allen Kent and Thomas J. Galvin (New York: Marcel Dekker, 1977), 225–77, and Martin M. Cummings, *The Economics of Research Libraries* (Washington, DC: Council on Library Resources, Inc., 1986), chap. 3.

13. Patricia Glass Schuman, "The Impact of Networks on the Profession," *New Zealand Libraries* 45 (December 1986): 69–73 considers cost savings as one of the myths of networks. On the other hand, Thomas Childers, "Do Library Systems Make a Difference?" *Library and Information Science Research* 10, no. 4 (1988): 445–54 contends that libraries participating in public library systems have few negative implications and, as well, gain additional resources.

14. Oliver W. Holmes, "The Problem of Federal Field Office Records," *American Archivist* 6 (April 1943): 95–96, and "The Evaluation and Preservation of Business Archives," *American Archivist* 1 (October 1938): 181.

15. William L. Joyce, "Consultant's Report: Historical Records Repositories," in *Documenting America: Assessing the Condition of Historical Records in the States*, ed. Lisa B. Weber (n.p.: National Association of State Archives and Records Administrators in cooperation with the National Historical Publications and Records Commission, 1984), 44.

16. Robert W. Arnold III, "The Albany Answer: Pragmatic and Tactical Considerations in Local Records Legislative Efforts," *American Archivist* 51 (Fall 1988): 475–79.

17. Isabelle Bruder, "Distance Learning: What's Holding Back This Boundless Delivery System?" *Electronic Learning* 8 (April 1989): 30–35.

18. Schuman, "Impact," 70.

19. Fleckner, "Cooperation as a Strategy," 456.

20. Chris Sugnet, ed., "Networking in Transition: Current and Future Issues," *Library Hi Tech* 6, no. 4 (1988): 103.

21. Schuman, "Impact," 70.

22. Michael Gorman, "The Organization of Academic Libraries in the Light of Automation," in *Advances in Library Automation and Networking: A Research Annual*, ed. Joe A. Hewitt (Greenwich, CT: JAI Press, 1987), 161.

23. For examples of these kinds of assessments refer to Susan P. Besemer, "Criteria for the Evaluation of Library Networks," *Resource Sharing and Information Networks* 4, no. 1 (1987): 17–38; Louella V. Wetherbee, "Employer Expectations: The View from One Network (AMIGOS)," *Journal of Library Administration* 11, nos. 3/4 (1990): 197–210; Beth Paskoff, "Networks and Networking: How and Why Should Special Libraries Be Involved?" *Special Libraries* 80 (Spring 1989): 94–100; and Thomas W. Shaughnessy, "Management Perspectives on Network Membership," *Journal of Library Administration* 8 (Fall/Winter 1987): 7–14. For the kind of needed research on the importance and nature of the organization of networks, see Betty J. Turock, "Organization Factors in Multitype Library Networking: A National Test of the Model," *Library and Information Science Research* 8 (1986): 117–54.

24. JoAn S. Segal, "Library and Information Networks: Centralization and Decentralization," *Information Services & Use* 8, no. 1 (1988): 9.

25. Steven A. Brown, "Telefacsimile in Libraries: New Deal in the 1980s," *Library Trends* 37 (Winter 1989): 343–56 provides a view of one aspect of the telecommunications world.

26. See, for example, Linda Hill, "Issues in Network Participation for Corporate Libraries," *Special Libraries* 76 (Winter 1985): 2–10.

27. Thomas Ballard, *The Failure of Resource Sharing in Public Libraries and Alternative Strategies for Services* (Chicago: American Library Association, 1986), 33.

28. See the existing case study by G. D. Byrd et al., "The Evolution of a Cooperative Online Network," *Library Journal* (February 1, 1985): 71–77.

29. Charles Phillips and Patricia Hogan, *A Culture at Risk: Who Cares for America's Heritage?* (Nashville: American Association for State and Local History, 1984), 82.

30. Paul Mosher, "A National Scheme for Collaboration in Collection Development: The RLG-NCIP Effort," in *Coordinating Cooperative Collection Development: A National Perspective*, ed. Wilson Luquire (New York: Haworth Press, 1986), 26.

31. Nancy E. Gwinn and Paul H. Mosher, "Coordinating Collection Development: The RLG Conspectus," *College & Research Libraries* 44 (March 1983): 129.

32. For some of the description of the benefits of this approach, refer to David Farrell and Jutta Reed-Scott, "The North American Collections Inventory Project: Implications for the Future of Coordinated Management of Research Collections," *Library Resources & Technical Services* 33 (January 1989): 15–28; Bonnie MacEwan, "The North American Inventory Project: A Tool for Selection, Education and Communication," *Library Acquisitions: Practice & Theory* 13 (1989): 45–50; David Farrell, "The North American Collections Inventory Project (NCIP): 1984 Phase II Results in Indiana," in *Coordinating Cooperative Collection Development*, ed. Luquire, 37–48; and David Farrell, "The NCIP Option for Coordinated Collection Management," *Library Resources & Technical Services* 30 (January/March 1986): 47–56. There have also been efforts to refine the conspectus as a collection analysis tool, such as in Beth M. Paskoff and Anna H. Perrault, "A Tool for Comparative Collection Analysis: Conducting a Shelflist Sample to Construct a Collection Profile," *Library Resources and Technical Services* 34, no. 2 (1990): 199–

215. There is other writing about coordinated collection development beyond the Conspectus, but the institutional archivist will be well served by starting with the Conspectus literature.

33. Jutta Reed-Scott, "Collection Management Strategies for Archivists," *American Archivist* 47 (Winter 1984): 27–29.

34. F. Gerald Ham, "Archival Strategies for the Post Custodial Era," *American Archivist* 44 (Summer 1981): 211–12.

35. Max J. Evans, "The Visible Hand: Creating a Practical Mechanism for Cooperative Appraisal," *Midwestern Archivist* 11, no. 1 (1986): 7–8.

36. Alan S. Mason and Gerald S. Saxon, "The Dallas Mayors Oral History and Records Project: A Program of Institutional Cooperation," *American Archivist* 45 (Fall 1982): 472–73.

37. Evans, "Visible Hand," 7.

38. The work on the appraisal of modern science and technology provides insight into the notion of cooperative appraisal and institutional archives. See Clark A. Elliott, ed., *Understanding Progress as Process: Documentation of the History of Post-War Science and Technology in the United States* (Chicago: Society of American Archivists, 1983) and Joan K. Haas, Helen Willa Samuels, and Barbara Trippel Simmons, *Appraising the Records of Modern Science and Technology: A Guide* (Cambridge: Massachusetts Institute of Technology Press, 1985).

39. Dan C. Hazen, "Preservation in Poverty and Plenty: Policy Issues for the 1990s," *Journal of Academic Librarianship* 15 (January 1990): 344.

40. For the historical context, refer to Pamela W. Darling and Sherelyn Ogden, "From Problems Perceived to Programs in Practice: The Preservation of Library Resources in the U.S.A, 1956–1980," *Library Resources & Technical Services* 35 (January/March 1981): 9–29.

41. John Dean, "Conservation Officers: The Administrative Role," *Wilson Library Bulletin* 57 (October 1982): 128–32.

42. Nancy E. Gwinn, "The Rise and Fall and Rise of Cooperative Projects," *Library Resources & Technical Services* 29 (January/March 1985): 80–86.

43. Ross Atkinson, "Selection for Preservation: A Materialistic Approach," *Library Resources & Technical Services* 30 (October/December 1986): 341–53. See also his "Preservation and Collection Development: Toward a Political Synthesis," *Journal of Academic Librarianship* 16 (May 1990): 98–103.

44. Lisa Fox, "The SOLINET Preservation Program: Building a Preservation Network in the Southeast," *New Library Scene* 7 (August 1988): 1, 5–9.

45. Margaret M. Byrnes, "Preservation and Collection Management: Some Common Concerns," *Collection Building* 9, nos. 3–4 (1990): 41.

46. "Strategies for the Future: The Preservation of Archival Materials in Canada," *Conservation Administration News* 29 (April 1987): 2.

47. New York Document Conservation Advisory Council, *Our Memory at Risk: Preserving New York's Unique Research Resources* (Albany: The Council, 1988), 29.

48. Joel S. Rustein, "National and Local Resource Sharing: Issues in Cooperative Collection Development," *Collection Management* 7 (Summer 1985): 2.

49. See Richard De Gennaro, "Library Automation & Networking: Perspectives on Three Decades," *Library Journal* 108 (April 1, 1983): 629–35.

50. Such sentiments have been presented by librarians like Michael Gorman, "Think-

ing the Thinkable: A Synergetic Profession," *American Libraries* 13 (July/August 1982): 473–74.

51. *A Statewide Archives and Records Database and Services: Background and Issues* (Albany: New York State Archives and Records Administration, 1989), 3.

52. The most dramatic illustration of this failure is in Avra Michelson, "Description and Reference in the Age of Automation," *American Archivist* 50 (Spring 1987): 192–208.

53. "Report of the Working Group on Standards for Archival Description," *American Archivist* 52 (Fall 1989): 451–52.

54. Donald E. Riggs, "Networking and Institutional Planning," *Journal of Library Administration* 8 (Fall/Winter 1987): 64.

55. Avra Michelson, "Description and Reference," 199.

56. See, for example, Lisa B. Weber, "Archival Description Standards: Concepts, Principles, and Methodologies," *American Archivist* 52 (Fall 1989): 504–13.

57. Chad Gaffield and Peter Baskerville, "The Automated Archivist: Interdisciplinarity and the Process of Historical Research," *Social Science History* 9 (Spring 1985): 167–184.

58. H. G. Jones, "The Pink Elephant Revisited," *American Archivist* 43 (Fall 1980): 483.

59. There are a large number of basic primers on library public relations, but a convenient way of gaining a sense of the librarian's perspective on this area is to look at Greta Renborg, "Library Public Relations," in *Encyclopedia of Library and Information Science*, ed. Allen Kent (New York: Marcel Dekker, 1984), vol. 37, supplement 2, 234–65.

60. See, for example, *Public Relations for Librarians*, 2d rev. ed. (Hampshire, England: Gower, 1982), chap. 5.

61. Edward G. Holley and Robert F. Schremser, *The Library Services and Construction Act: An Historical Overview from the Viewpoint of Major Participants*, Foundations in Library and Information Science, vol. 18 (Greenwich, CT: JAI Press, 1983) and Redmond Kathleen Molz, *Federal Policy and Library Support* (Cambridge: MIT Press, 1976) provide a good background on the importance and influence of library advocacy and the LSCA. For a counterview see David Shavit, *Federal Aid and State Library Agencies: Federal Policy Implementation* (Westport, CT: Greenwood Press, 1985).

62. Page Putnam Miller, "Archival Issues and Problems: The Central Role of Advocacy," *Public Historian* 8 (Summer 1986): 60-73.

63. Sugnet, "Networking in Transition," 103.

64. Segal, "Library and Information Networks," 3.

65. Harold Billings, "Governing Library Networks: The Quick and the Dead for the 1990s," *Library Journal* 114 (November 1, 1989): 49–54.

8

The Changing Contexts of Institutional Archives: Some Speculations

This volume has focused on the administration of institutional archives and primarily emphasized the appropriate foundational principles and practices. The stress on such principles and practices is both to make this book manageable in scope and to identify that there are such basic and pragmatic precepts in the daily operation of institutional archives. But archivists and their supervisors working in this environment need to realize that the contexts of these programs are constantly changing, with obvious (and numerous) implications for the administration of institutional archives. The purpose of this chapter is to introduce readers to some of these changes.

The first, more lengthy part of this chapter considers such changes in the way that the archival profession is redefining the nature of all archival institutions; this portion speculates on future directions and the specific implications for institutional archives. The second portion of this chapter ponders how information technology is possibly transforming the organization; such a transformation raises some serious challenges for the institutional archivist and the success of his or her program. It is deliberately more brief and speculative since the nature of the technological change is so rapid and since, therefore, the implications are both much greater and more difficult to pinpoint in any precise detail. It is, indeed, the subject for another volume.

EBB AND FLOW IN ARCHIVAL KNOWLEDGE

The North American archival profession has not sufficiently defined and described the basic principles underlying the administration of archival institutions, especially including institutional archives. This statement is not meant to suggest that the archival profession lacks such knowledge or even that there is some kind of grand theory guiding archival work and management, but it certainly seems that archivists have failed to describe systematically or usefully such basic knowledge.[1] This volume's effort is, at best, a preliminary one intended to provide introductory guidance, not to be the definitive reference. Archival knowledge—both principles and practice—is scattered about in journal essays, unevenly summarized in basic manuals, and inconsistently reflected in archival textbooks.[2] In fact, the nature of archival knowledge and its application to a broad diversity of settings make it difficult to summarize it effectively in any single volume.

The problem with archival knowledge affects the very institutions that employ archivists to carry out the archival profession's broader mission to identify, preserve, and make available for use the records of enduring or continuing value. Although the archival literature is filled with interesting and useful case studies of aspects of the management of archives and manuscripts in their respective repositories, there is relatively little, until recently, that strives to define what an archival repository is, what it should consist of, and the standards and guidelines that characterize such institutions.[3] One archivist's recent essay on organizational development in state archives commented that "archivists often overlook the organizational environment and processes in the institutions in which they work, institutions which ultimately permit them to carry out the profession's goals. For archivists to reach their professional goals, they must learn to successfully survive in and make the most of organizations; they must, as managers, create well-balanced, healthy organizations."[4] The question is, however, what is a "well-balanced, healthy" archives? What are archival administrators seeking to achieve in their management? Some recent publications provide clues to the answers to these questions, but this chapter is intended to carry the discussion in the profession even further and contends that more research, definition, and standardization are needed to answer such basic questions on the nature of archival repositories and how their managers and the profession can ensure their health and progress in documenting society.

Institutional archives will benefit from such a perspective. This chapter first considers what has been done in the area of defining archival institutions over the past decade. Then, and most importantly, it considers what needs to be done in the future regarding the strengthening of archival institutions. The purpose of these comments is to stimulate archivists' thoughts on some important issues and assist them to reevaluate what it

SELECTED EVENTS INFLUENCING THE DEVELOPMENT AND DEFINITION
OF ARCHIVAL INSTITUTIONS

1977   SAA TASK FORCE ON INSTITUTION EVALUATION

1981   START OF NHPRC FUNDED STATE ASSESSMENT AND REPORTING PROJECTS

1982   SAA PAMPHLET ON INSTITUTIONAL SELF-STUDY

1983   US MARC ARCHIVES AND MANUSCRIPTS CONTROL FORMAT

1985   SAA CENSUS ON ARCHIVAL INSTITUTIONS

1986   SAA PLANNING FOR THE ARCHIVAL PROFESSION

1988   NEW YORK STATE ARCHIVES SELF-STUDY GUIDE FOR HISTORICAL
        RECORDS REPOSITORIES

1988   JAMES GREGORY BRADSHER, ED., MANAGING ARCHIVES AND
        ARCHIVAL INSTITUTIONS

1989   SAA ARCHIVES ASSESSMENT AND PLANNING WORKBOOK

1989   DAVID BEARMAN, ARCHIVAL METHODS

is they do on a daily basis. This part of the chapter will provide a contrast
to what is going on in more general organizational change, the remaining
portion of this chapter.

RECENT EFFORTS IN DEFINING ARCHIVAL
INSTITUTIONS, 1977–1989

In the past decade the North American (as well as international) archival
profession has made considerable progress in answering some basic questions about its institutions, partly because the profession has become more
concerned with asking questions about such matters. The Society of American Archivists' Task Force on Institutional Evaluation was the primary
driving force in the North American work to study and evaluate archival
institutions. Formed in 1977, the task force continued its efforts until 1989
and produced along the way a brief pamphlet on evaluating archival institutions (1982), the most comprehensive statistical census of archival institutions ever undertaken in the profession (1985), and an archives
assessment and planning workbook to assist institutions to evaluate and
strengthen themselves (1989).[5] William Joyce, one of the key players in
the ambitious and extremely important work of the task force, recently
wrote an interesting description of this body's work. Joyce noted that the
task force declined to define archives, "owing to their daunting degree of
diversity of size, institutional placement, and other factors," opting instead
"to develop principles of archival activity by reviewing the range of activ-

ities that might be undertaken in archives. . . . "[6] This objective shaped all three publications that will influence subsequent work in the profession regarding the nature and evaluation of archival institutions. It seems, however, that the definition that this group eschewed could emerge from the self-study tools and programs that have been created. Already, for example, there is important work under way by the Association of Manitoba Archivists and Manitoba Council on Archives to utilize these and other products in just this way, setting forth the basic criteria for archival repositories to meet to qualify as archival programs. Depending on the success of this effort, it is likely that similar work will be undertaken elsewhere. These kinds of efforts relate to all types of archival programs, including institutional archives.

There is little doubt that the work of the task force was one of the most important efforts undertaken by the Society of American Archivists in the 1980s, an energetic and sometimes exhausting period in the profession's development. The task force's work was used by the SAA's Task Force on Goals and Priorities (GAP) in the definition of a long-range plan for the profession. Although the work of the two task forces, now both SAA standing committees, had very different purposes, their ultimate aims were very similar since the health of the archival profession is certainly greatly affected by the condition of the institutions that comprise it. One of the three goals developed in the GAP report related to the administration of archival programs. It noted, for example, that "a lack of *standards* for the care and preservation of archives has resulted in a proliferation of programs with inadequate facilities and staff," although admittedly what was meant by standards was not well described [emphasis added].[7] Still, the purpose of the GAP report is different from the purposes adopted by the task force's assessment workbook and the similar New York manual, both of which are user friendly texts intended to assist repositories to assess their strengths and weaknesses and to build upon their strengths to provide optimal care for the documentary heritage residing in these repositories. These guides have provided working blueprints for the content of this volume.

The questions remain, however, about what the archival profession and archivists now know about archival repositories and what they think they ought to do with them. A glance at the two recent self-study manuals for archival institutions is instructive. SAA's publication stated in the first line of its introduction that it is "designed to help you organize information about your repository, systematically evaluate it, and develop plans to improve that program."[8] It carefully and succinctly describes an evaluative process for repositories to follow. It also includes worksheets intended to support repository staff in looking at their "functional areas" or activities— legal authority and purpose, governing authority and administration, financial resources, staff, physical facilities, building archival and manuscript holdings, preserving archival and manuscript holdings, arrangement and description, access policies and reference services, and outreach and public programs. In these functions and activities, for example, an archives comes closest to being defined. Each includes a statement of principles, "amplification" of these principles, and a series of self-study questions that, in an interrogative manner, provide additional details, most of which are applicable for institutional archives. By necessity, of course, many of the statements are general. For example, under financial resources, it is stated that the "archives should have sufficient administrative staff, information systems, and equipment to process paperwork and maintain accountability of property and expenditures without detracting from the ability of staff to perform primary archival functions."[9] What is "sufficient" is not really described, and in a workbook of this sort it really could not be, but one is left wondering if what is sufficient for one institution is insufficient for another similar one because of other unexplained or unidentified factors. Clearly, the emphasis of this workbook is on institutional improvement, not institutional definition. With the SAA census data included, the idea is that staffs of archival repositories will be able to compare their programs with similar repositories and thus assess where they stand and learn what they need to do to improve.

The New York State Archives and Records Administration publication is very similar to that of the Society of American Archivists, a fact freely acknowledged in the New York publication.[10] This publication is one of many efforts recently undertaken by this state archives that built upon the findings and recommendations of the 1982–1983 New York statewide historical records assessment and reporting project. Stated simply in the foreword by state archivist Larry J. Hackman, the guide's "object is to improve the management of [New York's] documentary heritage by strengthening New York's historical records repositories."[11] Like SAA's workbook, the New York publication strives to identify the "basic elements" of a repository in five major areas—general administration, identification and retention of historical records, preservation, availability and use of historical records, and public programs and advocacy. Each element consists of a definition, description of the purposes and benefits, examples and explications, and a series of self-study questions that probe for more information about the element's status in the repository; in this way, the New York and SAA manuals complement each other and could be used side by side by archival institutions, including institutional archives, wishing to undertake self-study and planning. The New York guide also includes lengthy sections on fund-raising and cooperative approaches for administering historical records and a more detailed chapter on sources of assistance. While it could be argued that these two publications are not comprehensive regarding the management of archival repositories, together they may, indeed probably do, provide the most convenient information references for the administration of such institutions.

Assembling New York's guide was a process made considerably easier by the previous work of the SAA Task Forces on Institutional Evaluation and Goals and Priorities. Although the writing of this guide was not an easy task nor one that reassured anyone involved in it about what archivists really know about archival repositories, it was, nevertheless, an instructive process that led to reflection on the nature of archival programs; the guide turned out to be only a starting point, not a conclusion. It probably needs to be read and used this way by others; that is, it (and the SAA self-study guide) can be a useful starting point for additional analysis about the nature of archival institutions. This volume on institutional archives is also intended to be a starting point, not the definitive word, for individuals interested in the management of these kinds of archival programs.

The New York guide was a direct outgrowth of the statewide historical records assessment and planning work undertaken in the early 1980s by the New York State Historical Records Advisory Board with assistance from the NHPRC. The 1984 report of the state assessment project defined innumerable needs of the Empire state's historical records programs, not the least of these problems being lack of resources, lack of trained staff, poor facilities, and inadequately defined purposes. This report led to a variety of actions by the Advisory Board and the New York State Archives and Records Administration, including an ambitious New York Historical Records Program Development Project, again funded by NHPRC, that resulted in the self-study guide, a series of workshops on fund-raising, and a regional documentation strategy test.[12] Since the completion of the Historical Records Program Development Project, legislation has been passed to place professional archivists in various regions of the state and to provide grant support to historical records projects. Much of the early focus of this fledgling Documentary Heritage Program has been on promoting the use and evaluation of the self-study guide.

Producing a publication that could adequately assist the governing boards and staffs of historical records programs conduct institutional self-assessment and position themselves for improvement was a formidable task indeed. Except for the previous path-breaking work of the SAA Task Force on Institutional Evaluation and the SAA Task Force on Goals and Priorities, both of which pulled a lot of information together, there was little to guide such work. What was available was a maze of bits and pieces, made more complicated by the archival profession's lack of consensus about these institutional elements and a general preference for voluntary guidelines rather than standards supported by professional peer review, peer pressure, or other means. While there have been efforts to define elements of certain kinds of archival institutions, like those in colleges and universities,[13] such efforts had never gone beyond being wise counsel with little connection to reality or mechanisms for change. In other words, archivists still were not anywhere closer to defining what an adequate or quality archival repository should be. In fact, after the intense self-scrutiny of the early to mid–1980s, archivists knew a lot about the problems of archival institutions, but not necessarily how to resolve these problems and to improve the repositories. Requests for more resources for these programs were easy to articulate, but not so easy to defend or to obtain. How much money and staff were needed by a repository to meet its mission? Would archivists ever be satisfied with their resources no matter what they possessed? Were archival programs administratively placed in a manner that allowed their managers to be effective advocates?

The lack of energy devoted to defining quality archival programs is readily evident in looking at some of the basic elements defined in the New York guide. It is not difficult to contend that a repository should have a "mission statement," but where is there a model statement, or more importantly, evaluation of actual statements that have been drawn up, used, and refined? What is an "adequate financial system" for an archival repository? Although archivists know that archival operations cost money, the handful of costs evaluation studies undertaken by the profession prompts more questions than it provides answers.[14] Identifying cooperative programs as a basic element may appear to be a little risky, since, other than the archival community's experience with networks, there is little other than common sense suggesting that cooperation is essential. Even more revealing of problems is the identifying of qualified archivists to work in repositories. Not too many years ago, the archival profession even abandoned an effort to define an archivist; more recently, the profession has embroiled itself in controversy by commencing on a program of individual certification.[15] Whatever one's views are, it is still clear that there is only beginning to be consensus about whether all repositories require professional archivists or how individuals achieve the rank of being "professional." It is up to the archival profession itself to resolve such issues; they will not be resolved by accident or by someone else, and if they are, their resolution may not be favorable to the archival profession or its mission. Such problems have made the writing of this volume, of course, a difficult process.

To provide balance to what has been said above, it is necessary to state that there are many components of quality archival programs that have been adequately defined or described by the archival profession. Descriptions of a model collections policy, the US MARC AMC Format for description, and guidelines for disaster preparedness planning are all recent, excellent efforts by the profession to be more precise about what it does, and each has been incorporated into this volume.[16] Still, is the archival profession really sure how all of these fit together to form a program? For years the profession's attention on the small repository and the inexperienced or novice archivist has exacted, perhaps, a toll in the form of a lack of consensus about institutional components because it has seemed to lead archivists to focus primarily on common denominators. Perhaps the poor image of archivists, a subject of recent attention, is mainly the result of lack of attention on the archival institution since the profession is, after all, made up of individuals who are primarily employed in archival repositories. Do archivists' problems concerning the definition of what an archivist is or does actually extend from a decided lack of definition about archival institutions rather than any ingrained societal perspectives or prejudices regarding their work?[17] A question such as this deserves, at least, some attention.

The New York and SAA guides are both the result of educated guesses—or, to be kinder—informed opinions—about what an archival institution is or should be, rather than the consensus of the profession; the guides (and books such as this) will help to foster discussion in the profession that leads to the desired consensus. What is found in the New York guide, for example, is the best effort by a group of experienced archivists who have managed archival institutions, taught archival administration, and written about archival issues and concerns.[18] Because the guide is intended to assist archival repositories assess their strengths and weaknesses in order to plan for the future, it may not be important for it to try to define more precisely what an adequate or excellent program is; the assumption is that any program can stand improvement. But attentive readers will find at least a preliminary effort to go beyond a simple listing and describing of elements. In its introduction can be found the following statement:

Although all [the described] elements are important, a historical records program should always have at least the following: a well-defined mission statement; a written acquisition policy; adequate storage and reference facilities; and access to an individual trained and experienced in historical records administration. A written long-range plan of goals and objectives for strengthening the repository, including a strategy for acquiring adequate financial resources for the care of the historical records, is also important.[19]

It is not my intention either to describe in greater detail or to defend such elements, but rather only to state that they represent a kind of frustration by the guides' authors and advisers in desiring to have more precise definitions for archival programs. The real issue now is how, having this guide and the one published by SAA and other basic volumes such as this one, the archival profession can move toward more deliberate standards—agreed upon by the profession and enforced by example, education, and other means—that are helpful to the archival profession and its institutions that make it up.

THE CONTEXT OF RECENT EFFORTS

While there have been disagreement and confusion about the specific details of archival institutions, there has been growing consensus in the archival profession about what archival programs should be, that institutional planning and self-study are important tools for aiding these programs, and that professionwide standards and related issues are essential for strengthening individual archival repositories. All of these have been major topics in North America through the 1980s and are likely to set the professional agendas for the 1990s, nationally and internationally.

What should the archival programs, including institutional archives, be? They should have at least the following objectives:

- Preserve effectively their institution's and society's documentation possessing long-term research and other informational (archival) value
- Preserve the portion of the archival documentation in its original form that has symbolic, emotional, and cultural importance for understanding the relevance of the past
- Maintain repositories of archival and historical manuscript sources that can be used by any element of society to meet its informational needs
- Ensure that the archival records and historical manuscripts are used for understanding and dealing with important contemporary issues and concerns facing institutions and society as a whole

All of the archivist's planning and self-study efforts should be to acquire the necessary resources, facilities, staffing, and other support to meet these broad objectives.

Planning and self-study are especially important for archivists and archival institutions.[20] They help the archivist to define where his or her program presently is, to propose how to vision where it should be, and to set measurable goals for working toward that vision. Planning and self-study can help to build consensus about the archival program among the governing board members, parent agency, professional and other staff, and volunteers. They can provide a basis for enabling archival programs to cope with the typical change that they face. They can assist any program to make the best use of its limited resources and to determine where the new resources are needed and where they might come from. In the same light, planning and self-study can assist archivists to identify needed expertise for their programs and where they might find that expertise for their use. Regular evaluation, which is a standard aspect of self-study, and planning can also assist an archives to determine how its present staff is doing and whether any changes are needed.

The North American archival profession has committed itself to giving resources to the planning and self-study processes. In the 1970s, the American archival profession reached a major milestone in its development when the SAA agreed to a plan for professional staffing, continuing education, and a more expansive publications program. Supporting this effort was the numerical growth in the profession's size, as well as in the number of individuals working as archivists who first and foremost identified themselves as professional archivists, as well as concern about how to use better limited financial and other resources. These developments led to the beginning of a long period of self-reflection, manifested by debate about individual certification, accreditation of archival education programs, and the accreditation of archival repositories—all trends typical of any professionalization process. This period has come to be characterized as the "age of American archival analysis," and it has not been without implications for institutional archivists and their staffs.[21]

The second and successful effort to establish an individual certification process for archivists partly emanated from consulting and corporate archivists who were concerned about the quality of advice that businesses were receiving about what to do with their archival records. If successful, of course, the certification program should be one way in which institutions can identify and select qualified staff for their archival operations. But there are numerous other developments from this era that can help the work of institutional archivists, a few worth special merit. The US MARC AMC Format and descriptive standards have eased the way for the automating of descriptive programs. The efforts to strengthen graduate and continuing education programs have provided better opportunities for knowledgeable staff working at institutional archives. The program to sketch a detailed statistical profile of archival programs has given institutional archives a basis for comparing and measuring their progress. The establishment of the National Historical Publications and Records Commission and its State Historical Records Advisory Boards has provided both external funding and a network for planning, advocacy, and mutual support that institutional archives need to use.

The recent wave of professionwide planning, including institutional self-study, still is recent enough that the archival community is in a learning process in this area. Nevertheless, individual archivists have learned a lot more about self-study, coping with organizational and societal change, working with external consultants, and communicating with others besides archivists. The products of the late 1970s and 1980s—including basic archival manuals and textbooks, statewide archival assessment reports, and a professionwide plan—all constitute benchmarks by which the archival profession can measure its future progress. Institutional archives need to use these to build their own benchmarks.

LOOKING TOWARD THE FUTURE

What archivists should do in better defining and analyzing their institutions is not a question the archival profession has still really adequately asked, let alone answered. While the issuance of the two institutional self-study guides will likely prompt the correct asking of this and other related questions, it is still uncertain how the profession can best build on the knowledge contained in these volumes to aid archival institutions. At this time several avenues of action seem possible: promoting the use of the self-study guides and evaluation of the institutional and professional benefits of this use; strengthening the profession's management expertise, experience, and tools; and adopting a program of institutional accreditation. Each of these possibilities is important for institutional archivists and has been considered below in a way that promotes additional discussion by the archival profession. What follows is written in the sense of asking more questions, rather than necessarily providing answers. It is offered in the conviction that discussion in the profession of such answers will advance the archival profession's understanding of archival programs and the archivist's quest to document society and to preserve society's historical records. Institutional archivists need to participate in the process.

Self-study and Planning

Promoting the use of the two self-study guides is certainly something that needs to be done regardless of one's views on institutional self-study, planning, standards, or accreditation. There is little doubt that these guides can help any archival repository plan with useful benefits. But a number of questions emerge about such promotion. Will these guides be of consistent value to the wide range—in size, resource, and type—of archival repositories? How can a repository with limited or no professional staffing constructively use self-study? What kinds of incentives are necessary for the governing bodies and staffs of archival institutions to commit the time and energy necessary for successful completion of self-study? Given the obvious confidential nature of such self-study, what can the profession expect to learn about its institutions?

That these concerns are relevant and weighty can be seen from the 1977–1982 experiences of state historical societies' self-studies, supported by the National Endowment for the Humanities. Although there were many benefits found by those societies that conducted self-study, the process was immensely time-consuming, difficult, and, at times, controversial. During such efforts staff put themselves and their institutions under a microscope, and differences of opinions, communication problems, and problems with long histories readily moved to the forefront, and difficult "corporate cultures" blocked progress. The process of involving governing board with professional staff and administrators was also bound to generate some tensions. Working through such problems to focus on an agenda for improving the institution was found to be neither easy nor easily ignored.[22]

There are various things, nonetheless, that can be done to promote and justify institutional self-study. The SAA has taken the most obvious and logical step by creating a standing Committee on Institutional Evaluation

POTENTIAL FUTURE DIRECTIONS FOR ARCHIVAL INSTITUTIONS

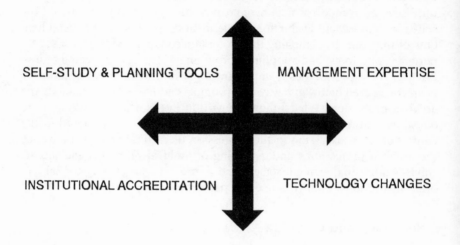

SELF-STUDY & PLANNING TOOLS   MANAGEMENT EXPERTISE

INSTITUTIONAL ACCREDITATION   TECHNOLOGY CHANGES

and Development and charging the committee to promote institutional self-study, using the SAA publication. But there must be, of course, other steps taken as well that help institutional self-study and planning to permeate the normal business of archival repositories. First, graduate and continuing archival education programs must emphasize a management of institutions and programs that introduces prospective and practicing archivists to the importance and value of self-study in a manner that assists repositories constantly to seek improvement and, at times, redefinition.[23] One way of bridging the gap between theoretical or knowledge-based education and practice is to have advanced archival students use the self-study guides to help smaller repositories evaluate and plan. This experience will assist future archival administrators to gain valuable experience in the management of archival institutions and programs, help to evaluate and refine the self-study tools that are now available, and build a set of case studies that can be used by the archival profession. Institutional archives, many of which are small, need to take advantage of such opportunities by working with graduate education programs to serve as test sites for such efforts. Institutional archives, graduate education programs, and archival students can all benefit from such an arrangement.

Second, the self-study guides should be incorporated into the much needed guidelines for archival consultants that many archivists hope will be developed at some point. Such guidelines should focus not just on who conducts such consultant work, but on what they do. As Virginia Stewart has suggested, although consulting is a basic and important archival function, there is a modicum of literature or guidance on it. She also indicates why more stringent guidelines are needed: "The archival profession may expect consultants to adhere to canons of professional practice in their work, thus advancing both the profession and the larger social goals of stewardship of historical documentation that the profession espouses."[24] The self-study guides provide a consistent basis for what these consultants should be doing, as well as advising their clients what to do. Institutional archivists, who make as much use of consultants as those in any kind of archival program, should work for such stringent guidelines.

Third, archival funding agencies, like NEH and NHPRC, should be encouraged to require completion of self-study for at least certain kinds of grant proposals. Such funding bodies already have certain requirements; requiring evidence of self-study, primarily in the product of a written, long-range plan for improvement, with substantial statements of support from the institution's parent agency and resource allocators, is perhaps the best manner to protect the use of funds from agencies such as NEH and NHPRC. The completion of a comprehensive self-study should provide evidence that the institution is serious about its mission, has committed to a certain path for improvement, and is not just forming its long-range goals around the prospects of acquiring outside financial assistance. It is likely that such requirements as these will become workable in the near future, and institutional archives should be prepared for this development.

Fourth, the results of institutional self-study and planning should be disseminated throughout the profession, in a manner that protects the institution's confidentiality. Archivists have not satisfactorily developed a consensus about what makes a successful or failed program. What now passes for descriptions of institutional life cycles and successes, in the archival literature and at presentations at professional meetings, is generally the result of individuals biased by their association with these institutions; although some of these efforts are well intentioned, others may be more the results of an institutional or individual boosterism. Building a set of case studies of institutional self-study that have been prepared by objective consultants and that can be evaluated by outsiders will do much to strengthen archival institutions, by increasing the archivist's understanding of how they work and, consequentially, how effectively the profession is working to accomplish its broader societal mission. This result would certainly assist the work of institutional archivists.

Strengthening Management Expertise

Improving the archival profession's management expertise, experiences, and tools, the second major area of action, has been on the minds of many archivists for more than a decade, at least as reflected in some seminal articles that have seemed to spell a new era for archival management.

Public administration has been shown to be a relevant course of study for archivists.[25] Other management techniques have also been demonstrated to be a legitimate and valuable source for archivists striving to build quality programs.[26] The management of archives has also been defined as an area mostly requiring a significant amount of research. In the most important article on the topic, Paul McCarthy stated that "there is a general lack of archival literature focused on the administration of archival programs; rather, archivists have tended to write about the administration of archival *collections*."[27] While archival collections are obviously an important part of an archival institution, there are other aspects of management that must be attended to in order to ensure that the repository holdings are well administered. Whereas librarians have tried to draw upon sociologists like Weber, scientific management theorists like Taylor, Gulick, and Urwick, systems theorists, and others for the analysis and management of their institutions, archivists have tended to draw on these same sources only for appraisal and other basic archival work.[28] Administrators of institutional archivists must also be good managers and be aware of the full arsenal of management principles and practices available to them.

Beyond the research areas that McCarthy identifies—individual competency, characteristics of successful programs, and the application and evaluation of management theories to archival work—the archival profession most profoundly needs tools to use for improving its managerial effectiveness. McCarthy suggested this need, as I have in this chapter, when he urged that "analytical profiles or case studies of successful archival institutions should be compiled in order to examine and evaluate organizational effectiveness and to determine the program and staff characteristics that contributed to the repository's growth and development."[29] What he is suggesting is that through study and the incorporation of such study into articles, books, case study packets, curriculum materials, and the like, the archival profession can begin to fine-tune its notion about the nature of archival institutions. The existence of the SAA's Archival Management Round Table gives evidence that there is interest here, and, in fact, offers one distribution point for such materials, as well as a possible source for generating the needed publications and other items. Institutional archivists need to get into this loop of activity, both to contribute and to learn from others.

Given that improving management expertise is the most voluntary and least controversial approach to the defining and strengthening of archival institutions, what kind of materials and actions are needed here? Archivists need to utilize the management literature better, either by preparing a bibliography of this literature tailored for archivists or by bringing attention to other existing bibliographic and online data bases. Archivists also ought to build on some of the management research by adapting its research approaches to the archival institution. Librarians have been extremely effective in this area, as was noted earlier. There should be a greater emphasis on this area in the continuing education opportunities for archivists, not only to make archivists better managers but to encourage them to conduct research, assign staff to doing research, and disseminate research results. Institutional archives are excellent laboratories for such work. Professional archival associations should assign a portion of their sessions to deal with the management of their institutions, rather than their collections; it is well known that a significant portion of the archival literature results from professional meetings. Finally, graduate archival students should be encouraged to conduct research into the management of archival programs that may produce some publishable studies that will better equip these individuals to take their place someday as administrators of programs.

Accreditation

A program of institutional accreditation, the third avenue of action, is certainly a controversial suggestion, probably at least as controversial as have been the early phases of the individual certification program. Mentioning an accreditation program for archival institutions is bound to elicit strong reactions from many archivists. The specter of additional financial burdens and institutional elitism is bound to appear quickly in any discussions about such a program. This reaction not only reflects considerable misunderstanding about accreditation (which I will return to later in this chapter), but ignores mounting evidence that the profession must look to the development of some kind of institutional evaluation and assessment that will assist individual archivists, archival institutions, and the archival profession to carry out the archival mission effectively. But the need for an accreditation program is generally shown by archivists' worry about the quality of archival institutions. Howard Lowell, for example, in writing about state archives, expressed the following concern: "A strong state archives program can be a positive argument for support of other archival programs in the state. A weak state program provides no model for other archivists to use when arguing for support of historical manuscripts or university archives program. Indeed it becomes a 'model' to overcome."[30] Would an accreditation program be of any assistance in eliminating the burden of weak institutions? Would institutional archives be able to use model programs in building support for their operations?

The most common form of accreditation, for postsecondary education, originated in the early twentieth century. As one authority on the topic has said, "Accreditation not only was a product of this period but also shared the characteristics of the society that spawned it: idealistic, self-motivated, reform-minded, desiring improvement, believing in both individual initiative and voluntary collective action, and distrustful of government (though seeing government as embodying the ultimate power to right wrongs). These characteristics still infuse accreditation."[31] Accreditation in this context has been defined to be "a process by which an institution of post-secondary education evaluates its educational activities ... and seeks an independent judgment to confirm that it substantially achieves its objectives and is generally equal in quality to comparable institutions or specialized units." The essential elements of accreditation are a clear statement of intentions, completion of self-study to assess how well these intentions are being met, on-site evaluation by a selected group of peers, and decision by an independent accreditation commission that the institution merits accreditation.[32]

The clearest kin to a possible accreditation program for archival institutions is the one administered for museums by the Association of American Museums (AAM). AAM's program has been in effect for 20 years and has become a major factor stimulating improved professional museum standards. Including a process of intensive institutional self-study as well as a visiting committee, the program is considered by many to be instrumental in improving the quality of museums. That the program has been successful can be seen in the comment by Patricia Williams and Allen Liff: "Originally museums were asked to meet 'minimum accreditable standards.' But the standards have risen, and the commission now uses the term 'currently acceptable professional standards.' "[33] Although museum accreditation has not been without its critics,[34] the process has continued to evolve in a manner that accounts for the diversity in this field.[35] In short, museum accreditation may be a prototype for the accreditation of archival institutions.

What could be gained from a formal archival accreditation program? The most beneficial result would be placing institutional self-study, for which the profession already has some adequate tools, in a larger process that would stimulate its use. The major problem the profession faces now is how to get archival institutions, their governing boards, and their staffs to use the various self-study guides and to commit the time, energy, and resources necessary to make self-assessment successful. Another benefit of an institutional accreditation program would be its stimulation to archival standards. SAA has had a Task Force on Archival Standards draw up a list of existing standards and make recommendations for additional ones. The profession also has a major effort under way on descriptive standards, driven by the need to make national data bases work and to build on the foundation laid by the US MARC AMC format. An institutional accreditation program could identify and promote the development of other standards relative to the administration of archival repositories. Finally, the accreditation program could help improve the public profile of archival institutions by recognizing institutions as accredited and by communicating to the public that there are recognizable criteria for determining quality, dependable institutions that safeguard society's documentary heritage. All of these activities would benefit the kinds of institutional archives profiled in this volume.

What would an archival institutional accreditation program look like, and how would it work? The AAM program provides the clearest model, although other fields' proposed and actual processes could also be instructive.[36] There would need to be acceptable guidelines for the process, and such guidelines are roughly available in the two self-study manuals described earlier. A structure would also be needed, a freestanding or independent committee that would govern the program, much as an independent Academy of Certified Archivists was established to govern the individual certification program. This body would have to develop a peer review process, outlining how site visits would work, what their reports would have to include, what would happen to these reports, and how the committee would make final decisions and handle appeals. It would appear that none of these steps would pose insurmountable obstacles greater than anything the profession has taken on before. The biggest obstacle might be the cost of this program.

What would an archival institutional accreditation program cost? There really are no reliable estimates, because the specific nature of the program has yet to be defined. But the program, which could be modestly developed, would also have to be self-sustaining. If there was a general governing body of five individuals administering the program and making accreditation decisions and institutional site visits in teams of three individuals each, then the cost to individual archival repositories should be able to be kept affordable. Each repository would have to support the expenses and costs of the site team plus some kind of general fee that went to support the work of the programs' governing body, including its meetings, legal expenses, publicity, accreditation materials, and the like. An individual institutional cost as low as $1,000 to 2,000, for a process needing to occur probably no more than once every five years, would probably be achievable. Some, of course, will view such costs as prohibitive or as additional evidence of an elitist process accessible only to the larger archival programs. These concerns can be overcome by a process that proves its contribution to the improving and sustaining of institutional archival standards and their actual use in these programs.

It must be stated, of course, that successful results of an accreditation process have not been easy to achieve in other disciplines and would not be easy for the archival profession either.[37] Archivists must realize that developing an acceptable institutional accreditation process will take time, careful planning, and hard work.

INSTITUTIONAL ARCHIVES, INSTITUTIONAL CHANGE, AND INFORMATION TECHNOLOGY: A FINAL NOTE

The information technology of the past half-century has wrought tremendous changes on the office, office workers, and organizations, all in-

stitutional aspects naturally falling within or affecting the responsibility of,
the institutional archivist. The degree and impact of changes on institutions
and their archives may be a debatable point, as is the future significance
of this technology for society and its organizations, but there should be no
debate that the institutional archivist's mission, work, and responsibilities
will be affected to some degree by these changes.[38] For the institutional
archivist, it is, in some ways, merely an extension from managing earlier
technology changes, such as the typewriter or the electrostatic photocopier,
and their shaping of the institutional record. Nevertheless, the modern
computer has speeded up the rate of change, altered expectations for the
management of records and information, and even transformed certain
fundamental concepts of information. Modern information technology suggests the need for a certain rethinking of the nature and roles of the
institutional archives and its staffing that should be carefully considered by
any individual occupying the archivist's position.

There is a vast body of studies and opinions about modern information
technology that should cause the institutional archivist to pause and to
reevaluate his or her program. The computer and its applications have
brought serious changes to the nature of such basic concepts as information
and documents. Some experts have talked of information refineries that
are "an electronic, computer-based process that takes undifferentiated volumes of raw information . . . [and] converts them into electronic form, ex-
tracts the content units and recombines them into a new form that can be
distributed in a variety of ways."[39] Another has noted that "hypermedia
environments make it increasingly difficult to define exactly what a document is."[40] Even authorship of documents, in electronic form such as
hypermedia, has become a questionable exercise.[41]

The transformations wrought by electronic information technology go
beyond just the actual information systems and their products and uses.
The ways that institutions function and look are also being affected. Decentralized work forces, increased specialization, flatter organizations, and
new ways of communicating and making decisions have all been attributed
to the technology.[42] If nothing else, the technology introduces a new concept of information retrieval for an institution's employees, that of self-
help; where individuals were generally accustomed to acquiring information through a professional intermediary, such as the librarian or archivist,
now they are increasingly able to search and find the electronic files conveniently from their own desk.[43] The implications for the institutional archivist can be suggested by noting the changes to the organization's mode
of operation and documentation that electronic mail, a relatively simple
use of the technology, seems to bring. Electronic mail reduces personal
interaction in an organization, leads to more informal and concise types
of communication, and speeds up communication. Electronic mail is also
used to transmit messages of a wide variety, including policy and decision-

oriented matters.[44] For the institutional archivist, the concern is how to review the generally large amounts of communications that are transmitted via electronic mail, how to relate these communications to other institutional records, and how to determine in what form these electronic mail messages should be preserved. Electronic information technology poses many additional challenges to the institutional archivist committed to documenting the organization and providing information that is vital to the organization's functioning.

On the other hand, the institutional archivist should take comfort in the fact that certain fundamental concerns have not changed very much despite the increasing utilization of expensive and sophisticated information technology. "Whether the information was spoken, handwritten, printed with ink, or recorded on wax, film, or magnetic tape," some observers have suggested, "the purpose has always been the same: To take whatever information was available and convey it to someone for social, informative, entertainment, educational, financial, commercial, political, or military needs. In this sense, nothing has ever changed."[45] In fact, many of the problems that archivists, records managers, and other information professionals have been concerned with for many years remain as obstacles with the newer automated systems. An analysis of long-term technological change in one organization concluded that problems of too many duplicate files, the inability to locate files that are needed, and an overload of information were still prevalent despite what other accomplishments had been made.[46]

One of the most serious obstacles for the institutional archivist to contend with is determining how to manage the information of archival value that is produced with the aid of the new technology. For many years the archivist has operated on the assumption that records that were meant to be preserved would be created in a form by their creators that was stable enough to be maintained by the archivist and that would not violate any of the archivists' basic principles.[47] There is, at present, however, considerable debate about the viability of basic archival principles as well as the role of the archivist in whatever organizational setting in which he or she might be found. Some have argued that there is little compatibility of techniques used for managing paper records that can be carried over to electronic records. Others have adopted more sanguine stances. Regardless of the degree of usefulness of older archival principles and methodologies, it is nevertheless the case that the institutional archivist should consider adopting some other approaches to meet their organizational mission.

The institutional archivist, working in the organization that has adopted the electronic information technology or that may be in the process of more fully embracing this technology, must consider taking a number of actions necessary to cope with the technology and to continue to play a viable information role in the organization.

First, the institutional archivist must be knowledgeable about these new technologies; in effect, the assumption about the accustomed educational background of the archivist in the humanities must be expanded to include more of the information sciences than has been hitherto deemed feasible or possible.[48] He or she cannot run the risk of managing only records that are in more traditional paper-based or other forms. Doing this will cut off the archivist from important groups of records and information that may be more vital to the organization than those found in other organizational management systems. Effective archival appraisal, for example, is possible only if records are examined in their functional and other organizational contexts, including their relationship to other records. To accomplish this and other ends, the institutional archivist must be able to communicate effectively with the organization's data processors, managers of information systems, and vendors supplying computer hardware and software.

Second, the institutional archivist must be in an administrative position that allows him or her to have a role in the design of key organizational information systems or in the purchase of off-the-shelf systems that the organization intends to adapt. Earlier in this volume the importance of the archivist's being proactive in the identification of institutional records possessing archival value at the point closest to creation of the records and having management's support to do this was mentioned. The archivist must be aware of information technology standards, how various computer systems work (at least to the degree that the archivist can point out specifications that meet the needs of the maintenance of the archival record), and, just as important, their own technical standards for archival records and their maintenance and use.[49] In some cases, it appears, encoding specifications into the information systems for electronic records possessing archival value may be the best route to take in ensuring that the organization's archival records, in whatever form, are identified and preserved.

Third, the institutional archivist must be open to a decentralized archival system for the organization. The complexities of, and requirements for, electronic information systems may make it impossible or undesirable for the archivist physically to move archival records in electronic form into the archival facility. This point is especially true for relational and other data bases that are archival in nature and that will not allow more than a snapshot of its files at any given moment to be preserved. Archivists might need to become "gatekeepers" to the organization's electronic records and issue guidelines and standards to the institution's employees to ensure that certain systems are maintained and accessible to others. This role requires, of course, considerable administrative support and authority, as well as a different philosophy of archival custodianship than is the present norm.

Fourth, the institutional archivist needs to be open to new ideas about the form in which archival information is preserved. Records that are now in standard textual forms might need to be put into digital forms that can be accessed by organizational staff from their own workstations. This measure, in effect, will enable the archives to deliver information from its holdings in a manner that will allow and encourage the archives to be used. As institutional workers become more accustomed to having access to information via the computer on their desks, the archives will be ensured of having a vital information role in the future. As one individual in the information technology field has suggested, a "shift in thinking" about the use of information technology has occurred. "It is now accepted that raw information, or even processing power is not enough. It is the ability to retrieve, communicate and share information that provides real advantage."[50] Institutional archivists need to be able to promote the use of the "raw information" that is in their holdings in the new high-tech environments.

All of this discussion suggests, of course, new prototypes and roles for the institutional archives. The administrators of these programs need to keep these in mind as they build their own programs and as they work for needed professional archival standards and principles. Institutional accreditation and other similar approaches mentioned earlier in this chapter must take into account the new information technologies and their impact, influence, and utility. Institutional archives in the twenty-first century may look very different from those that are now in operation.

NOTES

1. James M. O'Toole, "On the Idea of Permanence," *American Archivist* 52 (Winter 1989): 10–25. In fact, O'Toole's essay can be considered an effort to define more fully our basic archival knowledge. The interest in defining archival knowledge has certainly been evident in a series of essays on archival theory now extending over the past decade, but, it should be added, hardly resolved to anyone's satisfaction. See Frank G. Burke, "The Future Course of Archival Theory in the United States," *American Archivist* 44 (Winter 1981): 40–46, and subsequent responses to Burke published in the journal. The response that goes to the ultimate extreme, contending that there is little distinct archival knowledge, is John W. Roberts, "Archival Theory: Much Ado About Shelving," *American Archivist* 50 (Winter 1987): 66–74.

2. For one thing, there is no single textbook that archival educators and administrators can use that provides satisfactory descriptions of basic archival functions and the management of archival repositories while reflecting changing notions of archival principles and practices, as well as present professional issues and concerns. This problem is compounded by the general difficulty of access to the existing archival literature. The Society of American Archivists' new Archival Fundamental Series may improve this situation considerably, although it is difficult to measure the impact of such publications on archival practice. SAA's Basic Manual Series (1977-1985) certainly was a major influence on standardizing archival administration, although probably not as significant as the adoption of the US MARC AMC Format.

3. At least one archivist has been critical of the profession's preoccupation with such

"nuts-and-bolts" concerns; see Peter J. Wosh, "Creating a Semiprofessional Profession: Archivists View Themselves," *Georgia Archive* 10 (Fall 1982): 1–13.

4. "The Change Masters: Organizational Development in a State Archives," *American Archivist* 51 (Fall 1988): 441.

5. *Evaluation of Archival Institutions: Services, Principles, and Guide to Self-Study* (Chicago: Society of American Archivists, 1982); Paul Conway, "Perspectives on Archival Resources: The 1985 Census of Archival Institutions," *American Archivist* 50 (Spring 1987): 174–91; and Paul H. McCarthy, ed., *Archives Assessment and Planning Workbook* (Chicago: Society of American Archivists, 1989).

6. William Joyce, "Understanding SAA's Principles of Institutional Evaluation," SAA *Newsletter*, May 1989, 10.

7. *Planning for the Archival Profession: A Report of the SAA Task Force on Goals and Priorities* (Chicago: Society of American Archivists, 1986), 16.

8. McCarthy, *Archives Assessment*, 5.

9. McCarthy, *Archives Assessment*, 22.

10. *Strengthening New York's Historical Records Program: A Self-Study Guide* (Albany: New York State Archives and Records Administration, 1988).

11. *Strengthening*, vii.

12. For additional information about these other aspects of the project, see Richard J. Cox, "A Documentation Strategy Case Study: Western New York," *American Archivist* 52 (Spring 1989): 192–200, and "Fund-raising for Historical Records Programs: An Underdeveloped Archival Function," *Provenance* 6 (Fall 1988): 1–19, the latter of which was largely republished in chapter 6 of this volume.

13. See, for example, *College and University Archives: Selected Readings* (Chicago: Society of American Archivists, 1979). In one of Nicholas Burckel's contributions to this volume, he talked about the individual appointed to be university or college archivist who turns to the literature for help. "Unfortunately," he wrote, "relevant information is difficult to find: library journals traditionally eschew archival articles and the *American Archivist*'s articles on college archives are frequently no more than institutional case studies. The new archivist, therefore, conforms to his job with few guidelines or suggestions" (38).

14. For some of these studies see William Maher, "Measurement and Analysis of Processing Costs in Academic Archives," *College & Research Libraries* 43 (1982): 59–67; Terry Abraham, Stephen E. Balzarini, and Ann Frantilla, "What Is Backlog Is Prologue: A Measurement of Archival Processing," *American Archivist* 48 (Winter 1985): 31-44; and Uli Haller, "Variations in the Processing Rates on the Magnuson and Jackson Senatorial Papers," *American Archivist* 50 (Winter 1987): 100–9. While such studies are useful, what use the profession has made of them is questionable. On the one hand, they have not really been integrated into our overall concepts of archival management. The most recent volume on the management of archives, for example, hardly considers the financial aspects of archival administration despite the availability of such studies: James Gregory Bradsher, ed., *Managing Archives and Archival Institutions* (Chicago: University of Chicago Press, 1988). On the other hand, archivists have not really viewed the results of such studies against the larger background of their mission and professional nature. The first effort in this regard is David Bearman, *Archival Methods*, Archives and Museum Informatics Technical Report 3 (Spring 1989), which examines appraisal, preservation, arrangement and description, and use in terms of archival goals, assumptions, and realities; according to Bearman, for example, archival processing rates become unrealistic when

considered in the context of current archival positions, processing backlogs, and creation of new documentation.

15. William J. Maher, "Contexts for Understanding Certification: Opening Pandora's Box," *American Archivist* 51 (Fall 1988): 408-27; Maynard Brichford, "Who Are the Archivists and What Do They Do?," *American Archivist* 51 (Winter/Spring 1988): 106–10.

16. John P. Barton and Johanna G. Wellheiser, eds., *An Ounce of Prevention: A Handbook on Disaster Contingency Planning for Archives, Libraries and Records Centres* (Ontario, Canada: Toronto Area Archivists Group, 1985); Faye Phillips, "Developing Collecting Policies for Manuscript Collections," *American Archivist* 47 (Winter 1984): 30–42; and David Bearman, "Archives and Manuscript Control with Bibliographic Utilities: Opportunities and Challenges," *American Archivist* 52 (Winter 1989): 26–39.

17. David B. Gracy II, "What's Your Totem? Archival Images in the Public Mind," *Midwestern Archivist* 10, no. 1 (1985): 17–23.

18. A number of archivists, primarily Larry J. Hackman and Bruce W. Dearstyne, commented on drafts of the guide, which I principally wrote. In my opinion, the difficulties the profession has in viewing archival institutions were evident in the challenge of developing any agreement or consensus among these three archivists. These discussions were made more effective by the inclusion of a non-archivist, Judy Hohmann, who wrote the guide's chapter on fund-raising.

19. *Strengthening*, 4.

20. While extensive institutional planning efforts often require self-study, there are some major differences between the two processes. In the context of this volume, I am stressing that the two should go together, but it is still worth mentioning briefly some of the differences in this note. While planning is primarily intended to produce a document setting forth future directions, self-study is intended to determine the status of an institution against recognized and accepted standards. Self-study does not have to lead to a formal plan, although it often provides the basis for undertaking work on a plan and can be used as an initial step in a more comprehensive planning effort. Self-study provides an analysis of an institution's strengths and weaknesses. It also enables an institution to create a profile of itself that helps it to reevaluate its real working priorities.

21. For a description and analysis of this period, see Richard J. Cox, *American Archival Analysis: The Recent Development of the Archival Profession in the United States* (Metuchen, NJ: Scarecrow Press, 1990).

22. Suzanne B. Schell, "Self-Study," *History News* 38 (October 1983): 13–16 describes the NEH program.

23. Susan E. Davis, "Development of Managerial Training for Archivists," *American Archivist* 51 (Summer 1988): 278–85.

24. Virginia Stewart, "Transactions in Archival Consulting," *Midwestern Archivist* 10, no. 2 (1985): 115.

25. Andrew Raymond and James M. O'Toole, "Up from the Basement: Archives, History, and Public Administration," *Georgia Archive* 6 (Fall 1978): 18–33.

26. James C. Worthy, "Management Concepts and Archival Administration," *Midwestern Archivist* 4, no. 2 (1979): 77–88; Michael Swift, "Management Techniques and Technical Resources in the Archives of the 1980s," *Archivara* 20 (Summer 1985): 94–104.

27. Paul McCarthy, "The Management of Archives: A Research Agenda," *American Archivist* 51 (Winter and Spring 1988): 54.

28. Beverly P. Lynch, ed., *Management Strategies for Libraries: A Basic Reader* (New York: Neal-Schuman, 1985) reflects how these other fields have been used by librarians. Contrast how management specialists have been used by librarians to how archivists have used them in Michael A. Lutzker, "Max Weber and the Analysis of Modern Bureaucratic Organizations: Notes Toward a Theory of Appraisal," *American Archivist* 45 (Spring 1982): 119–30 and Jo Anne Yates, "Internal Communication Systems in American Business Structures: A Framework to Aid Appraisal," *American Archivist* 48 (Spring 1985): 141–58.

29. McCarthy, "Management of Archives," 51.

30. Howard P. Lowell, "Thoughts on a State Records Program," *American Archivist* 50 (Summer 1987): 398.

31. Kenneth E. Young, "Prologue: The Changing Scope of Accreditation," in *Understanding Accreditation: Contemporary Perspectives on Issues and Practices in Evaluating Educational Quality* by Kenneth E. Young et al. (San Francisco: Jossey-Bass, 1983), 5–6.

32. Kenneth E. Young, "Accreditation: Complex Evaluative Tool," in Young et al., *Understanding Accreditation*, 21.

33. Patricia Williams and Allen Liff, "Promoting Professional Standards in America's Museums," *Museum* 37, no. 3 (1985): 152; see also Alexander J. Well, "Demystifying the Accreditation Process," *Museum News* 60 (September/October 1981): 49 ff.

34. See, for example, Thomas D. Nicholson, "Why Museum Accreditation Doesn't Work," *Museum News* 61 (September/October 1981): 5ff.; Kenneth Starr, "In Defense of Accreditation: A Response to Thomas D. Nicholson," *Museum News* 61 (January/February 1982): 5ff.

35. Randi R. Glickberg, "Historic Sites and Accreditation," *Museum News* 60 (November/December 1981): 42–49; Joy Youmans Norman, "Reaccreditation: How It Works and How It's Working," *Museum News* 61 (July/August 1982): 63 ff.

36. An example is the latest proposal to accredit public libraries. See Margaret M. Kimmel and Leigh Estabrook, "Accrediting Public Libraries: An Update," *Library Journal* 113 (May 15, 1988): 54–55; Leigh Estabrook, "Accreditation of Public Libraries: An Outrageous Suggestion?" *Library Journal* 112 (September 15, 1987): 35–38; Ronald Dubberly, "Questioning Public Library Accreditation," *Library Journal* 113 (May 15, 1988): 56–58 and Terry L. Weech, "National Accreditation of Public Libraries: A Historical Perspective," *Public Libraries* 28 (March/April 1989):119–25.

37. See Mary F. Casserly, "Academic Library Regional Accreditation," *College and Research Libraries* 47 (January 1986), 38–47, which emphasizes that there is a definite lack of useful data used by librarians in this process, resulting more in public relations efforts rather than serious evaluations, and Delmus E. Williams, "Accreditation and the Process of Change in Academic Libraries," *Advances in Library Administration and Organization* 7 (1988), 161–207, which provides a convenient summary of some of the pros and cons mentioned in discussions of library accreditation efforts.

38. A good starting point for understanding the range of opinions about the extent of impact of information technology on archival work and the various responses by archivists is Marion Matters, ed., *Automated Records and Techniques in Archives: A Resource Directory* (Chicago: Society of American Archivists, 1990).

39. John H. Cloppinger and Benn R. Konsynski, "Information Refineries: Electronically Distilling Business' Raw Material to Make It More Usable," *Computerworld* 23 (August 28, 1989): 74.

40. Ronald E. F. Weissman, "Virtual Documents on an Electronic Desktop: Hypermedia, Emerging Computing Environments and the Future of Information Management," in *Management of Recorded Information: Converging Disciplines; Proceedings of the International Council on Archives' Symposium on Current Records, National Archives of Canada, Ottawa May 15–17, 1989*, comp. Cynthia Durance (New York: K. G. Saur, 1990), 42.

41. David Bearman, "Multisensory Data and Its Management," in Durance, *Management of Recorded Information*, p. 112.

42. See, for example, John Diebold, Jane Duffy, and Joel Levy, "Trends and Forecasts—OA and the Next Five Years," *Administrative Management* 48 (January 1987): 18–23 and Alan Radding, "Supporting the Flatter Organization," *Computerworld* 23 (August 14, 1989): 59–64.

43. See, for example, Kenneth E. Dowlin, *The Electronic Library: The Promise and the Process* (New York: Neal-Schuman, 1984).

44. See Esther Crawford, "Spoken into Print: Effects of Electronic Word Processing on Inter-Office Writing," Ph.D. diss., Texas Christian University, 1986, and Linda A. Kurth, "Message Responses as Functions of Communication Mode: A Comparison of Electronic Mail and Typed Memoranda," Ph.D. diss., Arizona State University, 1987.

45. Oswald H. and Gladys D. Ganley, *To Inform or To Control? The New Communications Networks*, 2d. ed. (Norwood, NJ: Ablex, 1989), 11.

46. T. K. Bikson, C. Stasz, and J. D. Eveland, "Plus Ca Change, Plus Ca Change: A Long-Term Look at One Technological Innovation," unpublished paper, Rand Corporation, 1990. See also *Management of Electronic Records: Issues and Guidelines* (New York: United Nations, 1990).

47. Hilary Jenkinson, *Selected Writings of Sir Hilary Jenkinson* (Gloucester, England: Alan Sutton), 322–23.

48. As it appears at present, the standard educational requirements of an archivist are to possess a master's degree (usually in history, political science or a related field, or library science) and some formal archival course work and/or experience. There are few requirements for technical knowledge of computer systems. There is a trend for many job descriptions to require a familiarity with computer applications in archival administration, but this primarily reflects automated description systems that employ the US MARC Archives and Manuscripts Control Format. There is little reflection of any requirements for knowledge of electronic records or any efforts to make this a standard for archival work.

49. Again, see the UN report, *Management of Electronic Records*.

50. Patrick Scott, "The Organisational Impact of the New Media," *Aslib Proceedings* 42 (September 1990): 223.

9

Three Case Studies in the Formation of Institutional Archives

This chapter is an in-depth look at three different types of institutions and their needs for establishing internal archival programs. The three organizations—a Catholic diocese, an educational institution, and a professional association—are diverse in purpose, structure, size, age, and other aspects, yet each shares common concerns in the establishment of internal archival programs that can manage its records and play a vital role in its organization's administration. Common themes and issues introduced in the previous chapters of this volume will be evident in these case studies, which are meant to reinforce both the importance of institutional archives and the elements that constitute effective and viable institutional archives.

The source of these case studies is recent consulting reports. While identifiers of the organizations have been removed, the flavor of the reports has been maintained to suggest the nature and importance of institutional archives.

A DIOCESE'S ARCHIVES

The Roman Catholic church in the United States has had a long tradition of concern for managing its records, especially its archival records, although the church has struggled (as most organizations have) with how best to preserve its most important records. There are many reasons for this tradition, including concerns for modern management techniques, celebration of significant anniversaries and events, and interpretation of the church's history and its larger role in society.[1]

All of these are excellent reasons the diocese should possess the best archival program it can attain. Its archival records provide valuable information for the administrative, fiscal, legal, and other continuing needs of the diocese. The records provide the primary source of information for documenting the diocese's important role in the Catholic church and the geographical area. Maintaining the archival records can instill a sense of trust among Catholics that important information relating to their church and their involvement in it is being maintained in a manner that their descendants can understand. A diocesan archives provides a public service by making available records vital to understanding both the sacred and the profane. Finally, an archival operation provides the main source of documentation for use in celebrating through research and exhibition the diocese's forthcoming anniversary of its founding.

Present Conditions of the Diocesan Archives

The diocese, like many parts of the United States and international Catholic church, has made some effort to preserve and provide access to its archival records. The fact that it has centralized some of its archival records, assigned some clergy and lay employees to work with its archival records, provided space in one of its important historic structures, and expressed interest in considering a renewal of the archival operation are all positive actions taken by the diocese. But the present archival program is but a shadow of what it must be in order to provide adequate care for its archival records and services to diocesan officials and other researchers needing access to them.

Although the diocese has had an official archivist for over 70 years, the diocese's archival program is in critical need of a drastic overhaul. There are at least six major problems that persist. First, the material in the current archives needs serious archival processing and preservation attention. Second, while these archival records are important to the diocese, there is a higher volume of archival records scattered about the diocese that have received little attention and that limit accessibility by diocesan officials and other researchers. Third, there is no system in place that provides for the regular and orderly transfer of archival records to the diocese archives. Fourth, the archival operation as it is presently organized can provide little archival assistance to the parishes and other bodies associated with the diocese; such assistance is desperately needed. Fifth, the diocese's archival program is underfunded. Sixth, present archival facilities are inimical to supporting an effective and useful modern archives program. Each of these problems is briefly described below.

Processing and Preserving Archival Records

When one enters the archives vault in the basement, it is easy to become impressed with the orderly appearance of the archives boxes, filing cabinets, and other storage containers. Indeed, the physical appearance is much better than is normally found in archival programs of similar size and resources. The appearance is, however, deceiving. There are no detailed or otherwise adequate finding aids to the diocesan archives, except for a brief listing of the records and an inventory of the records of one Catholic society prepared by a local graduate student. In fact, only about 10 percent of the current holdings of the archives has been thoroughly processed (arranged, described, and placed in acid-free materials), thus creating a formidable challenge to providing any substantive archival services to diocesan officials and other researchers. The portion of records that has received adequate archival attention is depressingly (even surprisingly) small for a program that has had archivists (even if part-time) for over 70 years.[2] Moreover, a large portion of the archives holdings has significant preservation problems—remaining in acidic folders and clamped or stapled with corrosive fasteners or residing on highly acidic and brittle paper. While some preliminary arrangement has been made of the records, there is still a decided lack of attention to some basic issues that are essential to the effective preservation of the diocese's valuable archival records.

Although there is greater protection provided to the archival records that have been gathered together, the larger quantities of records stored at diocesan administrative headquarters or the seminary possess similar (and greater) preservation and processing challenges. Records are dirtier and less secure either because they are stored in basements or garages or because they remain in office areas and are treated as current records, subject to daily and unregulated (at least according to archival standards) use. Even efforts at diocesan headquarters to provide better storage and control of the parish files are only a breeding ground for future problems since the storage materials are highly acidic and the microfilm lacks archival quality control (there are no reference copies, only negatives, and processing quality is an unknown factor since it is done by a commercial vendor with few guidelines provided).[3] These latter problems indicate why it is important for the diocese to secure the services of a professional archivist who can provide needed advice so that the diocese does not waste money or effort.

Scattered Nature of the Diocesan Archives

A primary purpose of any archival program is to identify and ensure the preservation and use of an institution's archival records. This purpose does not necessarily imply centralization of archival records, but meeting this mission does require intellectual and physical control over archival records wherever they reside.[4] While the diocese has made a start in this control with the archival records it has assembled, there are large amounts of archival or potential archival records located in various buildings owned by the diocese. The records of some of its defunct schools situated in the basement of one of the seminary buildings need to be brought into the archives. The same is true for the parish, property, chancery tribunal case files, and legal records stored in various locations of the diocesan headquarters. In fact, it is obvious that there are many gaps in the diocesan archival records in the period from the early twentieth century to the 1950s (especially in the bishops' records), gaps that prompt one to wonder whether these records are located in other diocesan buildings, held in private hands, or lost. This dispersion of archival records in the absence of a thoroughly integrated archival system is a disaster waiting to occur. At this point, it is possible for archival records to be lost or inadvertently destroyed without any notice (at least, not in a timely enough fashion to salvage the records). Archival records must find their own way to the archives, under the present situation, in the absence of any coordinated archival or records management system. The role of the present archivist seems to be too reactive, a role that cannot sustain the operation of an institutional archives.

An even greater problem is that there has been no analysis of the administrative offices of the diocese to identify additional archival materials nor any investigation about the archival records created by the parishes, their schools, and other organizations associated with the diocese. For example, with what degree of certainty can diocesan records be destroyed without some knowledge of these other records? Is it known if the diocesan records thoroughly document the history of Catholicism or even the diocese's own history in the geographical area? In other words, it is not possible at this time to determine to what extent the diocese's rich history can be thoroughly documented. The creation of a more comprehensive archives program is necessary for there to be any hope for providing such documentation. Without this determination, it is inevitable that important records will be lost, causing difficulties both for the ongoing administration of the diocese and for scholarly researchers and genealogists needing access to the diocese's archival records.

Lack of an Archives/Records Management System

The scattered nature of the diocese's archival records is further aggravated by two omissions. First, there is no records management program that provides for the orderly transfer of valuable records to the diocesan archives when these records' usefulness as current or active (frequently consulted) records needing to be maintained in the offices comes to an end.[5] A full-scale inventory needs to be completed, development of a records disposition schedule completed, and education of diocesan officials provided to ensure that records with archival value are transferred to the existing archives. The establishment of a records management program can also enhance the preservation of archival records before they come to the archives. Records of known archival value could be stored in, and/or produced with, acid-free materials and filing systems created in consultation with the diocese archivist to ensure that the records are in good condition and well maintained from their time of creation.[6] Taking such action would lessen the costs and other drain on resources of the archivist, archival staff, and volunteers once the records are taken into custody by the diocese's archives.[7]

Second, the present diocesan archives has no coherent acquisition policy (or mission statement). The archives seems to take whatever it is offered. It does not seem to distinguish clearly between official diocesan records, the records of quasi-diocesan entities, or the records of other Catholic organizations in the geographical area. Should the diocesan archives be reserved only for the official administrative records created by the diocese? Should it work toward becoming a central repository for records of area Catholic organizations and institutions? If such an acquisitions policy is adhered to, what is occurring to other valuable archival records documenting the history of Catholic institutions, people, and events? These questions must be considered soon in the reorganization of the diocese's archival operations. Some recommendations will be made later in this regard. The present absence of a coherent acquisition policy is indicative of the fact that there have been little systematic planning and analysis devoted to the diocese archives; it now operates, despite the good intentions of its archivist and volunteers, as a ship without a rudder. This situation seems contrary to a good statement of purpose for the diocese's archives—"the primary function of the diocesan Archives is to collect, preserve, organize, describe and make available for purposes of reference and research, all those administrative, fiscal and legal records of the Diocese which have permanent or continuing historical value"[8]—but the generally reactive perspective of the present archival operation definitely does not support meeting such a mission.

Archival Leadership by the Diocese in the Local Catholic Community

Closely related to the third issue is the relationship between the diocese's archives and other Catholic institutions and bodies in the immediate geographic area. Without question the 300 or more parishes in the diocese have played important roles in the Catholic history of the region. The present archivist has done an admirable job of collecting histories and other secondary materials about the parishes, and there are important records regarding the relationship between the parishes and the diocese in the diocesan headquarters. But these records probably do not represent adequate documentation about the history of the more important parishes. In fact, the careful gathering of secondary materials about the parishes has probably developed as a substitute for working on the more difficult challenges of preserving the official parish records; it is possible that this activity has diverted attention and resources from some of the more important activities of an effective diocesan archives and constitutes a mix of library and archival functions.

The diocesan archivist should provide assistance with archival expertise to these parishes to help them determine how best to preserve their historical records. The diocesan archivist should develop a strategy for identifying the most important or representative examples of the parishes so that their archival records can be preserved through the establishment of separate parish archives, microfilming of the records and centralization of the microfilm at the diocesan archives, placement of parish archival records in local public libraries or historical societies that can provide adequate care for them, or selective collecting of original parish archival records by the diocesan archives. The diocesan archives and archivist need to provide leadership by example and through workshops, advice, and other means to ensure that the history of Catholicism in the geographical area is well documented. This leadership seems in keeping with an amplification of the present mission of the diocesan archives that states that the "archives exists to collect and preserve records of permanent historical significance related to the history of the Diocese and the Catholic Church" in the area.[9] It is also in keeping with what has been done by a number of other diocesan archives throughout the United States.[10]

There is also the matter of other Catholic organizations, some of which have long and important histories and others of which have had shorter, but still powerful influences on the church. There are some of these records in the present archives, such as the records of the Council of Catholic Women and those of Catholic Charities, but these have come into the archives because of individuals' (associated with these organizations) interest in seeing the records preserved. The diocesan archives or archivist has not developed any proactive policy or program seeking such records despite their importance. Leadership in defining the role of the diocese's archives program is very much an issue to be resolved despite a long archival tradition.

Funding and Resources for the Archives

The present diocesan archives program is underfunded and undersupported. It is readily obvious that a modicum of support has been provided. One individual has been assigned part-time duties as archivist, and another has been assigned to provide clerical support. There is also little visible evidence of any sort of regular budget, with many of the current records in the archives still stored in highly acidic materials and inappropriate file cabinets and no evidence of any work by a professional conservator on the more valuable diocesan archival records that might need such treatment. The present vault where the records are stored is also probably subject to temperature and humidity fluctuations (despite the presence of a humidifier and dehumidifier), although efforts have been to made to provide some environmental controls, and there is probably poor air circulation or control of pollutants.[11] Conditions of archival records stored in basements and garages are, of course, more lamentable. The present archivist has little in the way of resources with which to work to rectify the situation. For example, there is no personal computer that could be used for word processing duties or for arrangement and description work (there are now a number of software packages available for both archival processing and records management functions such as records retention scheduling and inventory control of a records center). In sum, the diocese's archives program is losing ground in its efforts to identify, preserve, and make available its archival records.

Present Archival Facilities

The diocesan archives is located in a basement vault of the historic former chancery building constructed in the early twentieth century. In addition to the vault storage, the archives operation has two offices (one on the main floor and one outside the vault) for the present part-time archivist, a room where volunteers work, and a reception room on the main floor where the secretary works and can greet visitors coming to use the archives. While there are now other diocesan offices in the building, little of the available space for archival storage is being effectively used. The vault area is half-filled with inefficient filing cabinets, and there is inadequate space (both for security of the archival materials and for the comfort of researchers) in which to work. Moreover, the awkward division of the rooms in the basement provides a visual experience of the archives as an afterthought rather than a priority or responsibility of the diocese, in addition to creating problems for effective administration of researchers and proper security for the archival holdings.

The present conditions of the diocesan archives are made more problematic by the potential use of this historic building as an archives center. The beautiful rooms and spaces and the excellent location are not utilized to promote the diocesan archives. Neither is its proximity to local universities where archives students and researchers should be actively engaged in the life of the archives. Yet, at present, the diocesan archives seems to be known only by the local genealogical community and a few others who find it by accident and through word of mouth, with the resulting conclusion that "although a great variety of requests for information comes to the Archives, the majority pertain to churches and parishes, deceased clergy, and genealogical matters."[12] That the exterior sign on the building an-

nouncing the location of the diocesan archives is not very visible is evidence
of the inadvertent hiding of treasures here despite a succession of faithful
and dedicated archivists. It is time for the diocesan archives to come out
of the basement.

A Vision for the Diocese Archives

What the diocese needs to do is determine what its vision for its archives
is or should be. To provide some sense of possible future directions in the
development of a modern archives program, one version of what this vision
could be has been prepared. It provides the basis for recommendations
and suggestions for priority actions, as well as something that should lead
to discussion by diocesan officials as they decide on the future direction
for the archives.

The diocesan archives should be at the hub of the administrative activities
of the diocese and be regularly consulted as new policies are set, old policies
reevaluated, and relations with parishioners continued. The archives should
provide a mechanism for preserving the diocese's corporate memory and
be drawn upon for commemorative activities, for public relations, and for
an understanding of past activities and present trends. The archives should
also be the leader in the local Catholic community's efforts to preserve the
sources of its past and to understand the significance of that past. The
present archives facility should be a model showplace for this leadership
and serve as home for the archivist, workshops and other educational
activities to the Catholic community concerned with documenting its past,
exhibitions on local Catholic history, and other similar activities. Finally,
the archives should have close relations with area universities that both
train individuals to work as archivists and records managers and have
faculty and graduate students who are studying American religious history,
urban and local history, and other topics that might be enhanced by consultation of the diocese's archival holdings. To do this latter (and other
essential) work, the archives should be automated and employ other up-
to-date professional archival and records management practices.

Recommendations for a New Diocesan Archives

The recommendations that follow are, taken together, the primary actions needed to be followed for a modern, effective diocesan archives
program to be established, supported, and nurtured. Hiring a professional
archivist, refurbishing the archival facility, establishing a records management program, establishing a mission for the program, entering into an
arrangement with a local graduate archives program, and developing a
broader profile for the archival program in the Catholic community and
general public are all essential tasks that need to be accomplished for the

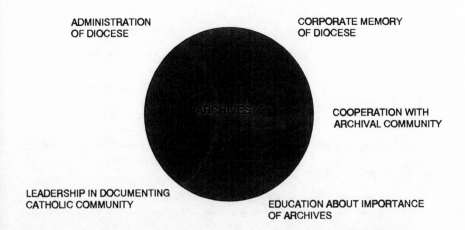

VISION OF A DIOCESE ARCHIVES

ADMINISTRATION
OF DIOCESE

CORPORATE MEMORY
OF DIOCESE

COOPERATION WITH
ARCHIVAL COMMUNITY

LEADERSHIP IN DOCUMENTING
CATHOLIC COMMUNITY

EDUCATION ABOUT IMPORTANCE
OF ARCHIVES

diocesan archives to function as a modern program. There are other, more specific tasks that also require attention, and these will be discussed in the next section. Of course, the diocese must provide more financial support to the archival program if it is to exceed its present limited scope; a concluding section on financial implications of these recommended activities is included.

Hire a Professional Director of Archives

The key ingredient to any successful archives program is having a professional director with appropriate education, knowledge of archival theory and practices, and a commitment to the archives profession. Not only will this position provide the necessary leadership for the development of an archives program, but it will be an addition that is attractive to granting agencies and for the placement of archival students. The National Historical Publications and Records Commission will not provide funding to programs that lack professional expertise. Conversely, the local university's new archives and records management program will not place fieldwork students in institutions that lack professional archival supervision.

The diocese should hire an individual who has graduated from a program that meets the Society of American Archivists' minimum guidelines for graduate archival education and who has sufficient expertise or demonstrates the ability to provide professional archival leadership and management skills. The entry-level position should be in a salary range plus the standard diocesan benefit package that will enable the diocese to attract an individual with the appropriate abilities, as well as demonstrate that this position is a high-level, professional one with diocesan support. In

STEPS FOR IMPROVING A DIOCESE ARCHIVES

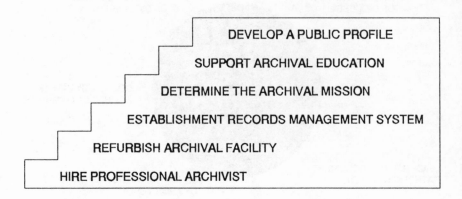

DEVELOP A PUBLIC PROFILE

SUPPORT ARCHIVAL EDUCATION

DETERMINE THE ARCHIVAL MISSION

ESTABLISHMENT RECORDS MANAGEMENT SYSTEM

REFURBISH ARCHIVAL FACILITY

HIRE PROFESSIONAL ARCHIVIST

addition, the diocese should provide enough funding for the new archivist to attend the annual meeting of the Society of American Archivists, the biannual meetings of the regional archival association, and professional seminars and workshops at the university and elsewhere; an annual professional development budget of about $2,000 will cover this necessary continuing education (necessary because of the rapidly changing nature of the archival profession). In addition to travel support, the archivist should have sufficient funds to acquire computer hardware and software, upgrade the microfilming facility, and properly house the archival records.

The diocese should also seek an archivist who has qualities essential to the task. The most important quality is the outlook of an archival manager. The diocese cannot hire an individual who sees the position as merely restricted to that of processing archival records. Rather, the archivist must see his or her main responsibility as being a program manager responsible for acquiring funding, building a comprehensive archives-records management program, and serving as spokesperson for the importance of archival and records management issues. This responsibility requires an individual who has general management skills, public relations abilities, grantsmanship, and the image of a professional (or the ability to develop all of these attributes), not just knowledge of archival and records management principles and practices. Obviously, the selection of the right person as diocesan archivist is crucial to the program's success.

Refurbish the Present Archival Storage Facility as an Archival Repository

This building has excellent potential as an archives facility for the diocese, although there are certain limitations that will need to be addressed in making optimum use of it. Its advantages are threefold: excellent location, more than sufficient space,[13] and interesting spaces that can be utilized for storage, reference room, exhibition areas, and processing and other archival offices. The building's limitations are likewise threefold: with one exception, although the overall space is sufficient, the small rooms limit efficient storage of archival and other records; lack of environmental controls throughout the building; and lack of elevator and other features that limit the building's effectiveness as an archives. These problems can be worked out in time, however, and improvements phased in as the archival program is developed under the direction of a professional archivist. What follows is a possible use of the building, although some decisions will have to be postponed until the diocese determines the scope of the mission of its archival operation, a records inventory is completed and records retention schedule is developed, and a thorough examination of the structure is completed under the guidance of an engineering consultant with the cooperation of the new archivist who can provide specific archival standards for heating, ventilation and air conditioning systems and archival security and access and who can oversee whatever work will need to be accomplished.

The main public aspects of the archival program should be moved to the first floor of the building. There are three main rooms in the front of the building. These rooms can be used for (1) an archival reference room for researchers, (2) a receptionist office for greeting researchers and providing archival services, and (3) an exhibition area for changing exhibits about the history of the diocese, Catholicism in the local area, and the role and work of the archival program.

The one large, open room should be shelved over and used for archival records storage. This largest room (although it has lower ceilings than desirable for such storage and the windows will have to be treated for reducing light and pollutants that can damage the archival records) can easily accommodate the approximately 1,000 cubic feet of archival records that will be moved into it and provide some room for growth in storage.[14] This will allow easy removal of records from storage to the reference room since it will all occur on the same floor and will also provide security for the archives; public visitors and researchers will be limited to the front rooms, and access to other parts of the building will be limited to staff and diocesan officials. There is also direct access to the room from the parking lot to provide the best means for records deliveries.

The basement floor, where the archives vault is presently located, could be transformed into a place for archival processing and other related work. The vault can be used for the storage of artifacts, records with intrinsic value, and microfilm of archival records of the diocese and other Catholic organizations and institutions that may be acquired as the archives program expands its operations. At least one room should be set up as a micrographics laboratory with microfilm equipment, including perhaps the electrostatic photocopier for convenience copying for diocesan officials, archives staff, and researchers.[15] The remaining rooms can be divided up for archival processing by regular staff, graduate students, and volunteers. One weakness in this scheme is the lack of a dumbwaiter or elevator to transfer records easily from one floor to another; the diocese will probably need to address this issue in the next few years to develop an optimum archival facility, but it should be reserved until a thorough study of the building can be made for determining the needs (and costs) of renovating the building into an optimum archival storage, processing, and reference complex.

The second floor of the structure can be used for three main purposes. First, one of the larger rooms should be transformed into a public meeting room that can be used as a classroom for archives classes, special lectures, and other public programs. The local university is interested in having its basic archives class meet there; essentially, this arrangement would provide the opportunity for these students to be taught archival principles and practices in a laboratory setting. Second, one of the smaller rooms should be used as a boardroom for meetings by the archives oversight committee and other special meetings by small groups. Another small room could be the archives director's office. Third, the remaining rooms could be used for storage of supplies, other archival records, and miscellaneous items; their use could be determined as specific needs arise.

One chief problem that the diocese will eventually face in the use of this building as an archives facility is the needed storage for inactive records, some of which will be eventually transferred to the archives and some of which will be destroyed after a period of storage time. It is unlikely that this structure has sufficient space for storage of both inactive and archival records. The diocese, however, could make use of one of the commercial records centers in the city for such storage. The diocese must be very sure of how it wishes to use such a service. The diocese will also not face this problem until it establishes a records management system, probably in the second year of the redevelopment of the new program, and should not move in this direction until the diocesan archivist has been hired, the diocesan archives mission determined, and a long-range plan for the archival operation worked out and approved.[16]

Establish a Records Management System for the Diocese

The only effective manner by which the diocese will gain satisfactory control over its archival records will be by establishing a records management system that is built on a comprehensive inventory of the records, a records disposition schedule, a records center (diocesan-owned and run or an arrangement with a commercial center), and ongoing relationships with the diocesan officials and office managers and staff most responsible for records creation and use. Every record series should have a specific scheduled time that it is maintained in the creating office and then transferred to the records center; from the records center the records are either eventually destroyed or finally transferred into the archives. Developing a records management program will require a number of essential elements:

1. An archivist familiar with records management
2. Support of the diocesan administrators to enable compliance of all managers and office staff with the approved schedule
3. An oversight committee of the diocesan officials (representing administrative, legal, fiscal, and historical viewpoints) that approves final schedules and sets records management policy
4. A facility to provide temporary storage of inactive records before their final disposition (the need of a records center has been discussed under the refurbishing of the facility).

There are, of course, numerous other advantages to records management programs beside ensuring the preservation of archival records. Such programs can enhance the efficient and effective retrieval of diocesan records, enable a convergence point for managers of information systems and other information workers to cooperate on information- and records-related problems and issues, and save the diocese money through the destruction of unnecessary records, cheaper storage in records facilities (such storage can be one-tenth or less of what storage in offices costs), and recycling of filing cabinets and other expensive office storage equipment.

Determine the Diocese's Archival Mission

There are, obviously, many possibilities for the breadth of activity that could characterize the diocesan archival program. This program could concentrate all of its activities on the official records of the diocesan administration, provide a broader leadership to the Catholic community, collect the records of quasi-diocesan organizations and other bodies, or accomplish all of these goals. What the diocese determines its mission to be will necessarily affect its activities, priorities, staffing, and financial issues. It is the foundation for what the diocese's long-range activities and short-term goals will be. The diocese can, however, wait until the professional archivist is hired (indicating to this person before he or she is hired, of course, that this work needs to be done) and charge this person first to do a careful internal analysis of records management and archival needs, present options, and then develop a plan of action. The most logical route to take, even if the diocese opts for the fullest archival program that is possible, is to phase in the program over a period of time by first focusing on the diocesan archival and records management needs (getting the house into some degree of order) and then moving on to broader issues and concerns.

This route makes sense from a variety of perspectives, including the judicious use of available resources and establishing an archival program that can serve as a model for the parishes and other Catholic organizations or be an inviting place to locate their archival records.

Become a Laboratory for Archival and Records Management Work and Education

The diocese has a unique opportunity, assuming that the program remains located at the present building, for becoming a laboratory for graduate students preparing to become archivists and/or records managers, as well as a model religious archives and records program for other Catholic organizations in the area. The building is closely located to a university that is developing a curriculum in archives and records management and that has related courses in rare books, special collections, and library and archival preservation. Moreover, the school is already offering short-term workshops and institutes on archival and related topics as well. Given this proximity, the opportunity to set up in the building a classroom for teaching, and a myriad of projects that could provide field-work opportunities for students, the diocese has the opportunity to become host to a variety of students who could perform valuable and needed work for the archival program.

The benefits to both the diocese and the school could be numerous, but since this report is focusing on the diocesan archives, it is worthwhile to consider potential benefits to it. Students could work on reducing the current, rather substantial processing backlog. They could work on projects such as analysis of users, preservation surveys, and other basic research efforts that could provide the diocese basic data that it needs to plan for and develop its archival program. Students could be of immense aid in special initiatives such as conferences, exhibitions, and preparation of publications that would assist the archives to reach a wider public. In all of these activities, both the students and the diocese would gain. If nothing else, teaching basic archives courses in the midst of archival records (where records could be easily accessible for providing examples of specific archival procedures and principles) would be an interesting and exciting environment for students, instructors, and, hopefully, archives staff. With all of this project work done by students, the diocese would save some money as well.

Developing a relationship with the university might also provide an opportunity to construct and offer a special topics course in religious archives, a ubiquitous feature on the American archival scene. Such a course could enable students to delve more deeply into one major type of archival institution that demonstrates both the operation of general archival principles and how those principles are applied to the records of a major type of institution.

Develop a Public Profile for the Diocesan Archives

Public programs have become a major preoccupation of most archival operations. Archivists now realize that merely gathering archival records together and processing them for access do not guarantee that the records will be as effectively used as they should or are hoped to be. Archivists now spend a considerable portion of their time and resources preparing publications, promoting use of the archival records, holding and hosting special events, and so forth. The diocese will need to do the same for its archival operation. These kinds of activities range from the public relations appeal of supporting an archival program to placing a sign on the present building that announces that it is the location of the diocesan archives.

It cannot be argued that public programming ought to be the first thing to do in the renewal of the diocese's archives, but the diocese needs to realize that this programming is an important component of a comprehensive archival system. The current archives facility encourages, in fact, attention to this kind of activity. The possibility of a classroom and an exhibition area in the building opens up opportunities for work of this sort that can be used to build greater awareness of the importance of history in the Catholic community, as well as the general public's sense of the importance of Catholics in their region. Possession of a fine auditorium/concert hall also provides opportunities for the diocesan archives to showcase its program and progress. Educational programs on religious archives and other archival topics could also be held at the building.

The diocese is already involved with preparation for the celebration of the anniversary of its founding. One of the early responsibilities for the newly hired diocesan archivist should be to work on an exhibition celebrating the history, perhaps in cooperation with the local museum. The diocese, however, needs to not let the anniversary overshadow the development of a comprehensive archives-records management program; the danger is that the celebration of the anniversary will delay the records program or undermine its full development. For this reason, the diocese should take several actions. First, it should set aside a sum of money for contracting with a professional exhibit designer (the costs will depend on the scale of the exhibition). This action will free the archivist from a time-consuming responsibility and ensure a professional exhibition (few archivists are also skilled in exhibit design, and a sloppily designed exhibition can do more harm than good). Second, the diocese should set up a special advisory committee to deal with this event. The archivist should be a member of this committee, but the committee should be different from the records advisory body. Third, the diocese should designate an individual other than the archivist as responsible for overseeing the preparation of the exhibition. The archivist's responsibilities should be limited to advising on selection of documents and artifacts for display and on making sure that these materials are displayed in a safe manner that enhances their preservation. The archivist's main responsibility should be in preparing a published inventory to the diocesan archives or some other form of publication that draws attention to the vital work of the archives in preserving the diocesan history and that provides a lasting contribution to the diocese's anniversary celebration.

Setting Priorities for a Renewed Diocese Archives

The initial year of the renewed diocesan archives program will be the most critical as this time will be devoted to establishing a suitable foundation for the program. There are many potential activities that could be undertaken during this time, as there are many potential pitfalls that could hamper the development of an archival program. The newly hired professional archivist will need to develop a long-range plan based on more intensive analysis of the diocesan records, the present facility, and other elements.

The activities suggested below are based on a one-year period. They are merely suggestive of a number of activities that a revamped diocesan archives program will need to become involved in as it expands its operations into a modern archives and records management program. It is difficult to determine a schedule of activities beyond this initial one-year period, since what occurs depends on diocesan action (and commitment and financial resources), the hiring of an archivist, and other variables. The schedule is based on the assumption that the diocese will hire a professional archivist and convert the present facility into an archival repository. If this action takes place, the diocesan archives program should accomplish a number of major activities during its first year:

1. Establishing an administrative structure for the new archives program

2. Shelving present archival storage areas

3. Completing a long-range plan for the archives

4. Transferring all known archival records to the present facility

5. Beginning work on the diocesan anniversary.

By the end of this first year, the diocesan archivist should be seeking additional funding support to complete a thorough analysis of the facility and to conduct a diocesanwide analysis of records to establish a records management program. Additional funding levels will depend on first-year accomplishments and decisions made about the program.

BUDGET FOR STARTING A DIOCESE ARCHIVES

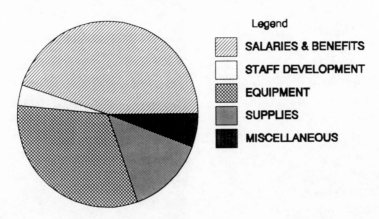

Legend

▨	SALARIES & BENEFITS
☐	STAFF DEVELOPMENT
▦	EQUIPMENT
▨	SUPPLIES
■	MISCELLANEOUS

Other Major Activities To Be Completed in First Three Years of Renewed Diocesan Archives

The following activities are the major initiatives that ought to be made as part of renewing the diocesan archives program. They are not listed in priority order since efforts to move forward in these areas will be concurrent. They are also closely related in scope and function. Since they have already been described, they are merely listed below.

1. Complete survey of diocesan records and information systems, leading to records retention and disposition schedule
2. Conduct analysis of the current facility for archival storage, including determination of environmental and security needs
3. Carry out survey of preservation needs of diocesan archival records and develop plan for appropriate action and acquisition of necessary funding
4. Evaluate diocesan micrographics program and facility and determine nature of micrographics services required by the diocese
5. Complete permanent exhibition on diocese and Catholic history that can be housed in the archives and toured elsewhere

Financial Considerations for the New Diocesan Archives: Start-up Costs

The following figures represent initial costs for starting a diocesan archives program. The figures are approximate, but a first-year allocation of $63,400 would provide a satisfactory level of funding for getting the program off on the right foot.

Salaries and Benefits	
Archivist's Salary	$24,000
Archivist's Benefits	4,800
Professional Development	
Travel, Workshops	2,400
Equipment[17]	
Computer	4,000[18]
Printer	2,500
Computer Software	2,000[19]
Records Shelving	12,000[20]
Supplies	
Acid-free Boxes	4,000[21]
Acid-free Folders	4,000[22]
Other Archival Supplies	1,000[23]
Miscellaneous	
Exterior Sign (Present Facility)	1,500
Consultants	2,000[24]

AN EDUCATIONAL INSTITUTION'S ARCHIVES

The report that follows concerns the care and management of an educational institution's archival and historical collections. This analysis is the result of a two-day visit to the institution and discussions with a number of individuals concerned with the institution's collections. The purpose of this analysis was to recommend ways that the organization could strengthen its archival and historical records program, although it must be stated at the outset that the institution also has the option of placing its historical materials with an existing historical records repository.[25]

Whether the institution fully develops its own archival and historical records program or not is a decision that its administration will have to make. The institution already has a good nucleus or foundation for developing such a program. A basic decision, however, has to be made. If the institution determines not to invest more resources into caring for its historical collections, there is no question that valuable materials will be lost and the administration of the institution itself harmed. Without such an investment, the institution should seek to place its historical collections in a historical records repository that has the sufficient funding, staff support, and facilities for maintaining such materials.

Mission: Setting the Scene

Although it is clear that the historical collections have been gathered to document the institution, there has been no effort to develop a mission statement that precisely defines the institution's archival and historical records function. This lack has had serious implications for the nature and support of the institution's historical collections. The significance of the collections is undermined by the serendipitous acquisition, arrangement, description, general care, and use of the archival records. Most of the records date from the earliest years of the institution, partly because there is no system that provides for the systematic transfer of the institution's records to its archives. There is also unclear administrative responsibility for the historical collections. This may account for the fact that the institution's financial provision for the historical materials is extremely meager and has prevented the archives from serving more useful roles in the ongoing administration and activities of the institution. Finally, there is no clear vision for the institution's historical collections, either for how these collections should be administered or for how they should be used in the administration and other programs.

Recommendation:

1. A mission statement should be developed that clearly defines the scope and purposes of the institution's archival and historical collections function. This mission statement should be drawn up in cooperation with the staff of the organization's library, the historian, and the appropriate administrative staff of the institution. The mission statement should be endorsed by the president of the institution.

Staffing of the Historical Collections

With the exception of the organization's official historian and one other part-time library employee, there are no staff resources to speak of. Part-time student help is sometimes available during the summer months for special projects, but whether this student help is provided adequate supervision or not is another issue that the institution needs to consider.[26] While the consultant was impressed with the enthusiasm and dedication of these individuals, it is also true that they have no relevant training that assists them in their duties of caring for the archival collections. Common sense and a strong knowledge of the institution's history are the main attributes that these individuals bring to their tasks. Many of the problems and needs discussed in this report are the result of the lack of archival knowledge and experience.

Recommendations:

2. The institution should create a regular, full-time archivist/records manager position and fill it with a well-trained and experienced individual.
3. The institution should use the professional archivist/records manager to train and supervise volunteers and student interns working with the historical collections.

4. The institution should provide additional funds to enable the archivist/records manager to attend appropriate professional meetings, conferences, and workshops.

Resources

Beyond the limited staffing and the physical space set aside for the archival holdings, the institution has apparently provided little in the way of resources to support the management, preservation, and use of these materials. Funds for the purchase of archival supplies come mainly from a private source of money, which provides about $400 annually. There are no other sources of funds, nor does there appear to be a separate budget account for the maintenance of the historical collections. In summary, there is without question insufficient financial resources to support the institution's historical collections, and the level of support provided by the institution itself is insufficient to foster the development of a quality historical and archival records program.

Recommendation:

5. In addition to creating and supporting the full-time archivist/records manager position recommended above, the institution should supply adequate funds for the regular maintenance of the historical collections. These funds should be initially used to purchase a sufficient supply of acid-free archival supplies and other needed storage equipment such as flat cases for oversized materials. Other areas requiring additional funds are mentioned in other sections of this portion of this chapter.

Appraisal of Historical and Archival Records

There is little sense at present of what records should go into the institution's archives. With older records, it is fairly easy to determine that they should be preserved, but more recent records pose greater problems. There is a lack of knowledge about basic archival appraisal criteria that would guide the identification of those records having continuing administrative, fiscal, legal, historical, and other research values. Decisions about what should be kept are often made in isolation, with little knowledge about the other kinds of information created and maintained by the institution. This problem is also exacerbated by the absence of any organization-wide records management program. Although the institution's archives and administrative quarters are separated by only a few hundred yards, there appears to be little coordination between the two operations. There were records of clear archival value in the vaults in the administration building that should have been in the archives. Moreover, the fact that any records come to the archives at all appears to be as much as by happenstance as anything.

The acquisition of nonofficial personal and family papers providing additional documentation on the institution is worth special emphasis. What is being done with the personal papers of people associated with the institution? What about the personal papers of leading administrative staff of the institution? None of these seem to have been given serious thought at this point. The newsletter recently started seems to be one excellent means by which to solicit such material and to report on its availability should the institution wish to use it that way.

Oral history is another aspect of the historical and archival records function that requires careful evaluation. Apparently, there have been some efforts to obtain oral reminiscences of significant individuals associated with the institution. There are, however, no standard practices being followed here, nor is there any clear sense of how such work should fit into the historical collections of the institution. For example, there does not appear to be any effort to connect the acquisition of an oral history with an underdocumented aspect of the institution. Furthermore, there does not seem to be any real facility for allowing researchers to use the oral history tapes.

Recommendations:

6. The institution should develop a coherent acquisitions policy to guide what goes into its historical collections.

7. The institution should establish an organization-wide records management program that provides for the orderly transfer of archival materials to the library.

8. The first task of the archivist/records manager should be to survey the institution's existing records.

9. A coherent plan for the use of oral history in documenting the institution should be developed and adhered to.

Arrangement and Description of the Institution's Archives

The scope of the institution's existing archival materials is impressive. There are extensive runs of the institution's publications, including annual reports, circulars, songbooks, magazines, and special publications. There are official files of presidents and other administrators as well as related organizations. Scrapbooks abound throughout the collections and provide supporting documentation regarding the institution's activities and individuals associated with it and these activities. A rich collection of photographs documenting the history of the institution is available. There is also an extensive collection of books about the organization or by staff, as well as some materials about local families and the history of the area. The collection of books used by the institution's clubs and related groups through the years represents a valuable resource for individuals interested in such groups.

Although the staff available to assist in the reference to the historical and archival collections has extensive knowledge of the collections, there is no satisfactory finding aid that a researcher could easily use when visiting the archives. The lack of any effort to organize the collections into their logical groupings or to provide a general description of the nature of these various components of the collections makes the use of these materials difficult at best and minimizes the capability of being able to discern gaps in the collections or to connect one group of records with related groups. There has also been no conscious effort to separate intellectually the institution's official records from books and printed materials about the organization and from personal papers and manuscripts (these are the three main groups of historical collections). Finally, the arrangement and description that have occurred have been somewhat ill-advised. One collection guide provided too much intricate detail on informational content, while the majority of the collections remained underdescribed. The continuing use of a library-type classification scheme for organizing archival and supplementary material developed a half-century ago encouraged the existence of these problems. There is no acceptable knowledge of current archival administration principles and procedures.

Recommendations:

10. The historical collections should be cataloged (arranged and described) following such basic archival principles as provenance and described using the US MARC AMC Format.

11. The institution should eventually seek to purchase a microcomputer and one of the software packages that provide for the use of the US MARC AMC Format.

Documentation of the Collections

Despite the extensive value of the institution's collections, there is virtually no documentation regarding how and why these collections have been assembled. This situation is partly the result of the lack of any systematic records management system that uses disposition schedules that govern when administrative records are either disposed of or sent to the archives. But the problem is more serious than that. The lack of documentation also reflects a lackadaisical attitude regarding the management of the historical materials that has resulted from meager resources, understaffing, and a lack of trained staff. Gifts to the collections are not regulated by any type of accessioning system, and, as a result, there seems to be no manner in which the provenance of an item could be determined.

Recommendation:

12. The institution should establish an accessioning system that indicates when collections or record groups are acquired by the archives and documents other pertinent information about the acquisition, such as originating office or source, restrictions, and so forth.

Facilities and Preservation of the Collections

At first glance, the facilities for the storage and use of the institution's records are quite pleasant. Several serious problems, however, plague the institution's historical collections in their current surroundings. First, the security of the collections is minimal. It is easy for the public to gain access to the areas where the collections are stored. This problem is compounded by having the museum on the same floor, inviting a larger public to want access to an area in which the historical materials are already generally insecure. Second, there are no environmental controls. The large windows bring in significant ultraviolet radiation directly on the collections and contribute to a space that must have widely fluctuating temperature and humidity readings through the year. An infestation of insects (wasps and bees) also indicated additional problems. Third, little is being done to provide physical care for the collections other than their storage in acid-free materials. Besides poor environmental conditions, some of the archival and historical materials are improperly stored on shelves; materials that should be stored horizontally are standing upright and the library-type shelving is generally inadequate for the archival materials and other historical collections. Finally, although an extensive quantity of the collection appears to have been microfilmed a decade ago, there is little knowledge by staff about what was filmed or desire to use that microfilm. The microfilm needs to be checked, and, if it is satisfactory, it needs to be used by researchers to save wear and tear on the original materials.

Recommendations:

13. The manuscript and archival collections should be moved into the rooms where the museum exhibitions and audiovisual collections are now located. This move will provide a more secure storage area for the original historical collections. These areas should also be shelved over and the windows treated to remove the damaging ultraviolet radiation. The reference area for researchers should be set up immediately outside these rooms.
14. The institution should acquire the services of a professional conservator to examine the facilities and to recommend actions that can be taken to improve the environmental conditions of the collections.

Reference

Although the consultant did not observe any reference activities, an impression of how reference is handled was gained through conversations with appropriate staff. Although the environmental conditions and security of the collections are problems, as described above, the actual working conditions for researchers are quite nice. The open, well-lighted room would be a welcome place for researchers to do their business. Yet, there are some problems that need to be addressed. There is no convenient summary of the collections or description of available finding aids. Researcher rules and regulations governing how the collections are used are nonexistent. The institution lacks a system of keeping records of who the researchers are, what they are doing, and what collections they have used (there is a short form that researchers complete, but it is unclear how this is used by the institution). There is no information about institution-related collections in other repositories, although some of the papers of past presidents have apparently gone to several universities. That the collections have been used by researchers is evident in the publications about the institution as well as the substantial number of dissertations (a number of which are available at the library) done through the years concerning the institution and its influence in American education, religion, and life.

Recommendations:

15. The institution should develop and use a policy governing the careful use of its historical collections.
16. A summary guide should be developed that enables easier use of the historical collections by researchers.
17. The institution should acquire copies of finding aids to other related collections located in other archival and historical records repositories.

Public Programs

It is obvious that the institution's historical collections have an especially important role to play in this organization's interaction with the public. One of the prominent aspects of the organization is its long and significant history. The public relations releases draw on this history, and it is obvious that one of the attractions of visiting the institution is to become part of its long and colorful tradition. Yet, it is also apparent that the institution is not utilizing this tradition in respect to its historical collections. The small museum has been unchanged since the institution's centennial 15 years ago, and there is little effort to relate that museum function to the other historical collections that are only a few feet away.

Recommendations:

18. The institution's administrators should be consulted to determine the best uses that can be made of its historical collections in publicizing the institution and in its educational programs.
19. A museum consultant should be used to determine the best nature of a museum

program for the institution and how such a program should relate to its historical collections operation.[27]

Other Concerns and Issues

One of the most interesting aspects is the movement that created educational institutions like this one around the United States. It seems that some of these other organizations have contacted the original organization to determine the preservation and management of its archives and what related material there is in this archives. This interest by related organizations represents an interesting opportunity to document the entire movement. If the institution could develop a model archives program, it could more readily provide advice to the other organizations and determine how the archival records of the entire movement should best be handled.

There is a large quantity of books and other printed materials that have no historical value to the institution and that are located in the middle section of the second floor of the library. Some of these materials may have monetary value and could be sold. One possibility would be to use the proceeds from such disposal to benefit the care of the institution's archival and historical collections, perhaps in the purchase of storage materials and equipment.

Recommendations:

20. The institution, provided it more firmly secures its own archival and historical records program, should seek to secure external funds to plan for the documentation of the movement.[28]

21. The extraneous books located on the second floor of the library should be sold and the proceeds used to support the care of the institution's historical collections.

Final Thoughts and Recommendations

Establishing, developing, and supporting an archival and historical records program are a serious and costly responsibility. The institution has noteworthy historical materials, facilities that could be prepared to provide optimum care for these collections, and innumerable reasons why it should have such a program. What it most clearly lacks at this point is archival expertise. To carry out all of the recommendations made above, the institution needs to commit itself first to creating a position of archivist/ records manager at a salary that will attract a well trained and experienced individual. This individual should have as his or her responsibilities the establishment of an organization-wide records management program that ensures the cost-efficient management of the records and information systems and the regular transfer to the archives of records possessing con-

STEPS FOR IMPROVING AN EDUCATIONAL INSTITUTION'S ARCHIVES

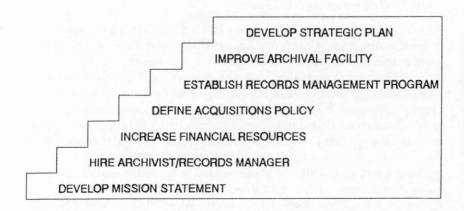

DEVELOP STRATEGIC PLAN

IMPROVE ARCHIVAL FACILITY

ESTABLISH RECORDS MANAGEMENT PROGRAM

DEFINE ACQUISITIONS POLICY

INCREASE FINANCIAL RESOURCES

HIRE ARCHIVIST/RECORDS MANAGER

DEVELOP MISSION STATEMENT

tinual administrative, legal, fiscal, and historical value. This individual should also be responsible for developing a quality historical records program that leads to the proper care and use of the historical collections. The archivist-records manager should also be able to seek external funding for special projects that enhance the organization's care of its historical collections; grants could be sought from a variety of sources to provide additional funds for preservation of the collections, special programs such as exhibitions and publications, and oral history. Finally, the archivist-records manager's first task should be to see that the institution's historical collections are the subject of a three-to five-year plan that incorporates all of the recommendations in this consultant's report in a logical manner.

Recommendations:

22. The institution should create and fill a position for a professional archivist/records manager.
23. The archivist/records manager should coordinate the development of a three-to five-year plan for the establishment of a quality archival and historical records program.

Costs

What follows are some very rough approximations of the costs of establishing and sustaining a quality archival and historical records program at the institution. Yearly costs would be about $30,000, including about $25,000 for salary and fringe benefits for a professional archivist/records manager, $2,000 for travel and education, and $3,000 for archival and other

BUDGET FOR STARTING AN EDUCATIONAL INSTITUTION'S ARCHIVES

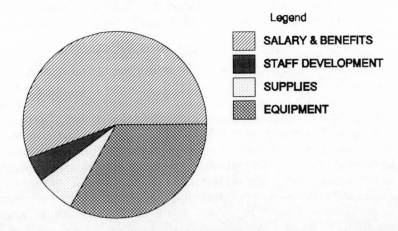

Legend

SALARY & BENEFITS

STAFF DEVELOPMENT

SUPPLIES

EQUIPMENT

supplies. Other onetime costs would be involved. These include $10,000 for metal records center shelving and window treatments, $5,000 for a microcomputer for word processing and supporting US MARC AMC Format descriptive software. Other costs, such as for exhibitions, renovation of the storage facilities, and the like, could be at least partially supported through outside funding.

A PROFESSIONAL ASSOCIATION'S ARCHIVES

Reasons for an Archives and Records Management Program

Like many professional associations, this association and its related organizations—the press, a certification corporation, and foundation—exist to promote professional standards, exchange information through publications and meetings, stimulate research, provide continuing education opportunities, encourage recruitment into the field, build a professional community, foster excellence by practitioners, and improve public image and government recognition of the discipline.[29] Essential to accomplishing such tasks are the effective management of the society's own records and information systems and the identification, preservation, and availability of use of the society's archival records and the archival records of the larger profession. Membership organizations, like the society, must often respond to membership needs and requests in a timely and effective manner, as well as providing and promoting a continued sense of the discipline's origins, traditions, and culture. Records management can assist the former, while an organizational archives program can support the latter. Records management and archival programs are also especially important for an organization like this that is the primary professional association for an important aspect of the broader professions and that has responsibility for work that is involved with one of the most significant problems of the late twentieth century.

Records management (or, as it is becoming increasingly called, information resources management) will provide an efficient and cost-effective solution to the society's information needs and will meet some of the association's other aims described above. Through records management principles and techniques, an organization can enhance the effectiveness of locating needed information. Effectiveness, as it is used here, refers to speedy access to the essential information required to resolve problems, make decisions, reevaluate programs, meet clients' requests, and generally assist the management of the organization. Through records management principles and techniques, an organization can also improve the efficiency of its information systems. Efficiency, as it is used in this context, refers to the ability to manage suitable information systems in a cost-effective manner and to be able to reduce or eliminate costs through the planned and regular destruction of unnecessary records, the storage of records in lower-cost facilities, and the recycling of expensive records storage containers. Security of vital records (those records that are crucial to the organization's functioning) is another typical benefit of records management programs.

Records management consists of a number of key components. Essential to the administration of records management programs is adherence to the life cycle concept of records or information. In this concept, records are viewed as following a standard sequence of viable use from creation through active use, then lessening use where records may be removed from the office into a less costly records center, to final disposition through destruction or transfer to an archives. Supporting the life cycle concept is the preparation of a records retention/disposition schedule in which every specific records series has been examined, described, and assessed according to its continuing importance to the organization; each records series is assigned a specific period of time for which the records are maintained and then destroyed or transferred to an archives. Such schedules become crucial tools for the administration of organizations. Needed in the preparation of such a schedule are the completion of an inventory of the organization's records and a systems analysis of the manner in which the organization utilizes information. Records management programs may also include forms design and control operations, responsibility for reports and directives management, supervision over information and records systems, and involvement with the mail (including electronic mail and facsimile transmission) systems. Records management programs are always responsible, if they are intended to be comprehensive in scope, for records' reprographic services and archival operations.

An archival program seeks to identify and preserve those records valuable for documenting an organization's continuing work through the years and for nurturing a sense of its own past. Such records are sometimes the organization's older or inactive records, but it is just as likely that the archival records will include records that are relatively recent in origin and that may be in active use in the office. For a young organization like the society, supporting a program that cares for its archives (and, as will be discussed here, for other records relating to the general documentation of the profession) can help to foster a sense of tradition and self-identity among its membership and the members' allegiance to their profession. An archival program can also fulfill other, more specific purposes as well. It can preserve records that can be used for educational and public relations activities. An archival operation can assist in the maintenance of certain records vital to the society's continuing programs and activities. It can aid in the protection of records relating to the society's membership. Finally, the archives can serve as a source of reference materials to support the kind of research that the society has been sponsoring and assisting in through the years, as well as help to preserve the results of officially sponsored research that has been completed.

An archival program supports a variety of specific functions. It is responsible for determining what records should be preserved (appraisal). An archival operation is charged with determining what aspects of an organization should be reflected in the archival records (documentation). Archival programs are responsible for the protection of the historical records in their care (preservation and security), facilitating access by researchers to the records (arrangement, description, and reference), and promoting their effective use (public programs). Supporting all of these functions is a well-articulated set of archival theories, principles, and practices that concern such matters as selection criteria, the description of records for use, and criteria for what records can be reformatted into microfilm or electronic form.

The purpose of this report is, then, to describe and recommend actions for the society and its related organizations to undertake to establish and develop solid records management and archives programs. The report is based on interviews with key personnel in the various departments, the press, certification corporation, and foundation and an examination of the records being created and maintained by these offices. Each interview sought information about the function of the office, the nature of records and information systems maintained by the office, problems regarding the administration of these records and information systems, use of the records, concerns, and concepts of the historical value of the records, and projections of the future development of the office and implications of this development for the office's records and information systems.

The Present State of the Society's Records

This time is a good point in the society's history to consider the establishment of records management and archival programs. At this time, the society has not been overwhelmed with its records, and most of the records have been retained due to the relatively small quantity that it is presently handling. There is, moreover, a long-term memory of staff evident in the organization's operation, due both to the society's founding only 15 years ago and to the presence of a number of employees who go back to or near the founding of this organization. The rapid growth and diversification of the society, however, provide evidence that the presence of a satisfactory corporate culture can be undermined in the near future. This is only one of many reasons the society should consider the establishment of records management and archival programs.

The threat to the present strong culture of the society can be seen in the number of existing records problems, enumerated below:

1. Duplication of records. Throughout the society there is evidence of the duplication of records. For example, nearly every department head holds copies of certain key documents, such as Board of Directors' minutes, for their own reference purposes. While this problem in itself is not serious, it appeared that in some instances there was uncertainty by the personnel about where the originals of these duplicated records were and the manner in which the originals were maintained. Since there are no specified retention periods for the maintenance of records and each department is left on its own to determine the retention of its records, there exists the distinct possibility that original and important records might be inadvertently destroyed. An equally serious problem is that an excessive quantity of records might be duplicated, adding unnecessary costs to the society in records creation and storage and creating additional problems in the retrieval of needed records and information.

2. Uneven decision making about records disposition. There is, without any doubt, uncertainty about how long records should be retained. This is the natural consequence of the lack of a records retention/disposition schedule that provides guidance in the retention of the records. The results are easy to predict. Some department heads are retaining all records, while others are regularly weeding out records that are not necessary for their administrative purposes. There are no criteria in use here other than the judgment by the department heads that the records have value or no value for their own needs and the existence of certain external record-keeping requirements, such as those imposed by the national professional association on the society for accrediting the latter's continuing education programs. For example, one department head maintains one "record" copy of certain society publications, while another keeps two copies.[30] While there does not seem to be any serious damage inflicted upon the documentation of the society, the present scenario provides the ingredients that some valuable records might be destroyed or that obsolete records might be retained at unnecessary cost to the society.

3. Unnecessary storage of records in a commercial records center. Because of the lack of a records management program with a retention/disposition schedule, the society may be wasting monies on storage in the commercial records center that it is using. The society's decision to store certain records off-site, out of the more expensive office space of its headquarters, is sound. It also appears, however, that obsolete records that could be destroyed are being stored in the commercial records center and that inactive records that should be stored out of the offices are still being retained in the offices. While the present costs are relatively modest (approximately $1,800 a year), the costs of $20 for each records delivery and pick-up easily reflect how expensive this service could become. These problems can be easily resolved by the formation and implementation of a records retention/disposition schedule.

4. Purchase of expensive filing equipment, rather than planned disposition, is used to resolve the problem of the growth of the volume of records. Because the society is a growing organization, its records are expanding in quantity. The society presently resolves this problem by purchasing additional filing equipment when existing filing equipment is filled. Not only is this equipment expensive, but it takes up equally expensive office floor space. The resolution of the society's records problems does not rest with adding filing equipment, but rather in determining what records should be retained, how those records should be retained, and where the records should be stored. For some of the society's records, their removal from filing cabinets to far more inexpensive standard records center cartons that are stored off-site in less costly space is the preferred action. For some other society records, their destruction is the preferred option. In both cases, the society will save money and reduce the number of expensive filing cabinets needed to be maintained in its various offices.

5. Lack of security copies of vital records. Many of the records being created and maintained by the society are, obviously, crucial to the effectiveness of the society's work and the meeting of its mission. There is, with the exception of making duplicate copies of computerized electronic financial records, little provision for the safeguarding of the society's records. A fire or other man-made or natural disaster could destroy many records that have no back-up copies and lead to serious problems in the continued functioning of the society. Nearly every department head the consultant talked with expressed concern with this problem. The resolution of this problem alone is reason enough to establish a records management and archives program.

6. Lack of knowledge about what records possess historical value to the organization. Because the society's staff is strongly committed to the society's mission, there is a well-developed sense of the historical importance of the organization and the profession that it supports and serves. There is also, however, a strong sense of frustration in being able to determine what records possess historical value. The department heads consistently asked in their interviews what records should be saved for this purpose, while also expressing a wide range of attitudes about what records have such value and the criteria used to identify these records. This finding is, of course, not surprising; there is no archivist/records manager on staff at the society at present to provide such guidance.

7. Lack of knowledge about how society historical records should be maintained.

BARRIERS TO EFFECTIVE MANAGEMENT OF A PROFESSIONAL ASSOCIATION'S RECORDS

GOOD
RECORDS
MANAGEMENT

RECORDS DUPLICATION

FAULTY RECORDS DISPOSITION

UNNECESSARY USE OF
   COMMERCIAL RECORDS
   CENTER

PURCHASE OF FILING
   CABINETS TO SOLVE
   RECORDS PROBLEMS

LACK OF SECURITY COPIES
   OF VITAL RECORDS

LACK OF KNOWLEDGE ABOUT
   ARCHIVAL VALUES

Throughout the society's headquarters, staff is struggling with how to store records it believes possess historical value to the organization. Due to the lack of training in this area, inadequate decisions are being made. Newspaper clippings are, for one example, maintained in their original form, when they should be either microfilmed or photocopied onto acid-free, archival paper. The Board of Directors' minutes are stored in looseleaf binders, when the originals should be maintained in archival folders and boxes and the original minutes created on acid-free paper. There are questions about other kinds of recording media, such as videotapes, throughout the society departments. In this environment, there is a high degree of likelihood that incorrect decisions might be made that threaten the society's archival records.

These problems are convincing evidence that without the establishment of a records management and archives program, the society's records problems and costs will grow and archival records will be ultimately lost.

The society possesses, however, a number of potential strengths that it can use to build an effective records management and archives program. These strengths are as follows:

1. The society's small and compact size and well-organized structure. Although the society has experienced rapid growth, it is a well-structured and well-run organization. The various departments have specific functions in which overlap is minimal. The creation of related bodies, such as the foundation and the press, has been clean and clear. Despite the growth, moreover, the society is still a compact organization in which communication occurs easily and decisions are readily made and carried out. All of these attributes provide the potential for an easily established records management and archives program because the

records functions are clear and distinct and the establishment of such a program has the possibility of easily evaluating information and records systems and making decisions about these systems and the retention/disposition of the records.

2. Possession of a strong mission statement and sense of mission. The society staff's sense of mission and commitment to that mission were impressive. This kind of attitude, essential to a strong, positive corporate culture, can be drawn upon to gain support for an organizationwide records management and archives program because this kind of program can be readily demonstrated to support such a mission and level of commitment. Concern for the historical role of the discipline, the image and importance of this discipline, and the mission to deal effectively with cancer as a major health problem can all be drawn upon to gain support and enthusiasm for an effective and efficient records management and archives program. The identification and preservation of the society's archival records can be explained as supporting the documenting of the society's historical role and the profession itself.

3. Good communication of society staff across division lines and "turf." One of the major obstacles to the establishment, development, and effectiveness of any records management and archives program is an organizational staff that is characterized by lack of communication or divided by concern over its department's prerogatives and responsibilities. The reason is that any records management and archives program crosses over and through organizational divisions, boundaries, and hierarchies. While such a program requires top-level support, it is also responsible for all of the records of the entire organization. The society seems to be an extremely hospitable environment for the location of such a records management and archives program. The society's staff seems to communicate very effectively and to cooperate across organizational borders. While this situation may explain why the duplication of records seems to be such a problem, the importance of this situation is that it would easily accommodate the work of a records manager and archivist.

4. A strong degree of professionalism. The professionalism and commitment of the society's staff have already been noted in several places in this report. It needs to be reemphasized here, however, that these strengths can help to guarantee the success of a records management and archives program if it is established by the society. First, it is easy to demonstrate how such a program can make the responsibilities of the society's staff easier and carried out in better ways. Second, a professional records manager and archivist will undoubtedly be greeted with acceptance as a peer and colleague.

5. Beginning of automated information systems. The society is already beginning to automate its information system in a comprehensive manner. The financial operations have already been done, and steps are under way to automate membership services and fund-raising activities by the foundation. This movement provides the opportunity to develop an automated records management system that allows all staff to determine easily when its records should be destroyed, transferred to a records center, or turned over to the archives. Likewise, the finding aid to the archival records could be automated, allowing society per-

sonnel to determine when there are archival records relevant to their own activity or research.

The society represents, then, an extremely hospitable environment for the establishment of an archives and records management program. The success of this program is highly likely, and its potential benefits to the organization are very great.

The remainder of this chapter provides more detail about what a records management and archives program should look like, how it can be phased in, and the potential costs of this program to the society.

What the Society Records Management and Archives Program Should Look Like

The purposes of records management are to allow for efficient, economic, and effective control of an organization's recorded information. In information resources management (the more recent manifestation of records management), the information contained in an organization's records is viewed as a resource much like equipment, facilities, and personnel. Information represents an investment. A lack of control over it can lead to poor business practices and services to customers and a failure to meet the organization's mandates. A loss of the archival records can lead to a faulty organizational memory that interferes with the organization's current activities and programs.

What does a society records management and archives program need to look like? What services does it need to provide to the organization and on behalf of its membership and the profession? What needs to be done to establish a successful society records management and archives program?

The society's records management program ought to include an effective records retention/disposition system, an archival component (which will be described in this section and in more detail later in the report), a facility for off-site storage of its inactive records, a standing committee composed of society staff and several other external representatives to oversee the program, a disaster preparedness plan for its records, and a staff person who is trained in, and knowledgeable about, records management and archival theory, principles, and practices. This program ought either to be a separate society department or to be directly under the executive director; the point is that the program needs to have visibility and authority to accomplish its objectives. The initial part of this section of the chapter discusses each of these programmatic elements in more detail. The remainder of the section considers how the program should be initiated and phased in.

The concept of a records retention/disposition system has been described briefly before. To develop such a system, the society needs to do a thorough inventory of its records and systems analysis of its information systems. The universe of the organization's documentation must be understood, including how that documentation is or is not used in the society's activities. The tool used to create this schedule is an inventory sheet that captures the following kinds of data for each series of records created and maintained by the organization: title of records series, span dates of the records, creating office, function of the records, description of the records formats and informational contents and other features, volume of records, related records, whether there are duplicated copies of the records elsewhere, audit requirements, legal requirements, administrative requirements, frequency of use, and historical value. These data are used to create a final schedule (which is updated as records series are deleted or added) that includes the title of the records series, creating office, and final disposition instructions; these instructions usually include noting whether the records will be retained in the creating office, transferred to a records center after a specified period of time, sent to the archives storage area after a specified period of time, destroyed, or reformatted for security or preservation purposes. This schedule is the backbone of an effective records management and archives program.

The society's archives program can consist of two major portions: one that cares for the actual records of the society that possess archival value and another that is responsible for documenting the profession. The first part of this archival component is the most straightforward in concept and execution. It focuses on the records created and maintained by the society.[31] The archival records are identified as the records inventory is prepared and the retention/disposition schedule developed. Each records series is assessed for its evidential and informational values, concepts that will enable the organization to determine which records not only possess value to the society's ongoing operation but possess information essential for documenting the historical evolution of, and main features of, the society or provide other information of value to individuals seeking to understand the history of the field. As these records are identified, they should be transferred either to a separate archival facility within and supported by the society or to another archival repository within close geographic proximity to the society.

The society might also wish to develop a broader mandate for its archival operation. The society ought to consider this because of its more general interest in the entire profession, the nature of the research that it has sponsored on the profession's standards and image, and related interests. Here the society might wish to follow the model of a "discipline history center" that has become a common feature in the science and technology fields. A discipline history center, usually associated with a research center or professional association, exists not to collect the archival records of its field but to ensure that these archival records are identified and preserved in appropriate repositories. Such centers seek to determine what aspects of the discipline should be documented, conduct surveys to ascertain the nature of the documentation that is available and that might already be in archival repositories, encourage the placement of archival records in the repositories or the creation of new repositories, and serve as a clearinghouse of information for researchers interested in the history of the field. The society should work toward becoming a discipline history center in its field.

The society has already committed itself to the use of an off-site commercial records center and utilizes the services of the nearby center for the storage of its inactive records, publication stocks, and supplies for its annual congresses. Such a facility is another essential aspect of any records management program, generally providing low-cost storage for inactive records. The society, however, needs to reevaluate at least two aspects of its current arrangement. First the society needs to determine whether the records it is storing in this facility even need to be maintained at all. Second, the facility needs to be assessed from a records management perspective for cost, security, environmental controls and protection, and other similar aspects. While in principle the use of this kind of facility is good, it needs both to be the right kind of facility and to be used in the context of an active, comprehensive records management and archives program.

The society also needs to establish a records management and archives committee that is responsible for oversight of the program and that ensures both what records are maintained and the wider aspects of the archival component. This committee ought to be composed of the key society staff, along with legal counsel and other society advisers who can determine the retention periods of the records from legal, financial, administrative, and historical or research perspectives. The primary responsibility of this committee should be establishing and maintaining the records retention and disposition schedule. Other responsibilities should include overseeing the society's relationship with the commercial records storage facility, evaluating requests for the purchase of records storage equipment, and approving staff training in records management and archival administration. The committee should be fairly compact in size, consisting of no more than six or seven individuals, and meet as often as desirable to establish the schedule and then quarterly or semiannually from that point. Given the present nature of the society's corporate culture, there should be little difficulty in this committee's freely interacting with the society staff in determining the maintenance of the records. If the society moves to establish a discipline history center, then a different kind of supervisory committee will be needed, consisting of historians of the field determining what components of the field should be documented and how they should be documented and maintaining liaison with the society's records management and archives committee. This latter committee should be separate from an internal records management and archives committee, although the activities of the two should be carefully coordinated.[32]

The society must also possess a disaster preparedness plan for the protection of its informational resources. Disasters, man-made and natural, can occur without warning and inflict serious damage to an organization's records. A disaster preparedness plan is one effort to ensure that the appropriate action is taken in response to such an event. It is based on the premise that quick and appropriate response can often ensure that an institution's organizational records can be saved. Such a plan is a natural outgrowth of a records management and archives program and includes several essential aspects. The society, to possess such a plan, would have to have a detailed location of all its records and have identified what of these records are vital to the society's ongoing work. Ideally, there would be off-site, security copies of all of the vital records. In addition, each staff person would have specific responsibilities in the event of a disaster, and the organization will need to have worked out plans with local fire departments and certain kinds of suppliers to ensure that prompt and appropriate responses are taken in case of such a disaster's striking the offices.

Finally, the society ought to have a person who is responsible for the records management and archives program. There are two basic alternatives that the society can follow here, depending on the scope and nature of the program that it wishes to implement. The first is a program that is restricted to managing the society's own records. In this kind of program, the society could have a part-time records manager and archivist by supporting a staff person's acquiring training in this area and using consultants at key points in the development of the program. Consultants should be used for advising on the development of the records retention/disposition schedule, the plan for an archives facility, development of a disaster preparedness plan, and other such activities. The second alternative is appropriate if the society decides to develop a discipline history center in tandem with a program for its own records and archives. If the society pursues this goal, it must seek to hire a full-time, professional archivist and records manager, an individual with appropriate education and experience.

Setting Up the Society Records Management and Archives Program

This and the following section are concerned with two areas. The first is a brief description of the steps needed to be followed in establishing a records management and archives program. The second area is a proposal for phasing in such a program. Both instances have been described based on the assumption that the society is moving toward a full-fledged records management and archives program and a discipline history center. The society should do so because of the benefits to the society and the nature of the society's mission and activities. It should be easy, however, to make revisions to the following recommendations if the society opts for a more limited program.

The following steps should be taken in establishing a records management and archives program:

1. Set up records management and archives committee. The purpose and responsibilities of this committee have been described earlier. This committee should provide oversight and coordination of all activities concerning the records management and archives program and should also be responsible for the development and implementation of a records retention/disposition schedule.

2. Complete records survey of the society. A complete analysis of the existing records and information systems needs to be done. This can be done in consultation with a records management and archives consultant who can advise on the development and use of an inventory sheet and provide training to staff to fill out the forms. If the society uses a consultant, it may also be possible to hire a records management and archives student from an area university to work with the consultant to complete the inventory. The student could complete the inventory through an inspection of the records and interviews with the society staff.

3. Establish and implement records retention/disposition schedule. This schedule is the backbone of an effective records management and archives program. Based on the analysis of the records and information systems, the records committee should analyze each records series and assign an appropriate retention schedule. Once the schedule is completed, the society staff should be introduced to it and trained in how it is intended to be used. A half-day training session, perhaps conducted by the consultant employed in the development of the schedule, could be useful in demonstrating to the staff what the schedule is, how it works, and its implications for the staff's work. By this time, of course, the society will need to have, at the least, designated an existing staff position as liaison to the records committee and as having responsibility for the use of the schedule. This staff person should oversee the destruction of records and the transfer of inactive records to the commercial records facility. Records that have been determined to have vital or archival value should be noted by this person, but the task of dealing with these records should be left to the time when the society employs an archivist/records manager.

4. Hire a professional records manager/archivist or assign existing staff person to this position and support that person's training. No later than this time, the society needs to invest in having a full-time archivist and records manager (again, this step is dependent on the society's determining to support a discipline history center). This person is essential to implementing the retention/disposition schedule, planning for the society's archives program, working with the records committee, and reevaluating how the commercial records facility will be utilized in storing inactive records and protecting vital records. The archivist and records manager, in tandem with the records committee, should also have the authority to control records related purchases such as filing cabinets and advise on other

STEPS IN ESTABLISHING A PROFESSIONAL ASSOCIATION'S
RECORDS PROGRAM

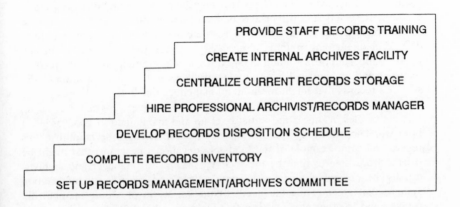

PROVIDE STAFF RECORDS TRAINING

CREATE INTERNAL ARCHIVES FACILITY

CENTRALIZE CURRENT RECORDS STORAGE

HIRE PROFESSIONAL ARCHIVIST/RECORDS MANAGER

DEVELOP RECORDS DISPOSITION SCHEDULE

COMPLETE RECORDS INVENTORY

SET UP RECORDS MANAGEMENT/ARCHIVES COMMITTEE

information systems and any other activities that need to be established to help an effective records management and archives program to be developed.

5. Consider establishment of a central current records filing area in the society's offices. One possible means of resolving certain records problems, such as duplication and retrieval, is to consolidate the files in a centralized area to which all staff has access. This solution is viable for the society, given its scale of operations. All that would be required is the assignment of several staff members to manage the records and to administer a program that keeps tab on the location of any specific file. Such an operation should be considered, however, only after the society has analyzed its records and developed a records retention/disposition schedule; this will indicate the necessity or scale of such a centralized records filing area.

6. Establish an internal archives facility and program. Using the records retention/ disposition schedule, the archivist and records manager should move to establish a facility for the storage and administration of the society's archival records. The schedule will provide the information needed for determining the scope of the facility based upon the volume of archival records. To establish this facility, an office area will have to be set aside to be shelved over for the storage of the records, acid-free archival storage containers and supplies acquired and the records placed in these materials, and an inventory of the archival records completed for use by society staff, society membership, and outside researchers. Guidelines for access to, and use of, the records will need to be developed, approved by the records committee (and in some cases, the society governing board), and put into effect. Publicity about the availability of the society's archives will also need to be done to ensure that the society membership and other external researchers are aware of the records and supporting program. Once the society's archival program is established, the records manager and

archivist should turn his or her attention to the development of the discipline history center.

7. Provide ongoing society staff training and guidance in the area of records management and archives. Once a records management and archives program is established, society staff will need to be given periodic orientations to the nature of the program and instruction in areas where needs develop or are identified. This kind of ongoing training is necessary because there will be, as in any organization, staff turnover and changes. Just as important, however, the records manager and archivist will identify new problems in the administration of the society's records that might merit additional educational efforts. For example, a basic problem in any records management and archives program is ensuring that active files in offices are initially set up and maintained in good order; a brief workshop on filing systems and administration could be helpful in this regard and is an example of the kinds of educational programs that might be offered from time to time by the society. The records manager and archivist can also be a resource person in assisting in developing records and information systems that are meeting the needs of the society in providing membership services and in other areas. This activity is especially important as the society continues along in its move to an automated, networked information system.

Phasing In and Costing Out the Society Archives and Records Management Program

In developing a records management and archives program (especially if the society opts for a discipline history center), the society ought to consider following distinct, carefully planned out phases. Below is a brief description of what these phases should look like and the time that these phases will require. The issue of resources will also be considered in this section.

1. Set up society records management program as outlined above. *Objectives:* This phase will require establishing the oversight committee, completing the records inventory and analysis, developing the records retention/disposition schedule, and implementing the schedule (disposing of unnecessary records and sending inactive records to the commercial records center). If an external consultant is used and an internal staff member is designated as liaison, accomplishing this important first step will require about six months. *Costs:* The main expense in this phase will be acquiring the services of a consultant to advise on the records inventory and analysis. Such a consultant would be responsible for an initial one-day workshop (retreat) for the society on the basics of records management and archives administration, developing the inventory form to be used in the survey, overseeing the completion of the inventory forms, working with the society in using the inventory forms to develop a records retention/disposition schedule, evaluating the relationship with the current commercial records facility and advising the society on alternatives, and investigating the possibility of the use of software for automating the records management program. The maximum

BUDGET FOR STARTING A PROFESSIONAL ASSOCIATION'S ARCHIVES

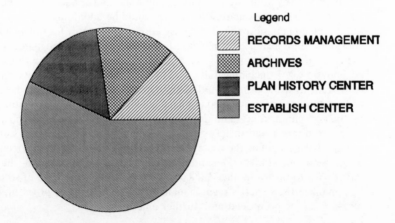

Legend

- RECORDS MANAGEMENT
- ARCHIVES
- PLAN HISTORY CENTER
- ESTABLISH CENTER

costs for the consultant would be approximately $10,000 (20 days at $500 a day), although the work may take less time than 20 days, especially if a student's services are used. There may be additional costs for travel for the society's records committee (if there are external members of the committee) and if the services of a records management student were utilized to help complete the inventory forms. These costs would be several thousands of dollars more (the student could be hired at $5 an hour, and his or her services would probably total about 200 hours). Total maximum costs are estimated at $12,500.

2. Establish society archives program. *Objectives:* This phase will require establishing a separate facility for the storage of these records, setting up this facility so that the archival records can be properly stored, removing the records to acid-free storage materials, developing a finding aid to the records, and publicizing the program. Another important aspect of this phase will be training an existing staff person to supervise this work and to work with the services of a consultant. This phase will take about one and one-half years. *Costs:* It is difficult to estimate these costs because there is no reliable information on the volume and nature of the society's archival records. It is reasonable, however, to assume that the society's archival records would probably total between 50 and 100 cubic feet of records, ranging from governing board minutes through the minutes of various society committees, main administrative files of the various department heads, society publications, key special interest groups' records, and other related records that might be acquired for this archives. The costs of archival supplies would be relatively modest, probably not exceeding $2,000 for acid-free boxes, folders, interleafs, and other similar supplies. The costs for the room where the archives would be housed would be more, however, requiring a space of 250 to 400 square feet for the storage of the archival records, tables, and chairs for archival processing and reference, desk and chair for the archival staff, library shelving for the storage of archival reference and society publications, records center shelving for the storage of the archival records boxes, and proper locks on the archives room door for security when the room is not

in use. The total costs of these additional furniture and shelving items would be about $2,000, while the room itself would have an annual cost to the society based on its rent per square foot. There would be additional costs for training a staff person in basic archival administration and probably for using an archival consultant until a staff person is hired. If a staff person is designated archivist, the costs of attending one or basic workshops and/or a university course would be about $4,000, including tuition costs and travel. If the society engages a consultant to work with this individual, at least for the first year, there would be an additional cost of $6,000 (12 days at $500 a day, based on a monthly visit by the consultant to evaluate progress and prepare brief written reports to the executive director and society governing board). The total costs of starting up this archives, excluding the rental costs for the space and the staff person's time, would be about $14,000. Depending on the needs of the program, the society might wish to invest another $3,000 to $5,000 in the acquisition of software to help manage the society's records management and archives program, but this decision can be postponed until further analysis is done.

3. Plan for the development of a discipline history center. *Objectives:* After establishing an effective records management and archives program, the society should turn its attention to the feasibility of establishing a discipline history center for the profession. To accomplish this, the society should have a two-day planning meeting in which it brings together experts in the history and present aspects of this nursing field, along with experienced administrators of other discipline history centers such as the American Institute of Physics and the Charles Babbage Center for the History of Computing and experts in archival appraisal and documentation. The purpose of this meeting should be to consider all the advantages and disadvantages of such a discipline history center for its field and to provide basic information that can be used for presenting a more detailed proposal to the society's governing board for the creation of such a center. The meeting could result, as well, in a publication on the approaches to documenting the profession and provide an additional outlet for publicity about the creation of the society's own archives program. The planning for, and execution of, the conference and preparation of final plans for the discipline history center would take about a year. *Costs:* The costs for planning for and holding this conference would be about $10,000 to $15,000, although the consultant would recommend that the society seek a grant to underwrite a large portion of the needed funding. Publication costs of the conference proceedings would be an additional cost, but this could probably be absorbed into the society's own ongoing publications program.

4. Establish a discipline history center. *Objectives:* If the society opts for the establishment of such a center, what would be needed to get such a program under way? Without question, this program would require the recruitment and hiring of a full-time, professionally trained, and experienced archivist and records manager to direct it. This individual would also require a fairly sizable budget to travel to society meetings and other meetings relating to the history of the profession and archival administration. There would be additional costs to support an advisory committee for determining documentary projects and overseeing the discipline history center. Ultimately, the center would need to

begin publishing a newsletter or, at the least, using a portion of the current society newsletter for disseminating news about the center's work and the availability of archival sources for documenting the field. The start-up phase of this center, including recruiting and hiring a professional archivist, would take six months. Another six months would be required to establish an advisory committee and get the center fully under way. *Costs:* In terms of 1990 dollars, the archivist of the caliber required would need to have an initial salary in the $30,000 to $35,000 range. Travel and related costs to support this position would require about an additional $5,000. Costs to support an advisory committee, which should meet at least twice a year, would range in the $10,000 to $12,000 area, depending on the number and geographic dispersion of the members. Costs for publications could be absorbed into the society's present support of the newsletter and journal. Initial start-up costs, in 1990 dollars, for a discipline history center would be in the $50,000 to $55,000 area, although the society could seek additional funds from external sources for specific projects.

Conclusion: Final Thoughts

These recommendations are intended for discussion and general guidance. If the society decides to embark upon the development of an institutional records management and archives program and, as well, the sponsorship of a discipline history center in the profession, every phase of development will bring new information that will revise the advice provided in this report. Several final points should be made in conclusion, reemphasizing ones made throughout this report. The establishment of a society records management and archives program will improve the work of the society in many areas. The establishment of a discipline history center will support the ongoing work of the society and enable it to foster a model program in this field. Both efforts seem to be natural consequences of the present nature of the society and will make it a better professional association.

NOTES

1. Peter J. Wosh, "Keeping the Faith? Bishops, Historians, and Catholic diocesan Archivists, 1790-1980," *Midwestern Archivist* 9, no. 1 (1984): 15-26 describes the nature of the tradition.

2. These individuals appear to have emphasized more their historiographical or librarian duties than archival responsibilities. The focus of the present archives is on providing historical and genealogical data and collecting mainly secondary historical materials (parish histories, newspaper obituaries and features, and other published articles).

3. There are very precise technical and quality standards that must be adhered to in order to produce archival quality microfilm and then use and store it properly. The diocese's present limited microfilming effort is succeeding only at reducing the space

required to store certain records. The informational content of the microfilmed records is at severe risk, greater than if maintained in their original paper form.

4. Archivists have long debated over the relative merits of centralization versus decentralization. The really important issue, however, is having the archivist in a position to ensure that records with archival value are properly identified and cared for and accessible, no matter where they are located. One present problem with the diocesan archives program is that the archivist does not appear to have the necessary influence to provide such advice.

5. This is not meant to imply that records transferred to an archives do not possess current value to an organization. Generally, records are transferred to an archives because their historical and other research values are greater than their values in the creating office, the frequency of use by the creating office has declined to a degree that suggests storage elsewhere, or the records require the greater preservation attention and security that an archival facility can provide.

6. Although the initial costs of taking such actions will be high, the diocese will in the long run save money as archival processing and preservation requirements are better managed.

The adoption of archival procrcessing and preservation specifications is also especially important as the diocese moves toward greater use of electronic information technology to store and use information. This technology requires the archivist to be involved as close to the point of creation of records as possible or face the risk of the information's being lost through erasure or obsolescent hardware and software.

7. The greatest portion of an archivist's time is taken up by arrangement and description (processing of holdings) responsibilities. Some of this time can be reduced by having the records management program in place in such a manner as to enable records to arrive at the archives in a condition that reduces processing requirements. Accomplishing this goal requires the support of the institution's chief executives and office managers and staff throughout the institution. The institutional archives must have a high profile within the organization, and the archivist must devote a significant portion of his or her time to educating individuals about the merits of records management and archival administration.

8. Unpublished "Statement of Purpose and Goals" of the diocese.

9. Statement of the present archivist.

10. Generally, diocesan archives have taken one or more approaches with parish records:

1. Collect parish records that were created before a certain date (a date selected because of some meaning associated with the history of the diocese and Catholicism in that area)

2. Collect sacramental and other vital records

3. Collect the records of parishes that have closed

4. Microfilm certain important parish records and maintain the microfilm for researchers at the diocesan archival facility.

This information is based on a conversation with James O'Toole, former archivist of the archdiocese of Boston and now faculty member in the Department of History, University of Massachusetts Boston.

11. There has been no systematic analysis of environmental changes in the vault, other than impressionistic notions. The consultant is convinced, upon examination, that there

is probably fair control of the environment but that it does not meet archival standards. At some point, more careful analysis needs to be done, especially before any resources are invested in expanding archival operations at the building where these records are presently stored.

12. Statement on the in-house listing of diocesan archives, n.d.

13. These recommendations are based on the assumption that the entire structure, with the exception of the meeting hall, is being turned over for use for an archives program.

14. The assumption is that the floor can support standard records loads of 30 pounds per cubic foot and other records center/archival facility standards and guidelines. Determining this support will require an engineering analysis of the building.

15. The degree of the microfilming program will be dependent upon the diocese's overall needs. The present limited microfilming does not justify the costs of a full-fledged internal program, but the diocese might wish to enhance its capability so that it can increase the quantity of microfilming of diocesan records and the records of related other organizations, such as those of parishes and other Catholic organizations. A full-fledged program will require the purchase of a planetary camera, engineering camera, microfilm processor, and at least one microfilm reader and printer. Other equipment will be needed to ensure sufficient quality control of the microfilm. It is probable, however, that the development of a micrographics program should be a second- or probably a third-year objective in the redevelopment of a modern records program.

16. The diocese can develop a list of these services close to it by contacting the Association of Commercial Records Centers, P.O. Box 20518, Raleigh, NC 27619 (telephone [919] 821–0757). Since the charge of these operations is based on the level of services provided on behalf of the records, the diocese should not become active in negotiating any agreement until it has analyzed its own records needs and developed a suitable set of needs.

17. No funds have been set aside for office furniture or classroom desks and chairs. It was assumed that the diocese could obtain this equipment from other financial sources or recycle the furniture from other buildings.

18. This figure is very approximate and is based on the diocese's acquiring a 386 computer with a hard disk storage capability (50–70 megabyte) that would allow it to use the computer for a number of applications, ranging from archival holdings management to records management, word processing, desktop publishing, and other functions.

19. This money should be enough to enable the diocesan archives to purchase software for archival management, word processing, spreadsheet, and desktop publishing.

20. This figure is approximate and is based on enough shelving units to house 1,200 cubic feet of archival records. Shelving prices vary widely, and the diocese may be able to reduce this cost significantly. The shelving needs to be reinforced steel shelving that is firmly secured and cross-braced. The large, open room in the present facility will hold more than this quantity of shelving, although floor load capacities and configuration of the shelving need to be planned carefully. The consultation recommends that the entire room be shelved over and that the shelving be installed in phases as the need arises and so that the costs can be phased in as well.

21. This figure represents about half of the total quantity of boxes that will be needed to house 800–1,000 cubic feet of archival records in the present facility's vault, diocesan headquarters, and the seminary. The diocese should plan on an equal quantity of such supplies for the second year and then a regular budget allocation for a smaller quantity

on an annual basis. The cost is for standard, legal-size (15.25″x10.25″x5″) boxes constructed of materials with alkaline buffering and lignin-free.

22. This figure also represents a phasing in of purchase of acid-free materials. This cost is for 10,000 acid- and lignin-free legal-size file folders.

23. This category is simply a catchall fund to provide some flexibility for the purchase of acid-free archival storage supplies. For example, there is a small photograph collection in the vault that will require special housing. Since the present diocesan archives has virtually no archival supplies, there need to be some additional funds set aside for contingency purposes.

24. The diocese should set aside some funds to engage additional consulting in a study of the present facility, micrographics program, conservation needs study, exhibitions, or some other area that it believes will require additional advice.

25. In general, the archival records of an organization ought to stay with it, provided that the organization is willing to invest the necessary resources into their care and management. For this institution, there are many obvious reasons it ought to develop its own archival and historical records program. The most important of these reasons are as follows:

1. The historical collections can support the educational functions of the institution.

2. The daily work of the institution is closely associated with its history.

3. A records management program could save the institution money and aid the use of its information in the institution's administration.

26. There is no professional archivist to ensure that the work on the historical collections is being done correctly and in a manner that conforms to archival standards and practice.

27. A logical plan would be having a small, permanent exhibit about the history of the institution on the second floor of the library with provision for small, changing exhibits that feature the archival and historical records. The present exhibition of materials is probably doing severe damage to these materials and is less educational than antiquarian in effect.

28. A small planning grant could be secured to bring together representatives of the various other organizations and other experts on the movement to consider what needs to be documented, where the existing records are located, and how these records should be best cared for. This work is an ideal possibility for external funding.

29. For the purposes of this report, references to the "society's records" are meant to include the records of these other bodies as well. While their records need to be retained separately, intellectually and physically, to adhere to basic records management and archival principles and to ensure that their different fiscal, administrative, legal, and other requirements are met, the records of all of these organizations could be managed well through one unified records management and archives program.

30. Ideally, in fact, three copies should be maintained: one for a "record" copy, one for reference purposes, and one for microfilming as a permanent security and reference copy. While microfilming has not been explicitly discussed in this report, it is a reformatting procedure that the society might wish to use for producing security and reference copies of certain key publications and records. Such reformatting techniques could be addressed as part of the process of determining the disposition of records in the preparation

of the records retention/disposition schedule. Microfilm could also be used for other educational and membership purposes; a microfilmed set of the newsletters could be offered for sale to the local chapters, special interest groups, and individual members.

31. At some point in the development of a records management and archives program, the society needs to consider what should be done with the documentation created by the society's local chapters and special interest groups. First, it should consider the nature of the records created. Second, the value of these records to the organization should be evaluated. Third, depending on the records' values, guidelines for their management should be established. Here the society could specify the preparation of annual reports of activities or more selective kinds of reporting. Clearly, however, the concern with the records of these organizations should be, at best, a secondary one; resources should be expended here only after the establishment of a records management and archives program and giving consideration to the development of a discipline history center.

32. This coordination could be accomplished through a staff records manager and archivist and through the placement of one or two individuals on both groups.

10

Sources for Assistance in Managing Institutional Archives

The purpose of this brief, concluding chapter is to provide information about publications and organizations where institutional archivists can go for additional assistance. The initial section of this chapter is a description of the essential archival publications. The reader needs to keep in mind that it is a very cursory description of this literature and that careful research will turn up many additional citations that might be of value to the institutional archivist. Furthermore, readers should remember that the first portion is concerned only with the archival profession's literature. There are helpful studies and articles in the library and information science literature, historical journals, records management periodicals, public administration publications, and the publication outlets of other such fields.

The second and remaining portion of this chapter is a brief description of professional associations that will be of aid to the institutional archivist in his or her work. Again, the emphasis of this chapter is on the archival profession. Institutional archivists will undoubtedly find additional assistance in other information-related professional associations or in the organizations that provide services to the type of institutions in which they work.

PUBLICATIONS

Basic Archival Administration Textbooks and Guides to the Literature

Institutional archivists will want to have a few basic volumes on their reference shelf for their own use and that of their staff. James Gregory Bradsher, ed., *Managing Archives and Archival Institutions* (Chicago: University of Chicago Press, 1988) is an interesting, if uneven, collection of essays that cover the full spectrum of the management of archival programs and the basic functions of these programs. Ann Pederson, ed., *Keeping Archives* (Sydney: Australian Society of Archives, Inc., 1987) is an excellent introduction to the fundamentals of administering archival records and historical manuscripts programs. It is more basic than the Bradsher book, but its writing is clear, its illustrations are excellent, and the editing to make a coherent volume is also outstanding. There are a number of earlier manuals, some of which are classic studies on archival administration, that the institutional archivist will find mentioned in Bradsher and Pederson and in the bibliographies and other references mentioned below. Institutional archivists will find it necessary sometimes to go back to writings by archival pioneers, such as T. R. Schellenberg and Hilary Jenkinson, to grasp the nature of archival administration as applied to their settings.

While the Bradsher and Pederson readers are noteworthy starting points for understanding the basics of archival administration and practice, neither volume is without its limitations; for some of their problems and strengths, see Richard J. Cox, "Textbooks, Archival Education, and the Archival Profession," *Public Historian* 12 (Spring 1990): 73–81. Institutional archivists should be prepared to use bibliographies and journals on archival topics for additional guidance. The most comprehensive bibliography ever compiled on archives was Frank B. Evans, comp., *Modern Archives and Manuscripts: A Select Bibliography* (Chicago: Society of American Archivists, 1975). The Evans compilation is, of course, extremely outdated, but institutional archivists might want to use the annual bibliographies published in the *American Archivist* from 1976 through 1980 and in 1986; Patricia A. Andrews and Bettye J. Grier, comps., *Writings on Archives, Historical Manuscripts, and Current Records: 1979–1982* (Washington, DC: National Archives and Records Administration, 1985); and Richard J. Cox, *Archives and Manuscripts Administration: A Basic Annotated Bibliography*, Technical Report 14 (Nashville: American Association for State and Local History, 1989).

There are occasional specialized bibliographies that will be of value to the institutional archivist. Two of the more pertinent ones for institutional archivists are Karen M. Benedict, ed., *A Select Bibliography on Business Archives and Records Management* (Chicago: Society of American Archivists, 1981) and the Society of American Archivists Religious Archives Section, comp., *Religious Archives in the United States: A Bibliography* (Chicago: Society of American Archivists, 1984). There are also shorter bibliographies on more focused subjects published occasionally in the archival journals.

More helpful to the institutional archivist will be a regular reading of the journals and newsletters supported by the archival profession. The *American Archivist*, published since 1938 by the Society of American Archivists, is the journal of record for the American archival community and a tremendous source for studies on archival theory and practice. *Archivaria*, published since 1975 by the Association of Canadian Archivists, is the other major North American journal. The *Midwestern Archivist*, published since 1976 by the Midwest Archives Conference, and *Provenance*, published since 1973 by the Society of Georgia Archivists, are other important archival journals published in the United States; both of these journals have published significant studies in the archival field. There are, of course, numerous journals on archival administration published worldwide that the institutional archivist in other nations will want to be familiar with and that publish from time to time articles on topics that institutional archivists from other countries will want to know about.

There are also other journals on specialized subjects that will be valuable to the work of the institutional archivist. *Archival and Museum Informatics*, published just since 1986, is an excellent source for news on automated techniques and electronic records in both archives and museums. *Conservation Administration News*, published since 1980, and the *Abbey Newsletter*, appearing since 1977, are important outlets for information about archival preservation; *Restaurator*, published since 1969, is a much more technically oriented journal on archives and library preservation, but the institutional archivist will want to peruse it from time to time. *Records Management Quarterly*, published since 1966 by the Association of Records Managers and Administrators, is the primary source for advice on records management and information resources management, essential activities for the institutional archivist.

There are, of course, numerous journals in other fields, such as library and information science, history, and the like, that publish articles on archival topics that will be useful to the institutional archivist. The main obstacle to discovering these articles and reports is that there is no existing bibliographic publication or data base that provides complete coverage to the archival literature. A valuable mechanism for resolving some of this problem is the Archives Library Information Center (ALIC) of the National Archives in Washington, D.C. ALIC is building a data base, primarily based on the extensive holdings of the National Archives' library, that can be searched on request. ALIC is also issuing occasional bibliographies on important or frequently requested topics. For more information about this important service, contact ALIC, Room 201, National Archives and Records Administration, Washington, DC 20408; the telephone number is (202) 501–5423.

Values of Institutional Archives

The importance of history and archival records can be found described in a number of places. Alan M. Kantrow, ed., "Why History Matters to Managers," *Harvard Business Review* 64 (January/February 1986): 81–88, has a number of interesting examples from the corporate world. There are also many personal testimonies, such as Harold P. Anderson, "Banking on the Past: Wells Fargo & Company," *Business History Bulletin* 1, no. 1 (1988): 9–12, scattered about in various journals and other publications. The broader importance of archival records can be seen in descriptions of their use in the classroom, such as Kathleen Roe, *Teaching with Historical Records* (Albany: University of the State of New York, State Education Department, Office of Cultural Education, State Archives, 1981) and Fay D. Metcalf and Matthew T. Downey, *Using Local History in the Classroom* (Nashville: American Association for State and Local History, 1982). Since many institutional archives are connected to educational organizations or have educational functions, these volumes will be useful for the institutional archivist building a case for his or her program.

The values of institutional archives can also be seen in the essays and other studies that focus on specific types of institutional archives. The nature and importance of business archives have been well described in Christopher L. Hives, "History, Business Records, and Corporate Archives in North America," *Archivaria* 22 (Summer 1986): 40–57 and Julia Niebuhr Eulenberg, "The Corporate Archives: Management Tool and Historical Resource," *Public Historian* 6 (Winter 1984): 21–37. An understanding of college and university archives can be gained from Nicholas C. Burckel and J. Frank Cook, "A Profile of College and University Archives in the United States," *American Archivist* 45 (Fall 1982): 410–28 and J. Frank Cook, "Academic Archivists and the SAA, 1938–1979: From Arcana Swish to the C&U PAG," *American Archivist* 51 (Fall 1988): 428–39. Museum archives can be understood through a perusal of William A. Deiss, *Museum Archives: An Introduction* (Chicago: Society of American Archivists, 1984). Religious archives are profiled in August R. Suelflow, *Religious Archives: An Introduction* (Chicago: Society of American Archivists, 1980) and in a number of interesting recent essays on the topic such as Mark J. Duffy, "The Archival Bridge: History, Administration and the Building of Church Tradition," *Historical Magazine of the Protestant Episcopal Church* 55 (December 1986): 275–87; James M. O'Toole, "What's Different About Religious Archives?" *Midwestern Archivist* 9, no. 2 (1984): 91–101; and Robert Shuster, "Documenting the Spirit,"

American Archivist 45 (Spring 1982): 135–41. The importance and nature of the archives of science and technology organizations can be glimpsed in Clark A. Elliott, ed., *Understanding Progress as Process: Documentation of the History of Post-War Science and Technology in the United States; Final Report of the Joint Committee on Archives of Science and Technology* (Chicago: Society of American Archivists, 1983).

The most useful, general introduction to the values of archival records may be James M. O'Toole, *Understanding Archives and Manuscripts* (Chicago: Society of American Archivists, 1990), a publication that also provides a concise introduction to the history of the archival profession and its mission.

Management of Institutional Archives

The basic importance of management for any kind of archival programs can be gleaned from the following types of articles and studies: Barbara Floyd, "The Archivist as Public Administrator," *Midwestern Archivist* 15, no. 1 (1990): 17–24; Susan E. Davis, "Development of Managerial Training for Archivists," *American Archivist* 51 (Summer 1988): 278-85; Michael Swift, "Management Techniques and Technical Resources in the Archives of the 1980s," *Archivaria* 20 (Summer 1985): 94–104; and James C. Worthy, "Management Concepts and Archival Administration," *Midwestern Archivist* 4, no. 2 (1979): 77–88. A publication that was not available to this author in the writing of this book but that promises to be a major step forward in the archivist's understanding of management issues is Thomas Wilsted and William Nolte, *Managing Archival and Manuscript Repositories* (Chicago: Society of American Archivists, 1991).

The recent preparation of self-study and planning how-to manuals has led to some interesting efforts to characterize the nature of archival programs. Paul H. McCarthy, ed., *Archives Assessment and Planning Workbook* (Chicago: Society of American Archivists, 1989) and Richard J. Cox and Judy Hohmann, *Strengthening New York's Historical Records Programs: A Self-Study Guide* (Albany: New York State Archives and Records Administration, 1988) are valuable resources for the administration of archival programs and are the publications to start with in the self-assessment of archival operations, including institutional archives. Another important reference for a comprehension of the legal aspects of archival administration is Gary M. and Trudy Huskamp Peterson, *Archives & Manuscripts: Law*, Basic Manual Series (Chicago: Society of American Archivists, 1985).

There has been some analysis of specific aspects of the management of archival programs that institutional archivists will find useful in the administration of their operations. William Maher, "The Importance of Financial Analysis of Archival Programs," *Midwestern Archivist* 3, no. 2 (1978): 3–

24; Terry Abraham, Stephen E. Balzarini, and Ann Frantilla, "What Is Backlog Is Prologue: A Measurement of Archival Processing," *American Archivist* 48 (Winter 1985): 31–44; William Maher, "Measurement and Analysis of Processing Costs in Academic Archives," *College & Research Libraries* 43 (1982): 59–67; and Uli Haller, "Variations in the Processing Rates on the Magnuson and Jackson Senatorial Papers," *American Archivist* 50 (Winter 1987): 100–09 are all pioneer efforts to evaluate from financial and other perspectives the basic work of the archivist. Since all of these studies are based on work in college and university archives, institutional archives should find these publications of particular value. A more generic evaluation is Thomas Wilsted, *Computing the Total Cost of Archival Processing*, Technical Leaflet Series, no. 2 (n.p.: Mid-Atlantic Regional Archives Conference, 1989). That there exists a need for more such studies in archival work is an understatement.

There are instances when it is better for institutional archives to be maintained by collecting historical manuscript repositories; see David J. Klaassen, "The Archival Intersection: Cooperation Between Collecting Repositories and Nonprofit Organizations," *Midwestern Archivist* 15, no. 1 (1990): 25–38 and Dennis E. Meissner, "Corporate Records in Noncorporate Archives: A Case Study," *Midwestern Archivist* 15, no. 1 (1990): 39–50. Another study in this realm is James W. Geary, "Catholic Archives in a Public Institution: A Case Study of the Arrangement Between Kent State University and the Diocese of Youngstown, Ohio," *American Archivist* 46 (Spring 1983): 175–82. Again, there needs to be more serious evaluation of the principles that should be at work in determining when an institution should decide to place its archival records in a historical records repository. Miriam Crawford, *A Model for Donor Organization and Institutional Repository Relationships in the Transfer of Organizational Archives* (Philadelphia: National Federation of Abstracting and Information Services, 1987) provides some useful guidelines, but it is clear that this subject requires considerably more thought, analysis, and discussion.

Some studies have more recently challenged the basics of archival administration. Institutional archivists should be aware of these professional debates and be able to ascertain how they might or might not affect their operations. The most noteworthy publication of this type is David Bearman, *Archival Methods*, Archives and Museum Informatics Technical Report, 3 (Spring 1989), which questions traditional approaches in appraisal, arrangement and description, preservation, and reference. Again, the primary professional archival journals will be the best source for these studies or for citations to other such publications.

Cooperation is an important aspect of administering archives, although it too requires more substantial study than it has received. For an introduction to this subject see John A. Fleckner, "Cooperation as a Strategy for Archival Institutions," *American Archivist* 39 (October 1976): 447–59 and Frank G. Burke, "Archival Cooperation," *American Archivist* 46 (Summer 1983): 293–305. Archival cooperation has been placed in its broader context in F. Gerald Ham, "Archival Strategies for the Post-Custodial Era," *American Archivist* 44 (Summer 1981): 207–16 and "Archival Choices: Managing the Historical Record in an Age of Abundance," *American Archivist* 47 (Winter 1984): 11–22, both statements concerning the impact of modern information technology and other aspects of modern society on the basic mission of the archivist. Multi-institutional and multidisciplinary approaches to appraisal have also recently appeared, with important implications for the cooperative work of archivists, including those responsible for institutional archives. See Helen W. Samuels, "Who Controls the Past," *American Archivist* 49 (Spring 1986): 109–24; Larry Hackman and Joan Warnow-Blewett, "The Documentation Strategy Process: A Model and a Case Study," *American Archivist* 50 (Winter 1987): 12–47; Samuels and Philip N. Alexander, "The Roots of 128: A Hypothetical Documentation Strategy," *American Archivist* 50 (Fall 1987): 518–31; and Richard J. Cox, "A Documentation Strategy Case Study: Western New York," *American Archivist* 52 (Spring 1989): 192–200. Archival networks, the pioneer form of archival cooperation, have been described well in "Archival Networks," *Midwestern Archivist* 6, no. 2 (1982): 85–240 and Richard A. Cameron, Timothy Ericson, and Anne P. Kenney, "Archival Cooperation: A Critical Look at Statewide Archival Networks," *American Archivist* 46 (Fall 1983): 414–32. There have also been a few case studies chronicling successful archival cooperation, such as Robert W. Arnold III, "The Albany Answer: Pragmatic and Tactical Considerations in Local Records Legislative Efforts," *American Archivist* 51 (Fall 1988): 475–79, and Alan S. Mason and Gerald S. Saxon, "The Dallas Mayors Oral History and Records Project: A Program of Institutional Cooperation," *American Archivist* 45 (Fall 1982): 472–74. Finally, Max J. Evans, "The Visible Hand: Creating a Practical Mechanism for Cooperative Appraisal," *Midwestern Archivist* 11, no. 1 (1986): 7–13 has a different slant from the documentation strategy process but has much to say about cooperative possibilities in this important function.

Appraisal of Institutional Records

An understanding of the basics of archival appraisal, useful for the institutional archivist, can be gained from reading Nancy E. Peace, ed., *Archival Choices: Managing the Historical Record in an Age of Abundance* (Lexington, MA: Lexington Books, 1984), which includes a convenient history of this archival function and a series of case studies. There are a number of other basic references related to this important function that the institutional archivist will find helpful. John A. Fleckner, *Archives & Manuscripts: Surveys*, Basic Manual Series (Chicago: Society of American

Archivists, 1977) remains the standard text on records surveying for the archivist. Maynard J. Brichford, *Archives & Manuscripts: Appraisal & Accessioning*, Basic Manual Series (Chicago: Society of American Archivists, 1977) summarizes thinking of a decade ago about the archival appraisal function. F. Gerald Ham, *Selecting and Appraising Archives and Manuscripts* (Chicago: Society of American Archivists, 1991), which the author of this volume did not see, will probably be a major updating and summarizing of the concept of archival appraisal as practiced in North America.

A number of essays have tried to show the needs for additional refinements of appraisal principles and techniques; refer to Richard J. Cox and Helen W. Samuels, "The Archivist's First Responsibility: A Research Agenda to Improve the Identification and Retention of Records of Enduring Value," *American Archivist* 51 (Winter/Spring 1988): 28–42 and Margaret Hedstrom, "New Appraisal Techniques: The Effect of Theory on Practice," *Provenance* 7 (Fall 1989): 1–21. These general discussions will aid the institutional archivist to understand the changing notions of archival appraisal approaches and suggest new ways for appraisal to be conducted in the institutional environments.

There are also specific case studies of appraisal that will be helpful to the institutional archivist, such as JoAnn Yates, "Internal Communication Systems in American Business Structures: A Framework to Aid Appraisal," *American Archivist* 48 (Spring 1985): 141–48; Dennis E. Meissner, "The Evaluation of Modern Business Accounting Records," *Midwestern Archivist* 5, no. 2 (1981): 75–100; Frank Boles and Julia Marks Young, "Exploring the Black Box: The Appraisal of University Administrative Records," *American Archivist* 48 (Spring 1985): 121–40; and Michael Lutzker, "Max Weber and the Analysis of Modern Bureaucratic Organizations: Notes Toward a Theory of Appraisal," *American Archivist* 45 (Spring 1982): 119–30. The most useful and detailed appraisal case study for the institutional archivist is Bruce H. Bruemmer and Sheldon Hocheiser, *The High-Technology Company: A Historical Research and Archival Guide* (Minneapolis: Charles Babbage Institute, Center for the History of Information Processing, 1989). This should be read in conjunction with Joan K. Haas, Helen Willa Samuels, and Barbara Trippel Simmons, *Appraising the Records of Modern Science and Technology: A Guide* (Cambridge, MA: Massachusetts Institute of Technology, 1985).

Institutional archives that might think it necessary to acquire records created on the outside that relate to the organization should be familiar with Faye Phillips, "Developing Collecting Policies for Manuscript Collections," *American Archivist* 47 (Winter 1984): 30–42 as a model for formulating appropriate policies.

A recently developed tool that could be adapted for use in institutional archives to determine the effectiveness of documentation of an organization is institutional collection analysis; see Judith E. Endelman, "Looking Backward to Plan for the Future: Collection Analysis for Manuscript Repositories," *American Archivist* 50 (Summer 1987): 340–53.

Other appraisal-related tools include sampling. See Eleanor McKay, "Random Sampling Techniques: A Method of Reducing Large, Homogeneous Series in Congressional Papers," *American Archivist* 41 (July 1978): 281–89; Frank Boles, "Sampling in Archives," *American Archivist* 44 (Spring 1981): 125–30; and Margery N. Sly, "Sampling in an Archival Framework: Mathoms and Manuscripts," *Provenance* 5 (Spring 1987): 55–75, for recent writings on this topic. Related to the concept of sampling is reappraisal, a process that calls for the regular and systematic reevaluation of records held by an archives; see Leonard Rapport, "No Grandfather Clause: Reappraising Accessioned Records," *American Archivist* 44 (Spring 1981): 143–50 and a rejoinder, Karen Benedict, "Invitation to a Bonfire: Reappraisal and Deaccessioning of Records as Collection Management Tools in an Archives—A Reply to Leonard Rapport," *American Archivist* 47 (Winter 1984): 43–49. The institutional archivist will find useful ideas in all of these writings and studies.

Preservation of Institutional Archives

There should be no question that preservation is an essential issue for institutional archivists. James M. O'Toole, "On the Idea of Permanence," *American Archivist* 52 (Winter 1989): 10–25 is an excellent introduction to the varying archival conceptions of permanence and the mission of preservation. There are also a number of basic, how-to guides for archival preservation that the institutional archivist will want to use. Mary Lynn Ritzenthaler, *Archives & Manuscripts: Conservation*, Basic Manual Series (Chicago: Society of American Archivists, 1983) is the publication that the institutional archivist will want to use first. Shelley Reisman Paine, *Basic Principles for Controlling Environmental Conditions in Historical Agencies and Museums*, AASLH Technical Report 3 (1985) will cover the necessary basics of this need for suitable environmental controls. Timothy Walch, *Archives & Manuscripts: Security*, SAA Basic Manual Series (Chicago: Society of American Archivists, 1977), while outdated in many respects, is still a useful place to begin when considering the issue of security. Disaster planning is well handled in John P. Barton and Johanna G. Wellheiser, eds., *An Ounce of Prevention: A Handbook on Disaster Contingency Planning for Archives, Libraries and Records Centers* (Toronto: Toronto Area Archivists Group Education Foundation, 1985) and Sally A. Buchanan and Toby Murray, *Disaster Planning, Preparedness and Recovery for Libraries and Archives*, PGI–88/WS/6 ED 297–769 (Paris: UNESCO, 1988). All of these should be read in conjunction with Alan Calmes, Ralph Schofer, and Keith Eberhardt, "Theory and Practice of Paper Preservation for Archives," *Restaurator* 9 (1988): 96–111, a fine introduction to the notion of preservation program phasing.

The use of microfilming or other methods of reformatting will confront every institutional archivist at some point or another. Nancy E. Gwinn, ed., *Preservation Microfilming: A Guide for Librarians and Archivists* (Chicago: American Library Association, 1987) will be of great value in considering this kind of reformatting. The process of selection for microfilming has been discussed in Richard J. Cox, "Selecting Historical Records for Microfilming: Some Suggested Procedures for Repositories," *Library & Archival Security* 9, no. 2 (1989): 21–41.

Arrangement, Description, and Reference Functions in the Institutional Archives

Although now considerably outdated relative to automated systems, David B. Gracy II, *Archives & Manuscripts: Arrangement & Description*, Basic Manual Series (Chicago: Society of American Archivists, 1977) is still useful for basic definitions and a description of archival processing. Equally useful is the SAA Committee on Finding Aids, *Inventories and Registers: A Handbook of Techniques and Examples* (Chicago: Society of American Archivists, 1976) for a brief comparison of these two traditional finding aids. Sue Holbert, *Archives & Manuscripts: Reference & Access*, Basic Manual Series (Chicago: Society of American Archivists, 1977) also provides a brief introduction to the concept and practice of archival reference. More recent descriptions of these functions can be found in Fredric M. Miller, *Arranging and Describing Archives and Manuscripts* (Chicago: Society of American Archivists, 1990) and Mary Jo Pugh, *Providing Reference Services for Archives and Manuscripts* (Chicago: Society of American Archivists, 1991); the author was not able to see the latter volume while writing this book.

Essays and studies relating to the fundamental purposes of arrangement, description, and reference can be useful to the institutional archivist reflecting on his or her program's mission and the nature of these functions in their setting. Some of these publications are Bruce W. Dearstyne, "What Is the *Use* of Archives? A Challenge for the Profession," *American Archivist* 50 (Winter 1987): 76–87; Lawrence Dowler, "The Role of Use in Defining Archival Practice and Principles: A Research Agenda for the Availability and Use of Records," *American Archivist* 51 (Winter/Spring 1988): 74–86; Elsie Freeman, "In the Eye of the Beholder: Archives Administration from the User's Point of View," *American Archivist* 47 (Spring 1984): 111–23; Mary Jo Pugh, "The Illusion of Omniscience: Subject Access and the Reference Archivist," *American Archivist* 45 (Winter 1982): 33–44; and Paul Conway, "Facts and Frameworks: An Approach to Studying the Users of Archives," *American Archivist* 49 (Fall 1986): 393–407.

Entry into the world of automated description and retrieval has caused the archivist to think more systematically about the arrangement and description functions. Lydia Lucas, "Efficient Finding Aids: Developing a System for Control of Archives and Manuscripts," *American Archivist* 44 (Winter 1981): 21–26 is a good introduction to this kind of more systematic thinking. Institutional archivists considering hardware and software acquisitions for automated arrangement and description (and the use of automation for other functions) should look at Lynn Cox and David Bearman, comps., *Directory of Software for Archives & Museums, Archival Informatics Technical Report* (Pittsburgh: Archives & Museum Informatics, 1990) and David Bearman, *Automated Systems for Archives and Museums: Acquisition and Implementation Issues, Archival Informatics Newsletter & Technical Report* (Pittsburgh: Archives & Museum Informatics, Winter 1987/1988). Issues related to the use of the US MARC Format are discussed in a number of studies, including Patricia Cloud, "RLIN, AMC, and Retrospective Conversion: A Case Study," *Midwestern Archivist* 11, no. 2 (1986): 125–34; Steven L. Hensen, "The Use of Standards in the Application of the AMC Format," *American Archivist* 49 (Winter 1986): 31–40; and most importantly, the report and working papers of the Working Group on Standards for Archival Description published in the Fall 1990 and Winter 1991 issues of the *American Archivist*. Another useful collection of essays is Anne J. Gilliland, "Automating Intellectual Access to Archives," *Library Trends* 36 (Winter 1988): 495–623. The standard manual for archival description and cataloging, in conformity with the US MARC Archives and Manuscripts Control format, is Steven Hensen, comp., *Archives, Personal Papers, and Manuscripts: A Cataloging Manual for Archival Repositories, Historical Societies, and Manuscript Libraries*, 2d ed. (Chicago: Society of American Archivists, 1989).

Introductory descriptions of the processing function can be gained from a number of articles, including Uli Haller, "Processing for Access," *American Archivist* 48 (Fall 1985): 400–415; Megan Floyd Desnoyers, "When Is a Collection Processed?" *Midwestern Archivist* 7, no. 1 (1982): 5-23; Arthur J. Breton, "The Critical First Step: In Situ Handling of Large Collections," *American Archivist* 49 (Fall 1986): 455–58; and Richard M. Kesner, Susan Tannewitz Karnes, Anne Sims, and Michael Shandor, "Collection Processing as a Team Effort," *American Archivist* 44 (Fall 1981): 356–58.

There are a number of essays that question the record group concept and the concept's utility that the institutional archivist might wish to consider. Frank Boles, "Disrespecting Original Order," *American Archivist* 45 (Winter 1982): 26–32 and Max J. Evans, "Authority Control: An Alternative to the Record Group Concept," *American Archivist* 49 (Summer 1986): 249–61 are good examples of this kind of literature.

The essential link between arrangement and description and reference is the principle of provenance. For a classic analysis of the importance of this principle see David Bearman and Richard Lytle, "The Power of the Principle of Provenance," *Archivaria* 21 (Winter 1985–1986): 14–27.

Institutional archivists should also consider the value of conducting user studies that can provide valuable information for the arrangement, description, and reference functions. Helpful discussions about the importance of user studies are Paul Conway, "Facts and Frameworks: An Approach to Studying the Users of Archives," *American Archivist* 49 (Fall 1986): 393–407; Lawrence Dowler, "The Role of Use in Defining Archival Practice and Principles: A Research Agenda for the Availability and Use of Records," *American Archivist* 51 (Winter/Spring 1988): 74–86; and William J. Maher, "The Use of User Studies," *Midwestern Archivist* 11, no. 1 (1986): 15–26. For examples of research done in this area, see David Bearman, "User Presentation Language in Archives," *Archives and Museum Informatics* 3 (Winter 1989/1990): 3–7; Diane L. Beattie, "An Archival User Study: Researchers in the Field of Women's History," *Archivaria* 29 (Winter 1989/1990): 33–50; Paul Conway, "Research in Presidential Libraries: A User Survey," *Midwestern Archivist* 11, no. 1 (1986): 35-56; Clark A. Elliott, "Citation Patterns and Documentation for the History of Science: Some Methodological Considerations," *American Archivist* 44 (Spring 1981): 131–42; Jacqueline Goggin, "The Indirect Approach: A Study of Scholarly Users of Black and Women's Organizational Records in the Library of Congress Manuscript Division," *Midwestern Archivist* 11, no. 1 (1986): 57–67; and Fredric M. Miller, "Use, Appraisal, and Research: A Case Study of Social History," *American Archivist* 49 (Fall 1986): 371–92. Although none of these studies relates to records held by institutional archives, the methodology and potential value for these kinds of archives should be obvious.

Public Programs and Institutional Archives

There is little literature on the ways that institutional archives can or should develop and use public programs. Institutional archivists will find Ann E. Pederson and Gail Farr Casterline, *Archives & Manuscripts: Public Programs*, Basic Manual Series (Chicago: Society of American Archivists, 1982) the most comprehensive introduction to this function. Gail Farr Casterline's *Archives & Manuscripts: Exhibits*, Basic Manual Series (Chicago: Society of American Archivists, 1980) is an in-depth exploration of this way of promoting greater understanding of archival programs. Other essays that may be useful to the institutional archivist in understanding how to apply public programs are Timothy L. Ericson, "Presence, Per-

spective and Potential: A Conceptual Framework for Local Outreach,"
Midwestern Archivist 6, no. 2 (1982): 149–61 and Jane Meredith Pairo,
"Developing an Archival Outreach Program," *Georgia Archive* 10 (Spring
1982): 4-12.

Records Management and the Institutional Archives

The success of an institutional archives program is dependent on its
relationship to a viable records management program. For a standard treatment of records management see Mary F. Robek, Gerald F. Brown, and
Wilmer O. Maedke, *Information and Records Management*, 3d ed. (Encino, CA: Glencoe, 1987). Records management has not always been applied successfully in environments where there are archival operations; see,
for example, Marjorie Rabe Barritt, "Adopting and Adapting Records
Management to College and University Archives," *Midwestern Archivist*
14, no. 1 (1989): 5–12. More unfortunately, records management textbooks
and articles have often ignored or misinterpreted the role of archives;
institutional archivists will find the records management literature informative, but they will have to use it with caution when considering their own
archival functions.

The two most useful records management-oriented publications for institutional archivists are studies that examine more broadly the role of
information systems in organizations. Richard Kesner, *Information Systems: A Strategic Approach to Planning and Implementation* (Chicago:
American Library Association, 1988) makes an effort to relate the work
of archivists to other information professionals in organizations. The Advisory Committee for the Coordination of Information Systems, *Management of Electronic Records: Issues and Guidelines* (New York: United
Nations, 1990) has much to say about the basic functions of records management in the electronic environment that an institutional archivist will
find helpful.

Special Records Forms and the Institutional Archives

Institutional archivists will often have to contend with special records
forms that challenge their basic approaches to management of their archival
programs. The most serious concern that has emerged in the past decade
is the growing use of office computer equipment. The United Nations study
on electronic records and the resource directory on automated records and
techniques mentioned above will be the best starting point for institutional
archivists needing to begin planning for how to administer archival records
in electronic form.

There are, of course, other special media that the institutional archivist
will encounter. Among the best references are Ralph E. Ehrenberg, *Ar-*

chives & Manuscripts: Maps and Architectural Drawings, Basic Manual Series (Chicago: Society of American Archivists, 1982); Frederick J. Stielow, *The Management of Oral History Sound Archives* (Westport, CT: Greenwood Press, 1986); David Bearman, *Optical Media: Their Implications for Archives & Museums*, Part 2 of *Archival Informatics Newsletter* 1 (Spring 1987); and Mary Lynn Ritzenthaler, Gerald J. Munoff, and Margery S. Long, *Archives & Manuscripts: Administration of Photographic Collections*, Basic Manual Series (Chicago: Society of American Archivists, 1984). One convenient, although uneven, collection of essays on various media is Cynthia Durrance, comp., *Management of Recorded Information: Converging Disciplines; Proceedings of the International Council on Archives' Symposium on Current Records, National Archives of Canada, Ottawa May 15–17, 1989* (New York: K. G. Saur, 1990). The reader will notice that this volume did not emphasize these kinds of special media but instead stressed basic principles and approaches needed for administering institutional archives.

Whither Institutional Archives

The archival profession is going through constant change. Many of these changes have or will affect institutional archives. For a summary of recent trends in the American archival community, read Richard J. Cox, *American Archival Analysis: The Recent Development of the Archival Profession in the United States* (Metuchen, NJ: Scarecrow Press, 1990). Other essays and studies that comment on recent debates and issues in the archival profession and that are worth a look by institutional archivists are Maynard Brichford, "Who Are the Archivists and What Do They Do?" *American Archivist* 51 (Winter/Spring 1988): 106–10; Paul Conway, "Perspectives on Archival Resources: The 1985 Census of Archival Institutions," *American Archivist* 50 (Spring 1987): 174–91; David B. Gracy II, "What's Your Totem? Archival Images in the Public Mind," *Midwestern Archivist* 10, no. 1 (1985): 17–23; and William J. Maher, "Contexts for Understanding Certification: Opening Pandora's Box," *American Archivist* 51 (Fall 1988): 408–27. Of course, the best manner for the institutional archivist to stay abreast of professional changes and debates is to read regularly the main professional journals and to attend professional meetings.

PROFESSIONAL ASSOCIATIONS AND OTHER ORGANIZATIONS PROVIDING ADDITIONAL ASSISTANCE TO INSTITUTIONAL ARCHIVISTS

There is a great variety of professional associations that institutional archivists can draw upon for help. A few of the most important ones located in the United States have been described below (many countries have their own professional associations). The main national professional association is the Society of American Archivists (SAA), 600 South Federal Street, Suite 504, Chicago, IL 60605, (312) 922–0140. This organization publishes a quarterly journal, the *American Archivist*; a newsletter that appears six times a year; and other books and special reports on archival topics. The society also has become a clearinghouse for other publishers on archival topics. The association holds an annual meeting in the fall and offers a number of workshops and institutes each year on a variety of archival functions and issues. There are also many special interest groups within the society that focus on specific types of institutional archivists.

The Society of American Archivists' counterpart in the records management field is the Association of Records Managers and Administrators (ARMA), 4200 Somerset Drive, Suite 215, Prairie Village, KS 66208, (913) 341–3808. Its range of products and activities is comparable to that of the society. Other national associations that occasionally offer publications or activities that would interest the institutional archivist are as follows:

American Association for State and Local History (AASLH)
172 Second Avenue North
Suite 102
Nashville, TN 37201
(615) 255–2971

American Society for Information Science (ASIS)
8720 Georgia Aveue
Suite 501
Silver Spring, MD 20910
(301) 495–0900

Both of these associations offer journals, occasional publications, meetings, and continuing education opportunities.

Institutional archivists will also want to be aware of regional professional associations and graduate archival education programs that are in their regions or states. There are over 50 regional archival associations, and the Society of American Archivists maintains a complete list of these associations and their addresses. The society and ARMA also publish education directories that will be useful for the institutional archivist wishing to take courses or to encourage his or her staff to take courses.

Institutional archivists can always turn to their state archival agencies for advice and referrals to other organizations and sources of assistance. The National Association of Government Archives and Records Administrators (NAGARA), Executive Secretariat, New York State Archives and Records Administration, 10A75 Cultural Education Center, Albany, NY 12230, (518) 473–8037 publishes an annual directory of these agencies. These state archives often have staff that can assist institutional archivists and certainly will be able to direct individuals to other organizations and individuals that can meet the needs of institutional archivists.

Finally, institutional archivists should remember the Archives Library Information Center (ALIC) of the National Archives in Washington, DC, as a source for hard-to-get archival and records management studies and searches on specific archival and records management topics.

Index

About the Author

RICHARD J. COX is Lecturer at the University of Pittsburgh's School of Library and Information Science. He has had nearly two decades of archival experience and is the author of many articles published in professional journals. Professor Cox was named a Fellow of the Society of American Archivists in 1989 and also won the 1991 Waldo Gifford Leland Award for "writing of superior excellence and usefulness in the field of archival history, theory, or practice." He has also recently been named editor of *The American Archivist*.